ALL MEN ARE ISLANDS

By the Same Author

POETRY
Postcards to Pulcinella
The Mongrel
The Solitudes
Judas

PLAYS
The Dull Ass's Hoof
This Way to the Tomb
Stratton
The Rape of Lucretia
Don Juan
Our Lady's Tumbler
The Death of Satan
Abelard & Heloise

PROSE
Journal of a Husbandman
Home-Made Home
Tobacco Growing in England
Where I Live
The Blue Fox
Jan at the Blue Fox
Jan's Journal
The Last Adam
Saint Spiv

ADAPTATIONS
The Eagle has Two Heads
The Typewriter
The Apollo de Bellac
The Rabbit Race
Beauty and the Beast

EDITIONS
The Selected Writings of Mahatma Gandhi
The Poems of Ben Jonson
The Songs and Satires of the Earl of Rochester

THE AUTHOR BY EPSTEIN

ALL MEN
ARE ISLANDS

An Autobiography

RONALD DUNCAN

RUPERT HART-DAVIS
SOHO SQUARE LONDON
1964

Printed in Great Britain by Richard Clay and Company, Ltd.,
Bungay, Suffolk

CONTENTS

CONTENTS

PART ONE

The Ceremony of Innocence

WE settle down to write our life when we no longer know how to live it. To pause is to admit defeat. When the present is interesting we do not bother with the past. We try to remember only when we've lost the vitality of doing anything worth remembering. The past is a wastepaper basket. We burrow into it only when we feel we have no future. I do not know what I will find in this dustbin. I have never kept a diary; I have never made a note in my life, believing that I could remember anything that was valuable, and what I couldn't was best forgotten anyhow. I had a notoriously bad memory.

Nel mezzo del cammin di nostra vita
mi ritrovai per una selva oscura
che la diritta via era smarrita.

Precisely. When we are lost and can't see the trees for the wood we can do little but look back at the path we have trodden. It has led nowhere. Nowhere is where I am.

It is factual but more or less meaningless to say I was born in 1914. In one sense I have not yet been born at all. No man is born of woman completely. There are as many kinds of births as there are deaths. Factually I was born in 1914, but even as a child I was acutely aware that this date was irrelevant. It was not that I felt I had lived before, but I always had access to experiences which I had never experienced. As a child I was constantly told things which I already knew. I could not explain this; it was something I took for granted. Only when I was made conscious of it did it begin to worry me. Most people describe their childhood wholly in terms of social environment and its effect on them. But with me this access to inherited emotions or experiences was more important than where or how I lived.

9

It is silly to say a man has only two parents, although, in a sense, I had only one. My father never saw me after I was three months old. He died when I was four. But not all the buried are dead. His absence throughout my childhood was more ponderable than a presence.

My sense of being different must have come from somewhere. I always felt it. No doubt my inability to conform was encouraged by the fact that when I was about eight my mother told me that even my birth had been a little out of the ordinary. Apparently she had had a sister who was on the stage. My father's family had heard that he was running about Skindles at Maidenhead with a Miss Cannon and assumed erroneously that it was with the girl who was playing in *The Merry Widow*. They did not bother to find out that my mother had in fact no connection with Shaftesbury Avenue, but had just left the convent in Belgium where she had been at school. My father was informed that if he persisted in marrying the actress he would be cut off. He did and was. They married in a register office and left for Rhodesia. This was the second time the family had frustrated my father. At Cambridge he had wished to read medicine, but his family considered a profession little better than a trade and he had not been allowed to study anything but Tattersall's. So he decided to take up farming and went to study agriculture at the Gwebi Experimental Station near Salisbury.

One day in Rhodesia there was a thunderstorm. It frightened a bull, which charged my mother. A few hours later I was born prematurely, under seven months, from a Caesarean operation. Appropriately the Great War was declared next day. "They did not think I'd live when you were born," I remember my mother telling me, "because of your enormous head. There wasn't anything else to you but your head. You looked like a tadpole with a very solemn expression. The moment you were born the doctor christened you Judge Jeffreys. You never cried; that would have been quite out of character."

Soon after the outbreak of war my father, who bore the German name of Dunkelsbühler, decided that it would be wiser if my mother returned to England with me. They never met again. Their marriage had lasted no more than a year.

Her journey home was not without incident. The captain of the boat wanted to put her and myself ashore at the Canary Isles because of her German name, though in fact my father was hardly any more German than she was. It is true he was born in Frankfurt, but he had lived in London as a child and had been wholly educated in England. At that time people did not bother to change their nationalities: the menace of passports had not been invented, and society had not marched so resolutely towards freedom. However, my mother refused to be dumped on any island and cabled her sister, who, through the impresario George Edwardes, managed to arrange her landing in England. These are the facts, but they do nothing to recreate the distress she must have felt. She was not only pregnant with my sister, and nursing a child a few months old, but she also knew now that my father had been interned as an alien, although he could not speak a word of German.

My father's family had not been inconvenienced in the same way. They were rich, and eventually they applied for a couple of hundred thousand pounds' worth of War Loan and then emulated the Royal Family by changing their name. The routine of the Dunkelsbühler household in Brook Street was not upset by hostilities. My granny still took her drive in the park every day alone—her husband had left her at my father's birth, when he had discovered that my father was the son of the Crown Prince of Bavaria. Nor was there any ruffle in the stately domesticity at my so-called grandfather's mansion in Park Lane. There my Great-aunt Henrietta lived also alone—except for ten stoical servants and two horrible Pekinese.

But my mother's life was not so easy. None of my father's relatives would see her. To them she was still an actress, for she had not bothered to tell them of their mistake. They now allowed her £25 a month, giving her to understand that this was a gesture towards me and not towards her. She took a cheap house in Clapham, which she shared with another sister and her husband and her two parents. It was here, at No. 9 Chelsham Road, that my sister was born and we spent our childhood. It was an ugly house with ten or eleven rooms, spacious and suburban. But it would be silly to pretend that as a child I wanted for anything. £25 a month in

1915 was quite a large income. I cannot claim the romanticism or the luxury of ever having gone hungry. On the contrary, one of my insistent childhood worries was how to eat what was put before me. It wasn't economics that had any impression on me, but emotional environment. I could not have been more than three years old when I became aware of two dimensions; my mother's beauty and my mother's sadness. She must have been very much in love with my father. Every time she picked me up or looked at me she would say, or some relative would tactlessly remark, how much I resembled my father. Sometimes she would stifle the tears; at others she would run from the room.

I remember one day being carried out into the back garden to see a German Zeppelin caught by the searchlights. My only other memory of the war is of a man whom I cannot identify. He was in uniform and took me on his knee. I started playing with the rings on his fingers; he had three. I asked him where he had got them and, I suppose because I was a child, he told me the truth. "I took them off some corpses in the trenches," he said. He little knew the "Judge" would remember.

A few months later—though I do not know what time means to a child—I was sitting at breakfast with my mother, sister and aunt. There was an air of celebration about the house. It was the 11th November 1918—Armistice Day. My mother was dressed to go out. We were going to see the crowds. I was excited, impatient for her to eat the boiled egg before her. She lopped off the top, then stopped to read a telegram which my aunt had just brought in. I protested. My mother read it and burst into tears. My father was dead. My mother was helped to her room. I followed her an hour or two later. She told me that there had been an influenza epidemic among the natives. My father, with his interest in medicine, had volunteered to help. He had got permission from the prison camp to do this, had then contracted the infection himself and died within a few days.

Between her tears I asked her what influenza was.

"An infection."

"What is an infection?"

"Something that comes from flies."

I promptly left the room, ran down the stairs to the kitchen and managed to reach for a tumbler from the dresser. Then I ran out into the garden and sat and waited. I wonder if there has ever been more hatred in a small heart. Eventually I saw a blow-fly on a plant. I pounced and had it beneath the glass. This was the creature that had caused my mother's grief. I did not think anything of my father. He never meant anything to me but what he meant to her. I sat in front of the tumbler watching the fly go round and round the glass and I began to curse. I have been cursing ever since.

But of course it was not all sadness. My sister and I had our boat. That was the kitchen-table, which we had upside down on the floor. One afternoon I would take her to Australia, another to Greenland. Sometimes we were hounded by sharks, sometimes shipwrecked like Robinson Crusoe. I always insisted that Brer Rabbit was rescued too. None, absolutely none, of the journeys I have made as a man were anything like so vivid as these fantasies across the kitchen floor. My sister used to make me describe the beach we landed on, and the impenetrable forests through which I led her, and the strange animals I would invent on the way. There was a dox: a cross between a dog and a fox; a geep, a half-goat, half-sheep; and there were cobras with heads at each end, and birds with the teeth of sharks. Sometimes these creatures would frighten her, and my mother would have to run into the room because a snake with fifteen heads was curled up in a corner, or a great panther was under the dresser.

My sister's revenge for being persecuted by my imagination was to insist that I should play her favourite game occasionally. This entailed going up into the drawing-room, where she would put a very scratched record of Caruso singing *Pagliacci* on the gramophone. Then I had to pretend that I was dead. I would have to lie there for half-an-hour, hearing Caruso again and again, being scolded every time I moved because I was not behaving like a proper corpse.

I suppose this macabre little game was my sister's way of redressing the balance. My mother favoured me: I was "the living spit" of my father. This preference showed whenever there were three biscuits or only one sweet.

We were living in Clapham but my address was the Land of

Make-believe. This was stimulated by Mr James Beale, by far the most interesting man I ever met. He was a retired bank-manager living in a sedate but dingy suburb in South London. I never discovered much about him except that he was a widower, and that most of his savings were invested in stamps. But, for all that, we must have had something in common to make up for the disparity in our ages. For Mr Beale was sixty-eight and I was only five.

I can remember our introduction vividly. I was on my way home from the little dame-school which I used to attend in the afternoon. The only thing I ever learned at this school was French knitting. One held a cotton-reel in one hand and a bent hairpin in the other, and poked the rainbow-coloured wool over four nails surrounding the hole in the reel. This produced a snake-like coil from the other end of the reel which my schoolmistress showed us how to make into reins. And with this home-made harness on my back, a pencil-box clutched in my hand, and a girl called Peggy, who lived a few doors away, acting as jockey, I was just coming into the home straight one day when I ran into Mr Beale.

That was because he was standing squarely across the pavement. He was our next-door neighbour and I had always looked upon him from a distance as a most forbidding old gentleman. But there he was now, still wearing his city uniform of black coat, over his highly polished shoes. He didn't move out of the way, but stood his ground, beaming benignly down at us.

"What are you doing, sonny?" he said.

"Playing horses. I'm Black Bess. Peggy is Dick Turpin."

"Indeed. Then I'd better be a five-barred gate. You see if you can jump over me."

So saying, he eased his trousers up at the knees to avoid creasing them, and knelt down on all fours on the pavement before me. This strange action frightened Peggy. She dropped my reins immediately and ran off up the road, calling for me to follow her. I pretended not to hear. Mr Beale looked such a tempting five-barred gate.

I took a run and jumped.

"Well done. You just managed to clear me."

14

He rose, dusted his knees and took me by the hand. Together we walked up the road. It was one of those hot dusty London evenings when every breath of air seems soiled. He led me right up to my gate, which adjoined his own.

"I suppose your mummy will be waiting to give you your tea?" he said, as if he had enjoyed our game down the road, and was reluctant to leave me. Somehow I sensed his loneliness.

"I daresay I could stay out and play for a bit if you'll be a five-barred gate again," I bribed.

He glanced up at my mother's windows. "No, I don't think I can do that again here," he said, "but I'll tell you what we'll do. We'll go and water my flowers. I've got two watering-cans. What do you say to that?"

"Yes, do let's do that," I cried eagerly, and let him take me by the hand again and lead me up his front steps. Then, as his front door closed behind me, I remembered that Mr Beale had no garden. I stood there in his narrow hall, wondering what I should do. But I forgot my fears immediately I heard the old man running the water in his back kitchen.

"Come and get your can," he called, adjusting the rose as he lifted a can out of the sink.

Mine was almost too heavy for me to carry. So Mr Beale took both, one in each hand.

"But where are the flowers?" I asked. "You haven't got a garden."

"Oh, haven't I?" he replied. "Just you follow me."

We went upstairs to his drawing-room.

"There," he said, "and I don't suppose you'll ever see such beautiful flowers though you live to be as old as I am. Mrs Beale loved lilies."

And with that, he began to water the fleurs-de-lis patterned on his carpet.

"You do one border. I'll do the other."

When we had emptied our cans, Mr Beale refilled them from the bathroom. After fifteen minutes the carpet was sodden.

"Haven't you any more flowers?" I asked, enjoying myself as I had never done before.

"I'm afraid not. And anyhow your mummy will be wondering

15

where you are. You'd better run along and have your tea; besides, I've got to get busy now and feed my animals."

"I didn't know you had a dog."

"I haven't."

"A cat, then."

"I suppose some people would call panthers cats," he said, "for they're the same species." Then he mumbled a latin name.

"I've never seen a panther," I pleaded. "Do let me help you feed your panthers. How many have you?"

"Two," he replied. "One is called Morning and the other is called Evening. And when they lie down together, the world is lonely as night."

He spoke in the most matter-of-fact tones, rather like a school-master.

I followed him out of the room where we had watered the flowers on the carpet; and, as he shut the door behind me, I noticed that it bore the inscription GARDEN painted neatly in the middle of one panel.

As we went downstairs to the kitchen we passed two other doors. One bore the word FOREST and the other SEA. Bank-managers are generally methodical.

Mr Beale collected a large knuckle of beef from the larder and we immediately returned and entered the forest.

This room was entirely bare except for a scurry of rats leaving a bone which lay by the fireplace. Mr Beale didn't seem to notice the rats, which had by now disappeared behind the wainscoting. He knelt down and placed the beef beside the bare bone. Then he stood up again and lit a nightlight which was on the mantel-shelf. He placed it in a saucer of water, just as my mother did every night when she put the nightlight by my bedside. But my friend placed his in the centre of the floor. They he drew the heavy velvet curtains which darkened the room completely.

"We must crouch in this bamboo-grass," he whispered. "If we stay absolutely quiet, the panthers will come down from the hills and drink from that pool."

"What pool?"

"Ssh," he said, pointing to the little saucer of light. "Night is

16

very thirsty of light. And it's because these panthers drink so much that all our days get drained away."

"You mean that if we gave them salt to eat," I said, "then they'd get so thirsty they'd drink so much time up that there'd be no tomorrow?"

The idea appealed to me. I never did like school.

"Exactly," he answered. "You at least understand. But of course you would. But you mustn't talk now or you'll frighten them away."

We continued to squat on the floorboards.

Suddenly Mr Beale took a jack-knife from his pocket and struck ferociously at the wall by his side.

"That's the second python I've killed this week," he confided. "They're easy to dispatch if you stab them between their eyes. Now look, the panthers are coming down now. There, beneath those mango trees. See how cruel the hard jewels of their eyes are—like emeralds of hate. And how sensuously they move on their silent paws, as though all the world were as soft as wood-ash."

"Are they drinking the light now?" I asked.

At that moment the nightlight flickered. Perhaps a down-draught from the chimney blew it out; but the forest suddenly became a blanket of darkness to me. And I screamed. Mr Beale picked me up and carried me out to the hall.

"That was a near thing," he said, mopping his brow. "It was just like a nightmare, only we both happened to be awake. That's the worst of life; it becomes so terrible, it leaves no terrors for our dreams. Now you must go home, or your mummy won't let you play with me any more."

"She doesn't know I'm here."

"No. And don't tell her either. Or she'll never let you come fishing with me tomorrow. It's Friday tomorrow. Friday's fishing."

It was easy for me to lie. I learned to lie as soon as I learned to talk. For I never could distinguish between what had really happened and what I had only imagined.

"We were kept late at school," I told my mother, "because we had to stay and learn the song we're to sing to the parents at prize-

17

giving; and we may be late again tomorrow," I added, thinking of Mr Beale's promise to take me fishing.

The room bore the inscription SEA, and of course I made the boat from his kitchen-table. We launched it by merely turning it upside down. Then we tied a teacloth across the legs at one end to serve as a sail. I remember these legs were splintered and rough where a cat had once sharpened its claws. Mr Beale, wearing a white seaman's sweater with a roll-collar neck, rowed with a couple of furled umbrellas as oars. I acted as coxswain and tried my best to keep the nose of the boat at right angles to the breakers, to prevent us from being overturned.

"Are you a good sailor?" Mr Beale asked, labouring against the current.

I nodded apprehensively.

"Better bale out a bit," he said, indicating an old enamelled saucepan in the prow of the boat.

I did as I was told, terrified lest we should sink and drown. And he rowed on for another ten minutes, until the sea seemed calmer, sheltered by a headland. Here we cast our lines, after baiting our hooks with imaginary bait which Mr Beale produced from a tobacco-tin in his pocket.

We stayed fishing for over half an hour. I began to feel bored. I even dozed, closing my eyes and letting my line go slack.

Mr Beale seized this opportunity. "Pull in," he cried, waking me, "you've got a bite." Frantic with excitement, I pulled in my line. Two smoked kippers were fixed on the hook. I chuckled with pride.

"Can we have these for tea?" I asked.

He nodded and we promptly beached our boat and went down again to the kitchen.

I had great difficulty in getting through the tea my mother had prepared for me that evening. "Peggy gave me a huge apple, and made me eat it on the way back from school," I explained.

For the next few days my mother took to meeting me herself. I fretted silently for Mr Beale; and as we walked past his house I could barely drag myself from all the magic inside his gate.

Then one Sunday afternoon about a fortnight later, while my mother was reading *Brer Rabbit* to me in the drawing-room, we heard a terrific row coming from Mr Beale's house. He was shouting and struggling. I wondered if the panthers had got him or whether his boat had capsized.

My mother stood up and went to the window. Outside Mr Beale's gate stood a hospital van. Four attendants pushed the raving maniac towards it, while smoke belched from one window of his house. Apparently poor Mr Beale had quenched the forest-fire which had flared within his brain by the well-known trick of lighting another.

As they bundled him into the back of the van, he saw me up at the window.

"Don't forget to give food to Morning and Night," he called.

"I wonder why he shouted to you?" my mother said.

"I don't know," I lied.

Then they slammed the door on him and drove away.

"About time," my mother said. "He ought to have been put away years ago."

My life was fulfilled on my fourth birthday. By which I mean everything that has happened since has been an anticlimax and has failed to match the joy and satisfaction I experienced on that day. My mother had taken me for a holiday to Bishops Hull, a small village outside Taunton. A farm-labourer, who lived in an adjoining cottage and who had lost an arm in the war, offered to take me fishing. I had been fishing before, but only for sharks from the upturned kitchen-table. I had never held a real rod or had my hook dangling in genuine water. Now the prospect alone of this expedition made me so excited that I ran a temperature and did not sleep at all the night before. I even forgot the grey hunter which I had discovered stabled in a pub opposite. The shutter of my mind must have been full open that day, for every detail of the river still remains in sharp focus. My cousin and I followed the man along the river-bank. It was my first river: then he stopped at a deep pool by a weir: it was my first pool; deep, bottomless. Branches of ash reached out so that half was in the shade; the sunlight shone on the other half, and the whole was so still that flies could walk upon the invisible skin of the water.

I watched the fisherman take from his pocket a small tobacco-tin full of worms. Then breathlessly I saw him hold his rod against his body with his iron arm and watched him dexterously fix a worm on the hook with the other. Then he cast his line, and for the next half-hour I sat too excited to speak, my eyes riveted on the scarlet float almost unmoving on the still water. But we caught nothing.

That evening I could not even eat my supper, I was too possessed. My mind was completely filled with the images of fish swimming beneath the water. I felt resentment against them for avoiding being caught. I lay in bed imagining I was a fish to find out how long it would be before hunger made me take the temptation of the hook.

That problem was promptly resolved the next morning by my mother who took me into Taunton to buy me a fishing line and one or two other pieces of necessary equipment. As soon as she got off the bus, I raced her towards the pool: found a worm and cast the float on to the water. Then I closed my eyes and prayed "Dear God, please make the trout hungry. Dear God, please make them like worms, not any worms, but my worm which I've put on that hook, for Thine is the Kingdom for ever and ever, Amen."

I have never prayed so fervently or succinctly. It was not a particularly odd prayer. As a child I always imagined God as a grocer, order-book and pencil in hand, giving me the courtesy due to a customer. I sat willing the fish towards the worm. My whole soul was screwed up into my eyes riveted on the float. I kept this up for half an hour or so, till my mother asked me to go and pick her some cowslips from the meadow behind her. Grudgingly I complied, running back with the flowers.

"Why don't you see now if you've caught a fish," my mother suggested casually; "it seems to me your float's quite low in the water."

"Yes, it is," I cried, hauling in, nearly falling into the water.

I can state, but I cannot express, the pleasure I felt as a great fish broke the water.

"You've never seen a trout as big as that, have you?" I asked my mother confidently.

"Never," she said truthfully.

20

"I shall eat it for supper," I said, "and perhaps I'll give you a bit for buying me the line. But tomorrow you can have all the fish. There's bound to be another tomorrow."

That evening I broke my fast and ate the whole of the fish. There was another fish on my hook the next day. And for every day that week. I never suspected that there was any coincidence in the fact that the fishes took my bait only while I was off picking flowers.

No doubt my mother's subterfuge was justifiable. I never suspected it and was seventeen before she punctured my boast about the trout I used to catch, by telling me they were herrings. But it was too late then. Consequently I have gone through life always sublimely confident that wherever I flung my hook an obliging fish would swallow it. And the incident has had other psychic repercussions.

I was allowed to play in the streets, always insisting on being the Red Indian if there were cowboys, always wanting to be the spy if it was a war-game, spending quite a good deal of my time being tied up, always the rebel.

And what I liked most were the street-vendors. I adored the man who came round with an extraordinary contraption which sharpened knives. I used to count the days to the weekly visit of a stall which was heaped with shrimps and winkles. Then there was the muffin-man on Sunday, with a flat cap and a tray of crumpets and a bell in his hand. There were gipsies with lavender; a butcher with a wheeled cart and a black horse; I loved his striped apron. But best of all was Friday. On Friday a man came down the street crying "Any old iron?" He pushed his barrow which contained a marvellous selection of wonderful shapes and mysterious things. I used to follow him, my eyes goggling at the variety of his treasures. One day, when he had stopped at the kerb to load on some more rubbish, a bird-cage fell off the barrow. He pushed on not noticing this. I waited behind a laurel-bush, fearful that he would turn round, then nabbed my prize. But I did not take the bird-cage home. I carried it to an old junk-shop where I sold it for sixpence. A few days later the owner of the shop sympathised with my mother for the death of her parrot and she thus discovered my

21

transaction. Being a broad-minded woman she congratulated me on my business acumen, and I now had another world; the world of this junk-shop. I am not sure whether three balls hung above it or not. All I do know is that the clutter changed, and sometimes I was able to buy something for my mother for twopence, a door-stop or some other hideous ornament which I would lug home.

This rather wild, ragamuffin background used to be interrupted. Sometimes, without warning, I would be hauled in from an exciting discussion with a gipsy or a vendor of winkles, only to be rushed to a bath and thrust into a black-velvet Lord Fauntleroy suit with champagne-coloured buttoned boots. My hair would be combed and we would sit there waiting for the Rolls-Royce to arrive. My father's brother did not wholly approve of his family's attitude to my mother, and he was quite prepared to make this dangerous expedition to the outpost of Clapham, so long as his mother let him have the car for the afternoon. I resented these occasional visits. Not only did I not understand the intrusions, but they always made my mother cry afterwards. My uncle looked like my father too.

And sometimes a really State occasion would occur. These were the days when my mother was summoned to the family solicitors, Bircham's, whose office is still there now, opposite the Cenotaph in Whitehall. Mr Danby had been detailed to keep an eye on my mother and see that she was not spending her allowance on her relatives, but on her children. I used to be taken into a large boardroom. There were a dozen black deed-boxes in a corner; they bore the names of various members of the Royal Family. I was treated, even by the commissionaire, with respect. They used to try and pretend my mother was my governess. The poor woman was constantly humiliated, especially by servants. She allowed this, or rather had no defence against it, not because she was uneducated, which she was not, or in any way socially inferior (she had been to a good convent), but because she was excessively timid and my father's family were as arrogant as they were stupid. Having driven my parents out of the country they now blamed my mother for my father's death. This did not stop my granny from collecting the money from his life-insurance. I did not know what life-insurance was. I thought it meant she had sold his corpse.

Some of my childhood is so remote that it seems to belong to somebody else: other parts are so immediate that I feel I am still living them. It is strange how much is entirely forgotten. Do we live if we can't remember? What a pity it is that so many memories are still painful. One particularly comes to my mind. Trivial enough, but I have never forgotten it. I suppose that means I have never recovered from it.

I had started to attend a local day-school. One afternoon as I entered the house I detected an atmosphere of intrigue. I ran into the sitting-room for my tea. As usual it was set out on a large table with a white cloth.

"There's a surprise for you today," my mother said, and pointed to an object on the centre of the table. It was a cake, or supposed to be a cake.

"I don't like the look of that," I said with childish frankness. "The icing is dirty and it looks as if it's been dropped on the floor."

"Try some," my mother said, cutting a slice.

"It's horrid." I spat it out.

Then I heard deep and terrible sobs coming from beneath the table. It was my sister's first cake. She had spent all day making it for me and had hidden under the table to hear my appreciation. Her hurt was horrible to see. When I say I never recovered from this incident, I mean that. It has turned me into a vacillating creature, unable at times to speak my mind to anybody I am fond of, if I think that "somehow they have tried."

And as I write this I am reminded of another Chaplinesque memory of a similar kind. An uncle of mine on my mother's side had a bungalow on the river at Hampton Wick. My mother had taken my sister and me and his two children there for a holiday. We were fishing for roach from the punt which was moored at the end of the garden. My mother came out from the bungalow with a tea-tray and set it on the lawn beside us. She was happy having the children alone. It was a holiday for her too. When she had put the tray down and called us from the punt, she turned, walked across the small lawn and up the three steps which led to the verandah of the bungalow. As she mounted the top step, we children saw one of her stockings fall down. We burst out into uncontrolled giggles. She turned to see what we were laughing at, saw it was herself, and noticed her stocking. I suppose she could have laughed too. She didn't. She ran into the bungalow crying. If insensitivity is the only sin, as Wilde said, I don't see how children can be innocent. My mother was always vulnerable; she had a saying which I heard over and over again, "It's the little things that count," and most of her time was spent doing these little things for us, which we either didn't notice or seldom appreciated. She never went out shopping without bringing us back a comic. It was generally last week's comic. And her elder sister, who lived in the house, was so infinitely more competent domestically than she was. It was always "Let me do that for you," even if "that" was dressing my sister or ironing my clothes.

I didn't realise how close and dependent I was on my mother until I was sent to my prep-school at Manor House, Clapham Common. I believe the school was something to do with Lord Macaulay. Perhaps it had been his house? At any rate it was too far for me to go home for lunch. I now learned what homesickness was. And I am learning still. The difference is I now know that it is possible to be homesick without a home. Homesickness was my first critical experience. My father's death did not affect me so much. He always remained an idea. Perhaps a hero, but no more a relative than Robin Hood. But when I first went to this day-school I was stunned with homesickness. I could learn nothing. I could do nothing but count the number of 38 buses which passed by, knowing that fifty-three of them had to pass the school before I could run out and jump on to one. The silver cord had not been severed. There are several kinds of birth. "Were we not weaned till then?"

I suppose one of the reasons why I was particularly homesick at this time was that my mother and I had entered into a conspiracy. Nothing makes us so close as a secret. She used to walk with me to school. It was two miles, and they were never long enough. Every morning for three months as we walked we talked about the same thing. She planned to have an enormous doll's house on a revolving table made for my sister's birthday. My mother and I became joint architects. For weeks we discussed the size of the rooms—whether the back should be hinged; whether it would be a town-house or a country-house. And when she left me at the gate I would run to sit at my desk, drawing some details of the doll's house, occasionally looking up to cross off another 38 bus as it passed. And after we had designed this house and given the plans to a local carpenter, we became wholly absorbed in furnishing it down to the last detail. We would walk miles after school, searching for miniatures and even matching materials, so that tiny curtains could be made to go with the suites of furniture. We could not find any small carpets, and the patterns on the linoleum were too big. I persuaded an uncle who was a draughtsman in the Ministry of Agriculture to design and make a carpet out of cardboard. It is impossible to convey now the sort of excitement I felt when my mother and I managed to find a tiny Dutch dresser and a tea-set which would fit on it. We talked of nothing else and thought of nothing else. No play or poem I have written has ever absorbed me as much as creating that doll's house. Eventually it was delivered. An entire room was set aside for it. We assembled the furniture there. The door was locked. It was to be a surprise for my sister. After she had gone to sleep at night I used to run to this room, and my mother and I would whisper to each other while we tried out various pieces of furniture. We had difficulty in assembling the bathroom equipment. We must have played like this for hours.

When the great day arrived, my sister was given her other presents, among which was a cricket bat, and then she was led upstairs towards the locked door, which I unlocked ceremoniously. No First Night as exciting as this. I opened the back of the doll's house, showed her the dining-room, complete even to a chandelier, and knives and forks set on the table; the bedrooms with silk eiderdowns and tiny pillows stuffed with feathers I had taken from a sparrow I had shot with my air-gun. But my sister wasn't even looking. It meant nothing to her. She picked up her cricket bat and ran into the garden. She never played with the doll's house once. I don't blame her now, but she hurt me then as I had hurt her when she had made the cake. After all it wasn't her doll's house; the toy belonged to my mother and me. The poor woman was having to live in a house full of relatives. This doll's house was her fantasy: the home she would have had if my father had not died. And I, who now stood in his shoes, had to play with the doll's house by myself. This was difficult. It had been collecting things for it that had been so absorbing.

I never knew whether my mother had filled her house with relatives or whether they had just moved in on her. I suspect that she was lonely and, after my father's death, was unwilling to live by herself. Anyhow the result was that my sister and I were brought up in a house full of adults. We did not have one mother but three: and although we had no father, we had uncles enough to help supply that image. And there were my mother's parents too.

I can't remember my granny's face, but vividly recall her black capacious lap. I suppose I couldn't have been very old when she died. I have a dim memory of my sister and me being packed off to stay with cousins and, on returning, my asking where Granny was.

"Gone up to heaven," I was told, and found it impossible to imagine her heavy form ascending anywhere. Nor, if that were true, could I understand why my grandfather dabbed at his eyes with a large red handkerchief when he looked at her empty chair.

"Why don't you go and join her?" I said, to try and cheer him up.

"You see, Granny has passed on," my mother would say.

"Where? You mean she's dead?"

"We all have to die," an aunt said gently.

"Then sitting here is like playing Postman's Knock," I concluded, gaily wondering which of us would be next.

From that moment I saw every postman as Death and worried every day I saw him call. Nothing persecutes or bullies a child so much as his own imagination.

A year or so after this my mother asked me what I wanted for Christmas. I told her a Meccano Set No. 6. I repeated the number—it was a size about three stages ahead of my abilities. But that was what I wanted. Wanted is too weak a word. Needed is nearer. Once my mind fixed on a desire it became an obsessional

26

necessity. As a child my desire for things, a new toy or somebody else's, was so fierce as to frighten people, including myself. Once gratified—and it usually was—the desire would disappear and I would show little interest in the object. This was not an unconscious game on my part, played to test my mother's affection for me. It was I think more sinister than that: a conscious exercise of my will.

My mother always took steps to comply with my latest whim, which, on the surface, didn't look so particularly perverse, and ordered this gigantic Meccano set from a store. But Christmas came and the set didn't arrive. I now found myself trapped between my will and my imagination. For to satisfy my will I had to sit by the window and wait for that figure I visualised as Death. Bravely I waited and watched for every post, but still the parcel didn't arrive. The poor postman began to fear coming to the house to see my face staring out of the window. And as the days passed and the Christmas season receded, my eyes grew fiercer, till Death who was frustrating my desire was, I am told, tempted to spend his week's wages in buying me a Meccano set himself. That would have pleased me. I would have found a sacrifice from Death most appropriate and succulent.

It is odd to recall the moments when we have been entirely possessed by our own capricious desires, and odder still to ponder what strange object has occasioned this identification. All I know is that I have never extended my will for anything as much as I did then for that Meccano set. And I had no interest in Meccano.

Fortunately if you look upon it as a sign of my trust, but unfortunately if you see it as a sign of my arrogance, I never for a moment doubted that my mother had ordered the set from the shop. She was exonerated. The battle was between me and Death. It was waged for three weeks. I became pale and my nights were sleepless as my small mind grappled with this mountain of frustration.

My mother had telephoned the shop. Enquiries were in hand. "They" couldn't understand: the parcel had been dispatched. Eventually they apologised. They were in error. They admitted the Meccano set had in fact been sent to Glasgow by mistake. An identical set was promptly sent over by special delivery. But my

27

distrust of "them" was now fixed. I have never trusted any corporate body, government or committee since. They sent my Meccano set to Glasgow; not even Death himself could be half as careless.

When the infernal thing did arrive—and I note that I am now bored recording that fact, whereas I enjoyed writing the previous paragraphs—the toy was only cursorily examined. I was too exhausted. My uncle took it over and constructed a large crane with innumerable pulleys and a clockwork engine to work the hoist. This my sister and I carried to the top of the house and for a few hours we enjoyed lifting a jug up and down.

This game was growing stale when my grandfather appeared in the garden four floors beneath. He was a kindly man of whom I was immensely fond. He was an engine-driver and used to hurry home every day to his garden or carpentry. He was really a countryman and I used to be fascinated watching the way he fondled his various tools, and how skilful his hands were; the nail he was hitting always went straight home; he could always find his screwdriver; his plane was greased before he put it away; even his spade was sharpened before he dug. And when he planted, he patted the ground with the back of the spade and then firmed the plant with his hands. He was a man who seldom spoke except with his hands. And when they had made this, or painted that, he would wipe them clean on a large red handkerchief. Of all the men I have met I respected him most: he was a simple man who never read and seldom spoke, but there was such understanding for things in his fingers. I used to watch him sharpen his chisel on an oiled stone, honing the blade by the minute, then wiping it on his hand, then casting his eyes down the edge, then back to the stone again. And as I watched the way he handled the tool I realised that his hands showed more fondness for things than other people's hands showed for people. As a man he was like his wood: straight-grained.

This respect for him occasioned my first moment of shame. My sister and I called down to him and asked him to fill our jug with water. Though he was doing something else, he didn't complain. We hoisted the jug to the window-sill. Then it occurred to me that it would be amusing to haul up the small garden-fork he was using. I nipped downstairs and put the hook round the handle when he wasn't looking. He turned round just in time to see his tool disappear over the ledge and came and stood beneath, looking up at us.

"Come, come," he said, which was his usual and only reprimand. Then he bent down to pick up another tool.

The temptation was too much for me. On an impulse I emptied the entire jug of water down on to the poor man's head. He was soaked—and he had filled the jug.

"Come, come," he said taking out his big handkerchief. "You shouldn't have done that."

But perhaps shame isn't the right word. I suppose we are ashamed only when we don't enjoy. It was one of the most pleasurable impulses I ever succumbed to, and my accuracy was especially gratifying from such a height.

This incident brought out the taste for bomb-dropping and sharp-shooting in my sister and me. Our downfall was the coincidence that Derby Day and the season for cherries invariably coincided. Every year we were taken as a treat to the roof of a public house overlooking Clapham High Street, to see the charabancs, coaches, carts, cars and even barrows trailing home full of toffs or pearlies after the great race. It was a festival, free like the Boat Race.

"Throw out your mouldies!" the children used to cry and scramble for pennies thrown by passing punters. But my sister and I were otherwise absorbed. We always came armed with a box of white-heart cherries. With our mouths full of fruit we would get down to the ammunition. Then from behind a window-box we would shoot the stones between our fingers at the passing carriages, or at the crowd on the pavement below. There was no lack of targets or ammunition. We used to keep a strict score: a cherry-stone at a policeman's face ranked as so many points, one at a dowager in an open car so many more. We became deadly accurate over the years and were wholly addicted to this annual sniping. Even now I sometimes succumb to this urge and find it difficult to pass a fruit-shop in June. Nobody who has ever owned a pea-shooter ever really recovers from the vice. Satire sometimes misses the target, but a well-aimed split-pea or lentil seldom. My mouth almost waters now as I think too of the pleasures I have derived from water-pistols—and not such a long time ago either. I could never vote for complete disarmament. Indeed I have often thought that if we all carried water-pistols to shoot straight into the face of the offending bureaucrat, tiresome waiter, or moronic theatrical producer, we should all be less belligerent beneath the skin.

One of my most secret ambitions as a child was to get my hands on a siphon of soda and press the lever firmly while I squirted it at one of the dozen fatuous faces I could think of. But my childhood went by, wasted by restraint. It was not until I was forty that the desire became stronger than my self-control. But that's another story. . . . How is it, I wonder, that people can handle these siphons every day of their lives, and not go gay with them, merely squirting the contents impotently into tumblers of whiskey, where it makes only a mild splash. What a tame timid lot we are that such a delicious invention can be on the market, and even in our hands, and nobody avail themselves of it. How is it that the smoke-rooms of clubs are not splashed by streams of soda? Have we not bores enough or sufficient courage?

And then there was my mother's elder sister, Arv. I don't know why I called her that when her name was Kate, but it stuck. I did the same for my mother whom I called Mole; and my sister, too, whom I nicknamed Bunny, though she'd been christened Bianca.

Arv fascinated me. She was a woman who lived for crime and never committed one. She was an Elizabethan; the sort of person for whom *The Revenger's Tragedy* was written. But instead of Kyd or Tourneur she had the reports of the Old Bailey trials, which she read out loud from the columns of the *People* or the *News of the World*. Licking her lips over the horrific details, she would occasionally put her paper down and say softly with infinite satisfaction like a caress: "The bugger!" or "The swine!" or "If I had my way I'd have him horse-whipped!" Then she would continue her Sabbath-reading in vain for something to shock her beyond credulity. It would be true to say that I was brought up on these murders, and that in a way Dr Crippen was one of my godfathers, and Marshall Hall another. Strangulation, rape, poisoning and the details of autopsies were imbibed by me before I was six. I knew that those poisoned by arsenic had traces of it in their hair which analysis revealed fifty years after death. I knew what precisely Jack the Ripper had done to his victims. No wonder I was a little bored when my mother tried to interest me in Grimms' *Fairy Tales* or *Alice in Wonderland*. I cannot recall any time in my childhood when the details of some current murder-trial were not the principal topic of conversation around me. Perhaps that is the reason why *The Ballad of Reading Gaol* meant so much to me when I read it in my teens. It is true, too, that when I read Poe for the first time in my twenties the *Tales* aroused a nostalgia in me for "the ceremony of innocence" of my nursery. But though Arv lived in this daydream of the hempen rope and the six-foot drop she was a kindly and sentimental woman. She would weep for every passing hearse, and celebrate with another Guinness every couple who got married in the church up the road. She was infinitely indulgent to me as a child and doubtless saw that I had a great future before me—in the dock.

It would hardly be accurate to say that this aunt had an appetite for gossip; what she did have was a compulsion to slander. While I was still playing on the floor I had one ear cocked listening to her reflections on her friends, relatives and neighbours. If she had nobody to talk to, then her ironing-board would be the recipient of this charitable soliloquy. "It's my suspicion that all the time he's leading a double life. I'd like to bet he's got another family tucked away somewhere." Then she would put her hand in a basin of water, flick the dry clothes, spit on the back of the iron, making the spit bounce on its hot surface, and continue. "Anybody can see she's not *his* daughter. Can't fool me. She's got eyes like her uncle's. The Pharaohs were like that too, they say." From my toy train I would look up and conclude that no woman had her husband's child; that all men were bigamists; and that a happy marriage was probably incestuous. I would then turn back to my train and deliberately lay my sister's doll on the track and run my Hornby into its china face to prove that I was a man. My aunt would beam down on me, and when I was particularly naughty and had dragged out my sister's hair by the roots, she would reward me by soaking a knob of sugar in gin and plopping it into my tea. Perhaps then I would doze a little, cuddling my teddy bear, indifferent to whether she saw any sinister seeds in the embrace. And on she would go with her meditations. She knew every Duchess by her christian name, and her knowledge of the Royal Family extended to their bathrooms. Nobody took her in; she was a kind of searchlight, and everywhere she focused succulent sin was illumined. Yet though I never heard her say a good word about anyone, I never saw her do anything unkind. She said the worst, did the best. What impressed me about her character was its inconsistency, its ambivalence. I remembered Arv when I came to write plays and people tried to tell me that characters should be consistent.

Her husband, Frank, was her one blind spot; she was fortunate in this. In her eyes he could do no wrong. He was a fairly innocuous individual who worked in the Ministry of Agriculture, and consequently a sedentary life caused his blue serge suits to shine. He liked to look well. This gave Arv her life's work. Most of her time was spent sponging his suits with vinegar, ironing them and polishing his shoes. He invariably wore a buttonhole and carried a cane. He was devoted to two hobbies: beer and crosswords. He would drink a gallon or two every evening, which made him sway on the stairs going past my room. But whatever his condition the previous night, he invariably did both *The Times* and the *Morning Post* crosswords before breakfast.

Their daughter, Margory, was about five years older than I and consequently acted as an elder sister to me. She was an amenable person, who behaved too well towards people to leave any impression on them other than gratitude.

My only association with Margory is something which may have nothing to do with her. But whether or not my memory is accurate, I know the experience was one of my most formative, or rather destructive. She and I had been taken to Bournemouth for a summer holiday. The adults, and I can't recall who they were, were sitting in deck-chairs on the beach. The sands were crowded. I had wandered off and suddenly realised I had lost my bearings. I remembered that the deck-chairs were near a pier. I started to run towards it and then realised there were two piers separated by about a mile. I was lost. I ran from one pier to the other, but couldn't find the deck-chairs. I was lost. There were thousands of people on the beach, all in deck-chairs, all anonymous, indifferent to the crying child who ran by, staring hopelessly into their faces. I remember, so vividly that my stomach turns as I write this, that it occurred to me then that I might be lost for ever, that I might never find the deck-chairs, never see my mother again, but run for ever—as I put it twenty years later in *The Rape of Lucretia*, "like a lost child with tireless feet." I don't think I have ever felt secure since that day. If I go away I am always looking over my shoulder, trying to secure my base, making certain the deck-chairs are still there. As it was, I ended in the Police Station. "Somebody will come for you, sonny," the Bobby assured me. I still don't believe him.

One way of describing a person is to say who they loved, or rather who their gods were. As a child I had two heroes; Napoleon and Steve Donoghue. These two figures had something in common: horses. I didn't see this connection at the time, but a large portrait of Napoleon mounted on his white charger was always above my bed. I think I picked it up at the junk-shop. And as soon as I could read I devoured Steve Donoghue's auto-biography *Just My Story*. I now see for the first time that both these heroes had another attribute in common to which I could relate myself; they were small. As soon as I went to my prep-school I was made acutely conscious of my size, by the boys mercilessly, the masters patronisingly. I remember saving up five shillings to send to the "How to Grow Taller Bureau." Their exercises did no good. I could see I had no future except to be either a dictator or a jockey. Mounted, a man has a different height. Perhaps this is why I have always been so found of horses.

The idea that children are not sexually aware until puberty must be incorrect. I don't believe I was abnormal or precocious in this respect. I could have been no more than four when curiosity about the opposite sex and even attraction to them became unrelentingly important to me. What a pity it is that the first budding of life should be bent back upon us, soiled with secrecy, bruised with guilt, made dirty with innuendo. I feel angry about this now, as though society had made me hobble to adolescence with one foot in a rabbit-trap. We worry about the malnutrition of the Chinese and the so-called backward races, but, as I observed later, Bantu brats are not lamed as we are lamed.

Like any small boy I asked the question. It is *the* question. If a child is not interested to know how he arrived on earth, he must be half-baked, unconscious and probably not fit to live at all. I didn't want to play with bricks. I wanted to know how I was born and where I had been before. I was told not to ask questions. The silly adults looked at each other. Their conspiracy didn't take me in. Nor did their ridiculous stories about gooseberry-bushes. I caught my aunt out on this by discovering from my uncle that gooseberries didn't grow in Africa. They all looked so shifty, as though I had been stolen from a store and they were ashamed of shoplifting. It was no use schoolmarms trying to interest me in elementary geography or mathematics while *the* mystery remained, not only unsolved, but unmentioned. I could see where I was going. I had learned that. I was going to die like my father, like the sparrow, like the fly and all the graves I passed every morning in the churchyard when I went to school. But to know where you were going and not to know where you had come from made the mystery only more acute. I did not connect my curiosity about the opposite sex or my attraction to them with this mystery. Instinct is the only means to knowledge when education forgets its derivation and leads us out of nowhere to facts that aren't worth knowing. Curse and blast our educational system which can leave a healthy, sane question unanswered and thwart a child's mind. I even became guilty about my curiosity. I was able to do quadratic equations and name the exports of Malaya years before I discovered the facts of life. I eventually discovered these by knitting several dirty stories together. I still cannot forgive a society that can make *the* miracle obscene.

Naturally I wasn't the only child of that era to be stuffed with statistics and deprived of mental sustenance. A friend of mine complained to me of the same thing. He was fourteen and just going away to school. His father, an Exeter lawyer, took him out for a walk, ostensibly to have a heart-to-heart talk with his son before he went away to school. My friend felt the importance of the occasion; the mystery was going to be revealed to him. They

34

walked a couple of miles in silence, then they came to a village green. His father stopped and stood looking at a pond.

"You see those ducks," he said, "well . . . people do it too."

They walked home in silence.

I was five. She was a year older and it was her sixth birthday. There was a party. We were playing hide and seek. In the cupboard I succeeded in removing her clothes. It was lucky we were not discovered. This girl became a famous musical-comedy actress. I used to attend her first nights. I always thought of the cupboard. I wonder if she did.

This incident gave me no sense of guilt, but the next distressed me for years. I suppose I was about seven when a boy who lived a few doors away and was about four years my senior started taking a sexual interest in me. It was always behind locked doors, in the lavatory. I knew this was wrong; the locked door told me so. This incident, which amounted to no more than revealing oneself, gave me an acute sense of shame which I carried as an invisible burden for over a year. I realised that the only way I could alleviate it was by telling somebody. Eventually, after months of worry and sleepless nights, I plucked up the courage to tell my mother. I went round and round before coming to the point, then suddenly I blurted out:

"Dennis makes me take my trousers off."

"Then don't let him," my mother said, very casually, as though the matter was of no importance. The let-down was like an earthquake to me. I had received no assurance. After this I knew I had to carry things myself. It wasn't that my mother was insensitive or unkind, but that she couldn't face a problem. She would turn away from any unpleasant sight.

I was six years old when I first saw the sea and the countryside. My mother took my sister and me for a holiday to Welcombe on the north Devon coast. I fell in love with the place immediately. I decided that was where I wanted to live. I had to wait another twelve years, but I have lived there ever since.

My first love-affair occurred there, though I didn't know it was that. She was a girl with three brothers much older than herself, staying at the farm where we were. She was called Rosemary Moon. Her father was a doctor in Croydon. Nothing happened except that I found that I would rather play with her than be with my mother or sister, and she would abandon her family to come up the stream with me. We did the same thing every day. The stream ran past the farmhouse, having emerged from a sort of tunnel in the hill. Our pleasure was to walk barefoot up the stream, our feet on the flat stones, turning them over to see if we could find any creatures underneath. Sometimes we found a small eel. I would shriek louder than she did. She was a tomboy. Both families started to tease us because we played together. She was my first companion apart from my mother. Then a sad thing happened, infinitely trivial, but it affected me for years. The holiday ended and I found very much to my surprise that I missed this girl acutely. One day a letter arrived for me. It was printed and I remember there was a drawing of an eel and the stream in one corner and it was covered with crosses at the bottom. She had missed me too. I put the letter in my pocket and took it out half-a-dozen times to read during the day. Then my mother and sister caught me doing this and started to tease me. I couldn't bear that. I ran to the lavatory, read the letter for a final time, tore it up and pulled the chain. As it flushed I felt I had thrown away something that I would not find again. I felt deeply ashamed of what I had done. It was an act of cowardice, an act of betrayal. There have been many, so many.

Of course I recovered, or, more accurately, thought I had recovered. We went to Welcombe again for a holiday the next year. My mother suggested that we should have a picnic on my beach for my birthday. This year there was a party of half-a-dozen girls who worked in a London bank staying at the farm. They used to go for walks together, singing "Old King Cole was a Merry Old Soul." I adored the song and insisted that all the girls should come to my party on the beach. I was very angry that some other people had used up most of the driftwood to light a bonfire. It was important that a kettle should boil. As I write this I see this incident started another compulsion. However, we found enough wood eventually, the girls came, and the tea-party was a great success. I announced that I wanted them all to visit me in London.

They promised to do so, and two or three weeks later they all arrived, each with a small present for me. I recall that I insisted on receiving these half-dozen girls in the bath. They sat around. I bathed. Somebody called me a pasha thirty years later.

Like many children I suffered from an acute compulsive neurosis. If only I had known the explanation then, but I didn't. For three or four years I suffered from a compulsion which was not only inconvenient but worried me because I could see that it was abnormal. It first developed when I was homesick at school in Yorkshire and writing a letter to my mother. When I had written the letter and sealed it up I had the urge to open the envelope and re-write it because my hands might have contaminated the paper. I was compelled to wash my hands and re-write the letter. Having done this and posted it, I then felt that I had to get the letter out of the box because the envelope might be contaminated. This compulsive pattern repeated itself. I would worry the school porter scores of times to open the box, so that I could take out a letter, re-write it not once, but sometimes several times. I would go and wash my hands, dry them with a towel and then, on leaving the wash-room, feel that the towel itself was contaminated. I would re-wash them and dry them on a clean handkerchief. This could repeat itself half a dozen times. My hands became sore. Anything I touched could be contaminated. If I resisted the compulsion, then something terrible would happen to my mother. This fear made me walk on the lines of the paving-stones, count telegraph-posts forwards then backwards, say my prayers at night in a peculiar way and, having said them, repeat them, just to propitiate the god who held the guillotine above her head. This morbid obsession stayed with me for several years. I think I must have been sixteen or seventeen when I succeeded in overcoming it. This I did by one day finding myself walking behind a woman who held a small child by the hand. The child dropped some toy into the gutter and went to pick it up; the mother slapped the child's hand because the object was dirty and she wanted him to leave it there. Immediately I remembered an incident in my own life.

When I was about four or five and going to my first school, my mother had given me a sailor's coat with brass buttons. She had told me that I was not to let the other boys tear the buttons off in the playground, and if I lost one I was to bring it back and she would sew it on again. I left for school imagining that the brass buttons were gold, and that I must not lose them. Two or three days later I went to the school lavatory, or should I be more accurate and describe it as a cesspit with a seat round it? As I was leaving I noticed to my horror that one of my buttons was missing. I looked for it and eventually saw the button lying in the lavatory-pan. It was not a clean lavatory-pan. I stood in terror, frightened by two alternatives; either going home without the button, or putting my hand into the filth. Eventually I did the latter. I must have washed my hands ten dozen times after this. But once having remembered the incident, by the accident of seeing it repeated, I forgot the whole problem.

From a very early age I became first frightened, then fascinated and ultimately embarrassed, by my own dreams. Up to the age of about ten I used to tell them to my mother: later I found it necessary to impose a censor: and as there was nobody to whom I could tell my dreams, I began to write them down. I bought a large notebook, inscribed it *Dream Diary*, and drew an eye asleep on the cover. This was the only diary I ever kept. The nocturnal adventures and journeys I recorded made travel-books dull by comparison. Even when I picked up *Gulliver's Travels* its fantasy seemed mild besides my own imagination. Later I found the same deficiency in Boccaccio too. So, instead of reading, I took to daydreaming. I would go off in a corner to indulge in this, but whereas my sister always carried a book, I enjoyed the pages and pictures of my own mind. Daydreaming was easy: like any child I had points of departure, such as, what would happen if I was the only man in the world (this dream came I suppose with puberty); how I would explore and farm the bottom of the Atlantic if I could bore a hole in the sea-bed to drain the ocean into the centre of the earth; what I would do if I were invisible, and so on. From any one of these jumping-off-places my mind would wander off for an hour. I don't suppose there is anything unusual in this. All children do it: artists keep it up, that's all. But my dream-diary interested me, not only as an escape, but because I wanted to know why I dreamed what I dreamed. I didn't know of the words conscious and unconscious, but I saw that I was, as I put it, two people: the me-awake and the me-asleep. I could see that they had almost separate identities, and that dreams were the language in which they tried to communicate.

I realised that the me-asleep would sometimes try to give the me-awake a dream to please. I didn't know the word compensation. But I now tried experiments to invert this procedure by seeing if I could do something deliberately during the day which would cause a dream. I found this easy: all I had to do to dream of water was to go to bed thirsty; the smell of leather by my bed made me dream invariably of horses. By the age of sixteen I had worked out a theory about dreams and was beginning to understand their language. I saw that this realm might absorb me for the rest of my life.

Then one day when I was about seventeen I picked up a book of Freud's. I read it in one sitting. My life's work had been anticipated. I was intensely disappointed that all my "original" work had been worked over, and the precious theories that I had hammered out were already in textbooks. I think this was the worst disappointment I ever experienced. It affected me deeply. For a year or two I feared that I might read in an anthology the poem that was still only half-formed in my mind.

Though my mother wanted me to go to Winchester, my father's family would not allow this. They insisted that I should go to the same school that he had been to, chiefly because the family solicitor was a governor of the school. So I was sent to a watering-place on the east coast of Yorkshire. It is one of those places which had an ancient foundation as a grammar school, but had been entirely rebuilt at the beginning of the century and now had aspirations to be regarded as a public school. The buildings were far too spacious to take anybody in. The classrooms and studies were airy, quite unlike the grubby burrows of Eton or the tatty warrens of Harrow. And the grounds were not at the other end of the town, but surrounding the imposing building.

One of the advantages of going away to school is that afterwards nothing in life can really be as unpleasant. You can be out of work, you can go bankrupt, you can go to prison, but always at the back of your mind you can console yourself with the thought that you are no longer at school. At any rate that's how it is to me. Perhaps there was nothing wrong with the place, and the trouble was all in me. That may well be so, since other boys seem to enjoy themselves there, and even attend Old Boy Associations and totter along to club-dinners wearing an old school tie beneath their grey hair. But I would as soon go back to an annual dinner at Wormwood Scrubs. I must admit I have often indulged in the fantasy of returning: in this dream I ride a bulldozer and hurl hand-grenades like confetti. To me this imposing pile, with its Latin motto, was a monument of unhappiness. Everything I learned there I had to try and unlearn.

But in fairness I can see that whatever the place had been like I would not have been happy there. To begin with, I was too homesick, and after the pain of that emotion had become deadened by habit, the only solid thing in my consciousness was the determination to undermine every aspect of authority and be the unrepentant rebel. I feel such hatred for this school even now that I find myself becoming almost inarticulate. But I must try to be objective.

The dormitories were light and airy. I daresay the school prospectus still shows a favourable photograph of them. I wonder if it shows the traditional initiation ceremony for the new boy. He had to go and kneel at every bed in the dormitory while the occupant placed a chamber-pot on his head, and finally, after enduring this humiliation half-a-dozen times, the last boy smashed the chamber pot on his head with a slipper. No, I don't think the generals and others who come back as Old Boys to give the prizes refer to that. Nor will they refer to another little tradition which was perpetrated against anybody who did not fit in. The victim was taken before a roaring fire. Boys held his arms and legs, his stockings were taken down until his calves were burned. I remember this happening to one boy—I believe he is in the House of Commons now. I wonder if the scars still show. If not on the leg they must be somewhere. This is supposed to toughen you up. It does. You become increasingly insensitive. I often thought of running away and would have done if I hadn't realised that doing so would worry my mother. And 230 miles is a long way to run. When I told her or anybody that I was not happy there they always replied that I would "settle down." I suppose that is what a judge could say when he sentenced you to fifteen years' hard labour. I felt I was enduring something like that. The difference was that I didn't know what crime I had committed that society or life should punish me so.

The first day of every term the entire school was assembled in hall. A few appropriate hymns were sung, whereupon the headmaster used to mount the hideous brass lectern and read a lesson, after which he stepped down and welcomed us back to a new term. After the usual string of platitudes punctuated with clichés, he would say—"And there is one other matter which I like to mention." Whereupon he held out his hand.

"If you do it," he would say—and we all knew what he meant— "your children will suffer. You will not have proper children."

Then he would put his hand in his pocket, re-arrange himself and strut from the hall. This piece of enlightened dogma was enough to persecute, bend and pervert the minds of all but those of us who were lucky enough to have some relationship with one of the school maids. And there were over four hundred boys and only ten maids. And they, bless them, had been chosen because they were either cross-eyed, fat, or moustached.

This school was, I daresay, no worse than any other. Of course the backward races and the heathen go in for child-marriages or such tribal obscenities as pregnant women being expected to initiate boys at puberty. I am not a sociologist, but clearly our educationalists are funking all issues unless they face this one. My own assessment is that eighty per cent of a child's intelligence is diverted and wasted by the worry of what to do with its own vitality. What we are living in now is a society founded on masturbation. And not only at adolescence; most of our literature is veiled emotional masturbation. A lot of our music is no better.

This feeling of resentment against society had the obvious repercussions on me. I had to get my own back somehow. I didn't co-operate with the masters. I read novels under the desk, cribbed my homework and spent the major part of my time hiding cigarettes and finding places to smoke. We were allowed out into the town twice a week and I would pedal down the hill where, from resentment at society, I would go from shop to shop stealing whatever I could when the shopkeeper was not looking. I must have become incredibly adept at this. I was never caught. Yet I remember lifting bottles of Yardley's scent from Boots in the market square and would snaffle razors before I could shave, face-cream, or anything that was on the counter before me. There was a sweet-shop at the bottom of the drive kept by a dear, dingy old woman, and my compulsion to steal, to commit the crime for which I had, as it were, already been punished, continued, even with her. I would lift slabs of chocolate, gob-stoppers and anything I could stuff into my pockets. Neither the town nor the school authorities ever suspected me. Indeed I was eventually appointed to serve in the school tuck-shop during the break. This was a position of enormous trust. The trust did not impress me: I availed myself of the opportunity. I now not only stole chocolate for myself, but failed to put a lot of the money into the till. This also went undetected. I think that the only reason I gave up thieving was that I found it so easy I became bored with it. Certainly I never experienced any moral scruple about it.

During one of the holidays the French master took a group of boys to Paris for a fortnight. We stayed in the Boulevard Haussmann. I was fourteen. We were marched off to the Louvre or the Luxembourg. But we had other interests. I met a very pretty manicurist in the Rue d'Hauteville. Odd that I can remember the name of the street. I followed her. To my disappointment she gave me a manicure.

My friend at school was a boy called Mortimer. It is strange but I cannot remember his first name. His father was a maltster and drove a racing Bugatti. The boy had a malformed leg and wore an iron clamped into his boot. Naturally the boys nicknamed him "Boots."

And about this time I had had the very considerable misfortune for a schoolboy of having Prince Victor of Cooch-Behar come up to school to see me. He had known my mother before she had married. He had lived with my aunt (the one on the stage) for years, then gone to India because the State would not allow him to marry an English girl. He had married, had two children, divorced his wife, and returned to set up house again with my aunt after she had been deserted by her husband. Uncle Viccy now became the father I had never had. In the holidays we were inseparable, going to Lord's or the Oval to watch Duleepsinjhi or Hobbs, and sometimes he would take me out of an evening, feast me on oysters and take me to a musical comedy. I was enormously fond of him and he used to come all the way up to Yorkshire just to give me a "blow-out" at an hotel for a couple of days. But I paid dearly for having a prince visiting me and lavishing presents on me at school. I was nicknamed "Lord Limehouse" and it seemed as if the entire school now had a purpose in persecuting me and "my faithful servant 'Boots.'"

To get away from the other boys I used to go to a field where there was a small stream. In Yorkshire they are called becks. It was a dirty little beck, filled with tins and refuse, but there was something here I needed, and I used to walk up and down it until the bell rang again. I suppose I may have been looking for the happiness I had found in another stream, but I didn't realise that until three seconds ago. I had to communicate my loneliness somehow, and so I started to write. I didn't think that anything I was writing was poetry, because the only poetry I had read was the impossibly dreary Milton in the form-room and the historical plays of Shakespeare, a few ballads, and the sonnets of Wordsworth. What I was writing was nothing like that, so it was not poetry. As soon as I had written it I used to make a paper boat of it and send it down the beck, watching it go under the bridge where the buses went. It was now that I became acutely conscious of being different: not only because the boys had isolated me. I was aware of things which I couldn't quite express, and I would often find I was crying though I didn't know why.

At the top of the field there was a small plantation of fir-trees which had been planted as a protection for some of the form-rooms from the east wind. I used to go there because I found the smell of the fir-cones fascinating. One day I saw a dead sparrow lying on the pine-needles. It was still warm. The death of this bird released something in me that I could not, still cannot, control. I think I cried over the little thing for half an hour and then,

43

oblivious of the school-bell, dug a grave with my hands and getting out my notebook wrote what I suppose was a dirge or a hymn or a black mass, which I buried with the bird and then covered with the pine-needles. Then I went back to be punished for being late for my Latin grammar. I hadn't the remotest idea what this incident meant to me or why it moved me. Even telling the story now has cost me more than anything I have written for years. It cannot be that I was less cruel than other boys, because I can remember that I owned an air-gun and would take enormous pleasure in shooting a sparrow, and had once done so to get the feathers for a pillow for my sister's doll's house. Could it be that I was ashamed of shooting that sparrow and therefore grieved for the next one? I don't know. It sounds an explanation, but what is the use of explanations when they do nothing to remove the emotion? We are all children, crippled children, and if there is any purpose in my writing about my childhood, perhaps it is to show some of the places where we become crippled.

I was about twelve years old when I met the influence in my life that has affected me more than anything else. I went to a theatre and heard Schubert. I had heard practically no music before this except for *Pagliacci*, and I have heard nothing since to equal it. The play was a sentimental musical comedy, supposedly based on Schubert's life, called *Lilac Time*. It contained a number of his songs. I was quite unable to keep away from the theatre. I went to it twenty-seven times. In the theatre I could not keep off the stage, and as soon as the curtain was down would run round backstage to meet the singer and persuade him to take me into his dressing-room and sing some of the songs again. My ambition at this time was to play Schubert, but I didn't know a note, and the only thing I could do was to persuade an aunt of mine to mark out the notes on the piano in numerical order, so that I could hammer out the melodies by following the numbers she had given me on a page. I used to sit for hours by myself playing these melodies over in this way. I cannot possibly explain why I found Schubert an irresistible influence at the age of twelve, or why he has always remained my favourite composer. Any attack on Schubert still produces fury in me.

My interest in Schubert and in him alone—at that time all
other composers bored me—made me start to take piano-lessons.
The idea that I would soon be able to play Schubert sent me back
to school one term even looking forward to it. The music-master
gave me one lesson a week during which he smoked a pipe and
read a detective novel. I used to amuse myself by playing the
wrong notes and even the wrong piece to see if he would look
up from his thriller, but he never did. Discouraged I gave up the
lessons.

I rose through the school, not through ability or character, as
you can see, but merely because of seniority. I was made a prefect.
This meant I had a dormitory with eight small boys to superin-
tend. One night I woke up to hear one of the boys, who was about
thirteen, crying. He was not a new boy, so I didn't dismiss it as
homesickness, nor was he the sort who got bullied; he was rather
the type that did the bullying. I got out of bed and asked him
what he was blubbing about? He said he couldn't tell me. I got
back into bed and forgot the matter, but it recurred a few days
later. This time I took the boy out into the corridor, to avoid
the sleepy eavesdroppers, and eventually he told me that he was
miserable because he did not like what the housemaster was
making him do every other day. I assumed that this was some
kind of chore, such as carrying in his coalbucket, and turned to
go back into the dormitory. But the boy's tears made me turn
back again.
"What precisely does he make you do?" I asked.
The boy broke down.
"He came up to our dormitory one evening before you had come
to bed, about a month ago, and gave us all a lecture about masturbation. He asked if we did, and when we denied it he said he
wanted to see me in his study next day to prove that I was not indulging in the habit. When I went there he made me take out my
penis and measured it with a ruler. He has done this every other
day."
"To other boys too?" I asked. He nodded.
It was too late to go to the headmaster, but I went to see him
the next day and told him that I wanted to report the housemaster

for assault. The headmaster, knowing I did not like the house-master, refused to believe me. Four boys corroborated the story.

The next term there was a new housemaster and I, who knew why he had left, was a danger, I suppose, to this "sound in mind and body" institution. That holiday my mother received a letter from the headmaster saying that my "Mayfair manner" was a bad influence in the school and, though I was not being expelled, it would be expedient if I were removed. I was delighted. I never returned.

After being asked to leave school, I spent several months in London. At this time I saw a great deal of a boy who had been at the same penitentiary. He was called Dyer and had run away from his home in York, where his father was an architect, to become a writer in London. For doing this his parents had cut him off. Uncle Viccy sympathised with him, bought him a typewriter, and helped subsidise him. At school he had been called "Dippy" because he suffered from some nervous ailment which caused him to turn completely round every ten paces. It was as if some clot went across his brain, forcing him to make this turn. However, his interest in becoming a writer introduced me to some of the authors that had not been set books at school. We used to meet in Lyons Corner House in the Strand and he would pass me poets of whom I had never heard. One day when I was about sixteen he showed me a Latin poem by Ovid—"Written in exile." It was a poem about homesickness. I remember looking at the Latin and without any effort whatever wrote a translation of the poem on the menu before me. My friend was impressed. I had unconsciously reproduced both the metre and the form. He got the poem typed out and submitted it: I think this was the only thing he ever got published.

We know what has happened to most of our friends, even though we no longer see them, but I have never discovered what happened to Dyer.

At this time I became ill with anaemia and bronchitis. I en-joyed this illness immensely. Not only did I have my mother to look after me, but it was a holiday to which there was no end, no term beginning the Saturday after next. And I now found a girl-friend who was about two years my senior. She was a secretary and used to look in on her way back from work and sit and play cards or gossip. She did this every evening and when I was a little better and able to go out she suggested one evening that I should go round to her house and spend the night with her.

"I will leave the window at the side of the house open," she said.

I was very attracted to her and hated her for what I thought was a tease. I didn't go; I didn't think she meant it. I was surprised that she didn't come round the next day or the next week. In fact I didn't see her again for five years, and when I did I asked her why she had stopped seeing me.

"I left the window open," she said, "and I sat up all night wait-ing for you."

"I thought it was a tease."

"What sort of a bitch do you think I am?"

This was a pity. It would have been a great help to me at that stage.

On my seventeenth birthday I was summoned by my trustees. Some future had to be found for me. I was far too young to go to the university. I had been sent away from school. I had failed to matriculate. They decided that the best thing was to send me to a school on the Continent. The way they said "on the Continent" sounded as though it was consigning me to purgatory. "There are plenty of good schools in Switzerland," they told my mother. "He and his sister had better go over there. Their grandmother won't raise any objection to the expense." I was now being treated as a very special person and I learned that my great-grand-father had left a large sum to be divided equally between my sister and me, and also that my grandfather had left us three-quarters of a million pounds. I gathered too that there was a protracted and costly lawsuit pending about the latter inheri-tance, but whatever the outcome I was being groomed for a life of leisure. It was suggested that, as I was showing no particular aptitude, I might take up breeding shorthorns, or perhaps even-tually acquire an orange-plantation in South Africa. But it was

47

made abundantly clear to me that I would never have to earn my living. This fact made no impression on me—just as well.

But before I left the solicitor's office I was to receive a shock, the memory of which has remained indelible. My trustee handed me an envelope which contained a letter. I opened it and started to read.

"I don't remember writing this," I said, recognising my own handwriting.

"You didn't write it," I was told; "it was written by your father with instructions that it was to be given to you on your seventeenth birthday."

It was not the contents of the letter that disturbed me. What was so alarming was that my handwriting was almost identical to his; though I had not seen his hand, here was proof that I was, as it were, a living extension of him. I never felt free after that. Always afraid that inherited traits would become manifest in me. The fear was not unfounded.

My mother took my sister and me to St Gallen, near the Boden-see. I was enlisted in Dr Schmidt's Institute which was an international college with boys from more than a dozen countries. My sister was sent to another school at Teufen, about ten miles away. Both schools were enlightened by comparison with the places where we had been imprisoned for the previous five years. The lessons were in German and we worked only during the morning. In the afternoon I used to ride, and during the evening we would go with a master from beer-cellar to beer-cellar, drinking the May brew. But even so I was unhappy. The lack of discipline, the occasional dance, to which my sister's school was invited, did nothing to relieve my homesickness; and it was with considerable relief that my sister and I learned that, owing to the financial crisis in England and our abandoning the Gold Standard, our trustees no longer considered it patriotic for us to be spending money in a foreign currency. We were therefore withdrawn.

My sister was despatched to the St James's School of Domestic Science to learn cookery, not serious cookery but decorations on cakes. For a few weeks I ate all her homework, doing my best to adjust the balance of that original cake.

But my trustees found me a greater problem. I was still too young for the university, only just seventeen. It was my mother who had the idea.

"Why don't you go round Africa?" she said one day. "It would broaden your outlook and the sun would do you good."

The trustees readily agreed. I was given £100 and told not to get up to too much mischief. I boarded the S.S. *Umtali*. It was a slow cargo-boat with a dozen passengers which was to take five weeks from Tilbury to Cape Town. But as the boat left the quay I found myself relapsing into homesickness again. I suppose my going off like this was an unconscious challenge to this predominant emotion. I would either break it or it would break me.

My fellow-passengers were adults, but I was neither boy nor man. This left me very much alone. I started to take up Latin again, knowing I would have to pass my "Little-go" to get to Cambridge. I can remember very little of the journey except that it seemed interminable; that I hated the sea because there was so much of it; that I detested losing the sight of land and longed to reach the Canary Islands.

At Teneriffe I rushed ashore, grateful for the earth. At that moment all earth was home to me. The sea is so damnably indifferent. I have never understood how anybody can love the sea. It hates men, that is quite clear. I went up the hill to the Cathedral of Santa Cruz, experiencing a kind of religious ecstasy, grateful to be away from the S.S. *Umtali*. Going into the church I saw the priest descending from the pulpit. I don't know what it was that made me go up there, but I remember being surprised to find it full of Guinness-bottles.

I don't know whether this broadened my mind. The rest of the voyage I spent sleeping on the deck, for two reasons. First, the man who shared my cabin now suffered from an outbreak of boils which revolted me, and secondly I found that lying beneath the Southern Cross made me feel nearer home. The reason for this was apparent to me. My mother had a brooch which my father had given her in the shape of the Southern Cross, with sapphires for each of the five stars. This symbol was of enormous significance to me. At this time I prayed to these stars.

I can recall nothing at all of landing in Africa; Cape Town left no impression on me; I was entirely self-absorbed. In a way the journey was proving a waste of time, as so many journeys have been since. I was only seventeen. I had discovered that you cannot go anywhere but to yourself and with yourself, that the destination is as bad as the company.

I took the boat on as far as Durban and then went inland to stay with some remote cousins at Johannesburg.

It was a bizarre continental household; a bit of Vienna or Salzburg transposed to a suburb on the Rand. It consisted of my cousin, old enough for me to call him Uncle, a cosmopolitan resentful at ending as a Colonial; his vacuous wife and her mother who never allowed you to forget that she was a Russian Princess or liked you to remember that she was a septuagenarian dipsomaniac. Her sole topic of conversation was the relative merits of singers she had heard in *Don Giovanni*, and she hadn't heard the opera for thirty years. Besides this trio from Central Europe, there were my cousin's two children; Fay a girl of my age and her brother Ross, a year or so older. They had been born and bred in Jo'burg, and even their parents despised them for it.

My first evening in this house is one of my most shameful memories. Soon after I had arrived my aunt informed me that a large dinner-party was to be held in honour of my arrival. My uncle invited me to sit and play a game of chess with him on the stoep. It was hot: I was thirsty; concentrating on the game, I failed to notice how often my relative filled my glass with whiskey. But as soon as I relaxed after he had checkmated me, I realised I was drunk. Even so, I had no idea how drunk until the Zulu servant came out and told me he had drawn my bath and I tried to get up to go and change for dinner. Perhaps it was the sun, perhaps it was half a bottle of whiskey: I was barely able to stand. The servant, Jan, carried me off and dunked me unceremoniously in a cold bath: but now, although I was aware of my state, it only worsened. I was unable to dress. I heard cars driving up and the guests arriving. Panic seized me, failed to sober me. The Zulu fumbled with my starched shirt and studs: he improvised a tie. Now fully dressed, I sprawled on the bed trying in vain to concentrate on an imaginary chess-problem. I was aware that the whiskey had had no effect on me while I had been playing. But this stratagem didn't help. Now even the bishops wobbled and moved in anything but straight lines, and the pawns wore an insolent leer. The Zulu applied an ice-pack and made me drink a cup of tea strong enough for a mouse to skate on. I heard them filing in to dinner. There was nothing for it. I followed with that slow and deliberate steadiness which is the gait of the hopelessly sozzled. I was introduced to women who had two heads, and their husbands who couldn't find their hands. Then we were all seated. Somewhere in the background I could hear my cousin singing my praises—anybody direct from Europe and who was not a Colonial received her snobbish approbation. And opposite I could hear her mother whispering in her bass voice to some man beside her, so that the whole table was regaled with the cast-list of *Don Giovanni* in Vienna in 1910. I decided to exert my will and concentrate on the pepper-pot. For a minute this seemed to work. It was my bad luck that soup was served. Bravely I fished for a spoonful. Then I was instantly and enormously sick on to the table and slithered as gracefully as an alligator on to the floor. The repetition of the cast-list continued: a dim lullaby or prayer as I passed out mumbling apologies to a pair of feet.

I did not regain full consciousness for thirty-six hours. Apparently my cousin had given me a couple of veronal tablets. When I did surface, prompted by diarrhoea, I discovered with some alarm that I was passing blood, and had a very bad attack of dysentery. For the next two days I was unable to leave the lavatory —not a very auspicious beginning as a guest. As I recovered from this bout my Zulu servant nursed me with massive gentleness. And my young cousin, a pretty girl of nineteen, popped in and out of my room. My dissolute behaviour ever since I had entered her house seemed to impress her in a manner I couldn't at the time understand. She used to come and sit on my bed. I talked. It wasn't that I was weak. I didn't understand. I thought she wanted conversation.

After a week I was well enough to stagger to my feet. I decided to take a tram into Jo'burg. The vehicle was crowded. Without thinking I gave up my seat to a middle-aged woman who had got on behind me. She hesitated: I insisted. The next thing I knew was two white passengers opposite me with the assistance of the conductor were hurling me off the tram: I landed head-first in the gutter. The coloured woman to whom I'd given my seat helped me to my feet. I walked along the pavement with her. I suggested that we should have some coffee. She refused, saying she didn't want to get me into any more trouble. I didn't understand. She explained. I took an instant dislike to the whole of South Africa.

That same day while ambling round the ugly city I noticed that a ball was to be held at the Carlton Hotel that night. To make some amends to my hosts I decided it might be a good thing if I took their daughter. I bought two tickets and went home. They approved: she was delighted. But their approval was somewhat strained six hours later when I returned their offspring. On leaving the ball I had taken a taxi. Quite an ordinary thing to do. But the tea-leaves were against me. A few minutes later the taxi swerved to avoid another car and overturned. I extracted my cousin. She had a black eye: her dress was torn: one shoe was missing: she began to cry. I myself was no worse for the experience except that I had lost my front stud, and my tails looked as if I had been rolling in the road. Having paid off the taxi-man, who was suffering from concussion, we hobbled home, to be greeted by her parents in the hall. My appearance told them I was drunk again. The story of the taxi was never believed.

After this unfortunate beginning I settled down to the trivial social life of the house and mugging up my Latin for the Little-go which I knew I had to sit for when I returned to England. I was still homesick, and used to get some relief by taking the train to Germiston where my mother's elder brother lived. He was a bachelor, who worked on the railways and had known my father in the Orange Free State. One day while wandering round the horrible slag-heaps of Germiston I happened to complain to him that I couldn't find a decent cigarette in the whole Union. He took me into a tobacconist. "When your father was out here," he said, "he'd never smoke anything but Flag. I've never tried them myself, but he swore by them." I bought a packet and was surprised to find they were only fourpence for ten. This was not like my father, evidence of whose expensive tastes could still be found in debts on two continents. I knew my uncle had an I.O.U. for £400 in his pocket which he had lent my father to pay some debts.

However, I tried these cigarettes. I liked them. I too found I could smoke no other brand.

After a couple of homesick months in Johannesburg I became restless and decided to go to the Orange Free State, to Frankfurt where my father had died. I knew this would please my mother: I had promised her to visit his grave. I wrote and booked a room at an hotel and set off on a tedious train-journey across the dusty Rand to this God-forsaken dorp.

Soon after I reached the scruffy hotel, I asked the proprietor if he could direct me to the cemetery. In conversation I revealed my identity and my father's name. His whole attitude changed. He announced that he was Mayor of Frankfurt and that I was to regard myself as the town's guest for the night. "There are one or two matters I'd like to talk to you about concerning your father," he said mysteriously. "We've often written to his mother in London but had no reply." Perplexed, I immediately set off for the cemetery. But I couldn't find the grave. I returned to the hotel and found the obsequious Mayor waiting for me beside a large car.

"It's such a rare thing for us to have such a distinguished visitor," he told me. "We've put our Beauty Competition a day forward and hope you will judge it for us."

I wasn't, and didn't look, very distinguished but I found myself bustled into the car. "I couldn't find my father's grave," I complained. The Mayor looked very embarrassed. "I'll show it to you myself after the Beauty Competition," he said shiftily.

The car stopped at a boat-house. Something like a reception committee greeted me. I felt an impostor. A motor-boat with a couple of policemen in attendance now conveyed me and the Mayor down the river to a restaurant where thirty or forty bathing-belles paraded before me, occasionally pulling their costumes down to prevent them riding up over their lower buttocks. I was not eighteen: I felt embarrassed. I had come to Frankfurt for a different purpose altogether. The Mayor beamed and started to make a speech; the girls grinned, pouting their breasts and ogling. I had never felt so shy of their whole sex. They paraded past me: I chose the least conspicuous and hurriedly awarded her the prize, now quite mystified as to why I was being so fêted.

Back in the hotel, the Mayor led me into his office and presented me with an ordinary white kitbag. "This contains your father's belongings," he said. "As you see, I've kept them in trust for you."

I opened the cords of the bag and fetched out a green vellum copy of La Rochefoucauld, a battered Nietzsche which my father had been reviewing for *The Times*, an enormous *Webster's Dictionary* and the manuscript of an unfinished play. That was all. I looked up at the Mayor. "That was all he left," he said. But his hospitality at lunch seemed to ease his conscience.

After the meal he led me across the cemetery to a little corner a hundred yards from the rest of the graves. "This is it," he said. "As you see, it's tidy. I personally have kept my eye on it." It was an unmarked grave on which a cactus grew. A simple stone edging surrounded it. "Why was he buried out here?" I asked, looking back to the graveyard. "A pauper," His Worship replied. "We didn't know who his family was when we buried him. I myself paid for this stonework, and though I've often written to London his family have never replied."

I stood there for some time, by this lonely pauper's grave, with its cruel kerb and gravel surface. I was overcome with loneliness. I remembered my mother's tears as she read the telegram at the breakfast-table. I recalled my efforts to capture a fly—and I felt myself turning into a statue, solidified by the futility of existence. The Mayor's fatuous and continuous commentary on the ephemeral quality of life was no help.

In the car he actually produced from his pocket-book the bill for the grave. "And there are one or two other unpaid accounts in my office," he said, making the most of his opportunity.

I paid His Worship in cash and immediately returned to Johannesburg.

The rest of my story in this sordid city, where nothing counts but money, and money doesn't count, was dominated by two emotions: moral indignation and sexual frustration.

I was so appalled by the way the coloured people were herded, segregated and humiliated, that I was constantly ashamed of being white. To live in Johannesburg is to participate in a crime: and to feel this and be unable to do anything about it gave me a sense of miserable impotence. This feeling was not alleviated when one day my Zulu servant told me that he was worried because there was an outbreak of flu in his reserve and his people were, as he put it, "dying like blacks." For a moment I was tempted to go there and nurse them as my father had done. But he had had some training as a doctor: I none. I felt I was treading in the old footsteps. The only thing I did was to buy a crate of medicines and have it sent to the village. A week or two later I was immensely touched to receive from Jan a snakeskin belt which his wife had sent to me. I wore this proudly: my relatives were not amused. But wearing it helped me to relieve my furious indignation.

As for my sexual frustration, which was now temporally fixed on my cousin, I took steps to relieve that too. And I don't suppose any man ever failed in his intentions so ignominiously or hilariously. She had been sex-teasing me for weeks: changing in my room, bringing tea and sitting on my bed, but always managing to avoid relieving me of the burden of my, if not her own, virginity.

One night I decided to do something about it. My room was on the ground floor: hers somewhere above me. Emulating Tarquinius, I mounted the stairs, then paused to take my bearings, not wishing to enter her mother's room. Or her granny's either. Gingerly I turned the handle of the door to my right. I tiptoed towards the bed and reached for her. Beneath my outstretched hand, I felt a yielding softness—and found myself, holding the sponge, face down in the bath. The noise had been appalling. I heard somebody stirring. I beat a hurried retreat to my room with sadly bruised knees. Oddly enough I don't think any breast ever after gave me the same sense of rapture I felt for that sponge.

A week or so later an event occurred which made me decide to leave South Africa immediately. A boy—aged twenty-five—was horse-whipped to death by his white baas. My hosts' feelings were not outraged: I could not stay there any more. They excused the white man, saying that the boy had probably insulted the baas's wife. But I had observed how these listless, bored white women flaunted themselves in front of their servants as if daring them to claim their own manhood.

I decided to leave next morning for Pretoria and then go up to Rhodesia. My cousin announced that she would come to Pretoria to see me off. But my mind had now switched from her. I was sensible of her gesture but quite unaware of its implications. On reaching Pretoria, she saw me to my hotel and offered to come up to my room and help me unpack. I allowed her to do this. When she had put my ties away, she sat on the bed for a while, then I saw her to the station. It was not until days later that I realised how I had rebuffed her. My mind had been elsewhere, but at least she had not bruised her knees.

Pretoria is a loathsome place of bureaucracy and stucco. I left within twenty-four hours for the Victoria Falls, where I was nauseated by the raw arses of the baboons in the surrounding forest (where it seems to rain for ever with spray from the falls) and captivated by two pretty twins from Bradford. They were doing a tour with their mother. To further my interest in nature I invited the two girls to accompany me up the Zambesi, ostensibly to photograph crocodiles. They accepted and collected equipment. I hired a boat and servants. Unfortunately their mother came too.

I had decided to return to England via the East Coast. This necessitated catching a boat at Beira in Portuguese East Africa. I left Salisbury for the coast a couple of days before the boat was due. After travelling for some considerable time, the train stopped at a halt named Umtali. I peered out. There was no station but a galvanised-iron hut. I was hot, tired, thirsty and longing for a bath. Then to my delight I saw a group of African women going up the train selling bottles of milk. I ran down the corridor and reached down for one, which I drank at a draught. It was cool, sweet, utterly delicious. I decided to buy another bottle for the journey and left the train in search of the native vendors, who had temporarily disappeared. I located these ladies behind the galvanised hut, all hurriedly and gaily milking themselves straight into the bottles. I was so fascinated watching this pretty ceremony that I did not hear my train go off. I bought another bottle, drank it and congratulated the vendor on the delicious beverage and the shapely container she swung before me. Then I approached the one official at this halt and asked him casually when the next train for Beira was due.

"Some time next week," he replied gruffly.

His remark took a minute or two to sink in.

"I can't spend a whole week in this place," I announced, finding my imperious manner.

"What else can you do?" he said.

I can remember nothing of that week except that it was the most unpleasant month I ever spent in my life. I was crucified on the hands of the station-clock. And the girls didn't return until there was another train.

When I did reach Beira I was told that there would be a boat within a week. My impatience was not allayed when I learned that it was doubtful whether there would be a berth in it.

The temperature in Beira was 126 in the shade: it is a figure I shall never forget. The shipping-agent, a man with a satanic sense of humour, recommended the International Hotel. It was the only hotel. It was no hotel, but a brothel in which the only whore was the proprietress, a Portuguese woman aged about forty-five, sodden with gin and depressed by some eighteen sweaty stone.

The town was swarming with insolent rats, the hotel infested with lecherous insects. In my room there was nothing but an iron bedstead enveloped in a mosquito-net. The heat was such that it was impossible to move from the bed until the sun went down. By day one could do nothing but drink gin with Fat Margot or lie turning with prickly heat on your bed. As you did this there would be a plop every five minutes as another lizard fell heavily from the ceiling to the floor bloated with insects and flies. The hotel advertised a shower-room. In this one stood on a duckboard while a servant held a holed bucket above your head and allowed the tepid water to drop over you. Then you wiped the rust from your eyes. At night I used to prowl the town. It shook with copulation. But the image of Fat Margot acted on me more effectively than a vow of chastity.

To finance my trip to the Victoria Falls I had cashed in my first-class return-ticket and consequently had to return home steerage. This proved more arduous than I feared. I found myself sharing a filthy little cabin with an immigrant to Israel who was so enthusiastic about the Promised Land that he produced a revolver to defend it whenever an Arab approached our end of the boat. The rest of the time he was absorbed in spreading blue butter over his private parts.

It was a relief to reach Zanzibar. Almost inevitably I found myself led off by an Arab pimp, who, having offered me intercourse with a boy, a young girl of six and a goat, had with some resignation taken me to see some exotic Arabian dancing. We sat in a cellar lit by candles. Six young Arab girls shuffled in listlessly: a cracked gramophone-record revealed its corrugations. I was angry that it was all so badly staged. And I was furious and sad that there was no other outlet for me. But I was seventeen, and curiosity overcame other emotions. I had never seen a naked girl: now six stood before me: I don't know what I had expected, but I remember being disappointed. One of the girls took me by the hand and led me into a tiny cell where there was a simple iron bed covered with a stained mattress. She was a very pretty girl about my own age. She waited for me to make a move, then made one herself. But I could see she was only doing it for money, so I gave her the money and nothing else. I don't know what I expected, but I know I was disappointed. Of course my fastidiousness hadn't been lessened by watching my cabin-companion with his ointment every morning.

After I'd given the girl the money I turned to go out, smiling at her to show there were no hard feelings. She looked puzzled, almost unhappy at the sense of her own inadequacy. She had had no complaints before. I was overcome by something I can only call compassion. And knew I had to do something to give this girl back the only security she had: the belief in her own body. "I'm impotent," I said, as though making a fervent prayer. The whites of her eyes showed her disbelief and her quick hand confirmed her suspicion. This had only made matters worse. She now looked completely bewildered and miserable too. I had to think of something quickly or risk the blue butter. "The fact is," I said, taking her hand, "I like you too much to use you." For a second she lay there working this out, then she sprang up and danced up and down on the bed with glee. Nothing I have ever said or done (or not done) has ever made any woman so happy.

On the way to Kenya I ran out of Flag cigarettes, then found that this brand wasn't stocked on board. That discovery merely irritated me, and it was only when I realised that no other brand could allay the craving that I became panic-stricken. Even while inhaling a cigarette of an ordinary brand I craved for a Flag. Almost whimpering with need, I watched the other passengers to see if I could find anyone with a packet of Flag. I was unlucky. I endured a day with a raging headache, then cabled my uncle in Germiston to post cigarettes to Marseilles and London. Fortunately I found a few packets in Aden and so managed to limp across the Mediterranean.

I had wandered round Dar-es-Salaam, Mozambique and Mombasa, but they left no impression on me. My next brush with what passed for life occurred on the boat itself.

There was a small lock-up bar in the third-class smoke-room. The barman, a perspiring fellow of forty-five with a wife and three children in Southampton, often used to play poker-dice with me for drinks. One evening when he was locking up his bar he asked me round behind, saying he'd got something interesting to show me. I watched him close the shutters and then he handed me a pile of photographs of himself which he said friends had taken in Sussex. Without much interest I glanced at the first, expecting to see the usual family platitudes. To my horror I stared down at an enlargement of an orgy between the barman and a couple of youths. Then suddenly I felt his hand upon me. I was being assaulted. "Let me out," I said, "and I won't report this. If you don't, I'll call and report you to the Captain." The barman cringed with fear and passed me the keys. The man was clearly at the mercy of his own perversion, and his perversion had no mercy. I felt sorry for him, yet sickened by him. It was terrible watching his apprehension for the rest of the voyage, wondering whether I would keep my word. But there was nothing I could do to reassure him.

This sordid incident bruised my mind till I ran into the next, which left me with more immediate fears than the barman's.

As we approached Port Sudan my cabin-companion asked me if I would help him ashore with his luggage. I agreed: he then suggested that I should carry one case off and meet him in the town later with it while he went through the customs. Before I could demur he disappeared: I tried to lug this heavy wooden box along the jetty. I asked a policeman to find a taxi: he helped me load it himself. An hour later my companion appeared sweating profusely. "Have you got the box?" he asked. I pointed to it. "There's a thousand pounds in there," he grinned. "In gold?" "No," he said, "but just as good." He opened it. I peered into racks of revolvers and clips of ammunition.

Then the gun-runner gave me a drink and I asked him where he was going. "To Tel Aviv," he said, "and as soon as I get there into hospital. As you've seen I've got a nasty dose of syphilis. The bitch!"

These were the days before penicillin. I was terrified, realising that I had spent a fortnight with this man in a small cabin, using the same washing-place, drinking from the same glass and occasionally observing him borrow my razor. And the irony of my predicament didn't escape me, because I had, as it were by default, been living like a monk. Shall we say of a mendicant order?

I rushed back to the boat and told the doctor of my predicament. "It takes some time to incubate," he told me. "Can't say yet whether you've got it. Give it a fortnight, then have a blood-test."

I lived in a state of funk and misery. I waited to go deaf like Beethoven or die like Rochester: hundreds of gruesome images tore at my mind. I felt I was finished. I was only seventeen.

The worry whether or not I had syphilis was alleviated by having a worry that was even more acute: would the next consignment of Flags arrive before my meagre supply ran out? I began to study Lloyd's sailings. Even the weather which might delay the boat concerned me. Eventually, when I was down to my last twenty Flags, headaches of apprehension assailed me. My doctor questioned me, and had one of these cheap cigarettes analysed.

A few days later my parcel arrived from Johannesburg. Now quite gay again I went to the doctor almost careless of the result of the blood-test.

"I've got the result of the analysis here," he told me. "You're a heroin-addict: but we'll soon deal with that. And by the way, the test is negative. You haven't got syphilis."

PART TWO

All Men are Islands

Two or three months after returning from Africa I went to a private tutor, Dr Seldon, who lived at Shelford on the Trumpington Road just outside Cambridge. This crammer took three other pupils, all swotting for their Little-go. He was an applefaced man who gave you the impression that he'd just had a cold shower and enjoyed it. His energy was so excessive that he wore his pupils out by making them accompany him on brisk walks before breakfast, or he would polish us off with a couple of sets of tennis after luncheon. He had two hobbies: spiritualism and giving up smoking. He indulged regularly in both; attending séances every week and giving up smoking every fifth week. During these terrible periods of self-restraint we pupils suffered unendurably, for the doctor's energy was such that the two-mile pre-breakfast walk would be turned into a canter. And to prove his will-power to us he used during these bouts of abnegation to keep a large box of cigarettes on his desk which he would offer to each pupil during their tuition. We would protest; he would insist, obtaining some masochistic pleasure from the torture we inflicted on him. After a week of this sort of tension the pattern was always repeated. He used to march into our study and announce that he was prepared to make a sacrifice for our peace of mind.

"Oh no, Doc, don't do that," we used to plead.

But he always insisted, "I don't think I'm right in giving you boys a guilt-complex about smoking, so, for psychological reasons, I have decided to smoke again, in moderation, so as to relieve you of that burden—or the temptation of your insufferable smugness."

We would then offer him our cigarette-cases simultaneously, and thank him for the gesture. Three weeks later he would renounce the degrading habit again. We could do nothing but sympathise with his wife during these sad times.

63

She was a neolithic-looking woman. Webster would not have had to use much imagination to see the skull beneath the skin. The bones prominent, her hair straight. But she had a good figure and was addicted to raw carrots. She supported her husband loyally in all his enthusiasms and foibles. And together they made a happy "progressive" pair, always in the forefront of any minority movement. Both made a fetish of being unconventional, and in this conformed to the Cambridge convention. They held it a principle that sex should be discussed openly. And like all their other beliefs they carried it into practice ruthlessly. Indeed they were so revealing about their sex-life to us that the experience itself must have come to them as an anticlimax.

Soon after I arrived there, my tutor informed me that I was "almost illiterate as far as mathematics went, your Latin and French are hardly up to prep-school standard, your history mainly fiction, while your divinity marks you a heathen. As for your English—I daresay you could take your Tripos in that right away." But he was undismayed and a brilliant teacher. With individual tuition even mathematics became less obscure to me. After a couple of terms the Doctor became confident of my getting into the university, and suggested that I should help him edit a dictionary of Psychic Terminology which he had been commissioned to write. I began to go to séances myself, posed before psychic photographers and placed my paws on innumerable planchettes. But I remained unconvinced; the book unfinished.

It couldn't have been mental tiredness, nor was worry about examinations the cause, but it was while I was at this crammer's that there occurred my first bout of the absent-mindedness for which I subsequently achieved an undesired reputation. One summer afternoon immediately after lunch Mrs Seldon came into the study and asked me if I would care for a game of tennis. I accepted gratefully and told her I would go up and change and join her on the court. She went off to wait for me. I immediately went upstairs to my room, took my racquet from the cupboard, then went to the chest of drawers for my flannels. Mrs Seldon waited on the court half an hour and then, as I hadn't turned up, came to my room to see what had happened to me. She found me in bed in a deep sleep. Slightly indignant, she woke me up to demand an explanation. For a moment I was as surprised as she. Then glancing down at myself I observed that I was wearing pyjamas. "I suppose what happened," I said, "was I went to the drawer to get my white flannels and found a pair of pyjamas lying on them, and so I must have absent-mindedly put them on instead, and then of course got into bed as one normally does after one's put on a pair of pyjamas. . . ." The door slammed.

My year at Dr Seldon's was uneventful; that is if we think of an event as something dramatic happening to us. The months passed without external incident. Dr Seldon gave up smoking regularly; his wife informed us she had the curse fairly regularly. It was supposed to affect her tennis. As usual I did the minimum amount of work and the maximum amount of day-dreaming. I learned to drive a car and bought a violin after reading Verlaine's lines:

> Les sanglots longs
> Des violons
> De l'automne
> Blessent mon cœur
> D'une langueur
> Monotone.

I intended, but never tried, to play it. I read very little. It was not that I preferred my own imagination to reading novels or poetry. It was simply that few authors could hold my interest; my mind would fly off the page. And it is still the same. With shame I confess that I have read fewer than a hundred books in my life. The more potent a book, the more it stimulated my own imagination. One page of one of my favourite poets—Ben Jonson, Donne, Pope, Rochester or Dryden—was enough to ignite the fuse and send my mind into orbit. I used to wonder how other people read a whole chapter or a whole book. I still don't know.

But there were events occurring in me. Though my consciousness was not given any new direction, it was becoming more defined. And as I write this aged forty-seven I am aware how little it has altered since. I don't know whether that is a confession or a boast. It is a fact. Whatever I was at eighteen, I am now. I suppose the only difference between a young man and an old man is that one has hopes and the other disappointments, but they are the same man. We don't grow up, we grow old. As I've said, we are all children, crippled children.

When I was ten I tried to join in other kids' games: I played Red Indians so long as I could be an Indian and not a cowboy. At that time I endeavoured to participate, to belong. But at eighteen I was becoming aware that whatever the games were that the adults were playing around me, I didn't want to join in; they were not for me. I felt acutely and uncomfortably detached from the whole hierarchy of their values. My seriousness could not take them seriously. I felt unidentified, a visitor, somebody passing through. I had the impression I had lived before, but I didn't believe it. I became fascinated by two legends: the Wandering Jew and the Flying Dutchman.

What people said was important seemed trivial to me. Things I thought fundamental were not subjects they cared to discuss. All men are islands: there seemed to be no bridge for me.

Basically the difference lay in this: I was, and am, acutely aware that life is ephemeral, limited and brief. I never wake up in the morning without being surprised at being alive: I never go to sleep without wondering whether I shall wake up. Death to me was the reality. Yet everybody I met and saw seemed unaware of it. They seemed to live as if they would live for ever. How else could they spend forty years marking exercise-books, going to an office to earn the money which would enable them to go on going to an office to earn the money which would enable them to—. I could see a skull beneath every bowler hat. Perhaps I should have been an undertaker. But I must make this point if no other: I was obsessed with the feeling that I was a small boat floating on an ocean, and the ocean was death. Nobody I knew would admit this sea that supported and surrounded them. This made communication difficult: the language was the same, but I could not share their values. I envied their insulation. I was jealous of their indifference. But I could not emulate them, however much I tried.

During this year at Dr Seldon's, I went with my mother and sister to Welcombe for a holiday. We had not been to Devon for several years, but I still thought of it as home. Though we had no house there, it was the place where I always wanted to be. Almost as soon as I got there I was out playing with the small stream which runs through the combe and makes a waterfall over the cliff —precisely as I had done when I was four, exploring and damming it up with my playmate Rosemary. I was not aware of any repetition, only of the immediate fascination of turning the smooth stones over in the bed of the stream. One afternoon when I was indulging in this almost compulsive act, I disturbed a large trout, which took cover beneath an ash-root in a pool. I watched the trout for some time, fascinated by its stillness when it had previously moved so quickly. I pointed the fish out to a farm-labourer who was grazing his horse by the stream while he collected an odd toll or two from cars parked by the beach. He suggested that we should catch the trout. I told him I had no line.

"We don't need a line," he said, plucking a dozen long black hairs from his horse's tail. Then he plaited these hairs together and made a hangman's noose of them, which he tied on the end of a small stick he cut from the hedge. "We'll soon have that trout out with this," he said, lying on the bank and leaning over in the shadow of the pool. "They fish are spry, but they'll never see this black noose in the water."

I watched him gently lower the noose through the water till it was a couple of inches in front of the trout's head. The fish darted forward into it. With a flick of the wrist he landed the trout on the bank beside me.

Nothing had ever delighted me so much. The farm-labourer had also caught me. There and then I told him that I wanted to live in Welcombe. He suggested that I should go with him and look at a derelict cottage on his father's farm at Southole, a couple of miles away.

"What would be the rent of it?"

"Twelve pounds a year."

"I'll take it," I said. "I think I know the cottage."

This impetuous deal delighted my mother. She would never have made the decision herself. With it she had the doll's house again which we had once had made for my sister. This time my sister did not turn away from the toy. Together we all renovated and furnished the place. My mother had spent her own childhood in a similar cottage at Addlestone: this one was now linked with her pleasant associations. And she was happier than I had ever known her.

I returned to Cambridge feeling reassured that I now had my toe firmly in Welcombe. When you suffer from homesickness it is at least a help to have a home.

About this time I received a letter from my trustees enclosing a cheque for £5. 16s. 8d. This sum was the residue of my grandfather's estate after the legal fees for the case claiming my inheritance had been paid. It had been estimated that his bequest to my sister and me was worth something like three-quarters of a million. Apparently the bulk of his property had consisted of an aluminium mine in the Pyrenees which the French Government had confiscated during the war because he was an enemy alien. My trustees had expended the rest of his estate on a protracted court case claiming the return of the mine: they had failed. Oddly enough neither my sister, who had received a similar cheque, nor I was disappointed: we had lost what we had never had; we treated the matter as a joke. And we still had my great-grandfather's inheritance. But my mother and trustees now began to question me about what I would read at the university, and what I would do when I eventually got some sort of a degree.

My Aunt Henrietta suggested the Stock Exchange and offered £5000 to buy me a partnership in some firm. To encourage me several brokers were asked to dinner. They talked about margins and commissions and tried to interest me in this game, but it was no use.

"If some people make money at stocks and shares," I told them, "it's only because a like amount has been lost by somebody else, so what's the sense in that?" My question wasn't answered. My aunt apologised for me. But there was one broker who did intrigue me. He was a very respectable figure who was a member of the Stock Exchange Council. He was a bachelor and used to dine with my aunt once a fortnight to play bridge. Half way through the meal he used to turn to whatever woman happened to be sitting beside him and casually ask her in a conversational way if she could smell violets. The person generally sniffed and then

68

said something or other to the effect that she thought perhaps she *could* smell violets. "Yes," the broker would whisper confidentially, "it's me." This was his only idiosyncrasy.

My mother, to pay out my father's family for frustrating his ambition, encouraged me to become a doctor. But since I always felt sick at the sight of blood, and invariably fainted if touched by cotton-wool, I never bothered to enquire further about that profession. I disappointed her in this, and consequently she never took any further interest in my career.

On the other hand my tutor got nearer to my inclinations. He suggested I should become a barrister because "You've got a logical mind and great facility in articulating an argument." Encouraged thus far, I decided to attend a trial at the Old Bailey. Some wretch was being tried for strangling his wife. I listened attentively to the points of law and walked out of the court and caught a bus back to Cambridge.

"Well?" asked Seldon hopefully.

"The law ignores circumstance," I said. "Besides, justice doesn't interest me."

"What does?"

"Mercy," I replied.

It's clear I was what is called a prig, spiritually arrogant and intolerant of compromise. I rushed about my adolescence with a verbal whip. The world seemed cluttered up with money-changers. Important things seemed to be excluded, essential values discounted. My predominant moods were incredulity that the temple was being used as a fish-market; indignation that the fish they were selling was putrid; and anger because nobody seemed to notice the fraud. They seemed to enjoy sucking their rotten offal and decorating themselves with fishbones. Naturally I was certain I could do something about it. I was confident that with my lash in my hand—at this time Swift was my model—I could do something to scourge mediocrity, which I saw as a solid unshiftable fog squatting on the country throughout the four seasons. Despair at what I saw alternated with moods of ridiculous optimism that something could be done about it. This is a fairly conventional portrait of youth. The trouble was that my youth lasted till I was forty-five.

The amount of energy I had was like a disease. I don't know anything about metabolism, but whatever gland it is that generates energy worked overtime in me. I doubt if the fact that I was a vegetarian had anything to do with it. I don't think I had much physical strength. I wasn't tough but wiry. The wattage came from my mind. Not only did I attempt to burn myself up, but everybody around me was fuel for the conflagration. These moods of frantic visionary activity alternated with fits of melancholia and lethargy. The conventional manic pattern.

In spite of going round Africa alone as a challenge to my terror of loneliness and homesickness, I still suffered from them. Even at Shelford, where the conditions were friendly and congenial, I found myself counting the buses that went along the Trumpington Road. But they went to London. I used to catch one home every week-end. For the rest of the time the umbilical cord was stretched fifty miles like a piece of elastic. Like every mother, mine used to celebrate these week-ends by getting in some delicacy which she knew I liked: they were always beyond her means, inevitably out of season. She indulged my eccentric tastes even to burning her saucepans. I enjoyed nothing quite so much as scraping burnt custard out of the bottom of a saucepan and eating it straight from the spoon. The stumps of celery were another favourite: my mother used to buy several heads to obtain the stumps, and sometimes when she came to Oxford Circus to see me off on the bus to Cambridge she would hand me a surprise packet of celery or one of my favourite cheeses. I daresay every mother and every son have this sort of traffic between them: all I know is I couldn't bear the pain of such tenderness. I used to shove the packet in my pocket, thank her casually and get into the bus. She would always wait till it moved off. Sitting in the bus I would see her standing alone on the pavement. She looked so much alone. It used to rain behind my eyes.

People who knew me at this time—including my mother—probably saw me as a normal young man concerned with neckties, his first motor-car, or his next girl-friend. I certainly tried desperately hard to interest myself in the things I was supposed to be interested in at that age, and I believe I succeeded in giving the impression of being more than usually extrovert and level-headed. But it was false, a masquerade.

The truth is: it rained behind my eyes. I felt a river of sadness flowing inside me, and like a frantic beaver worked day and night to erect some sort of dam to prevent the flood that I knew could wash my life out to sea. I was to spend many years trying to evade this centre to my being, trying to objectify it. I believe I got somewhere near it in a poem I wrote when I was about thirty, called "The Mongrel." But writing that poem did nothing to prevent this feeling.

I realise that I am not explaining it very well. If I could there would perhaps be little to explain. All I know is that there was something internal in me which I could not control, but which took possession of me. I was, and am still, a paper boat borne helplessly on its back. It is a flood, a great undammable river of sadness.

I suppose I first became aware of this river when I buried the little bird behind the form-rooms at school. By which I mean that finding and burying the dead bird had had a reaction on me which I couldn't stem or explain. I can see the psychologists jumping in here, bless them. And I am aware of the Freudian symbolism about dead birds. No, my sexual frustration at this period doesn't explain everything. Which is not to say that it wasn't an aggravation.

All I know is that I now became frightened of my eyes and terrified by my ears. On the bus going up to Cambridge I used to try and stare at the ashtray in front of me. I was terrified of looking at what I knew my eyes would see if they glanced at the passengers beside me, at the pedestrians in the street. For I knew it was impossible to look at people without seeing their sorrow, which would then release that river and drown me. It was as if I had X-ray eyes. I did not notice a person's face or clothes; such superficial details entirely escaped me. What I saw was the bone, the essential pathos in every person. Not their tragedy, nor their misfortune, but the pathos, the pathetic lost child in every being. Perhaps I was doing nothing more than project on to them the feelings I had for myself. But I became frightened of my eyes: it rained behind them.

Nor would I dare to listen to music. To me music—I think I love it as much as the sun—is such a potent, immediate thing. I am a born coward. I find music much more frightening than a machine-gun. When I was eighteen I found it would take me a whole week to recover from the experience of listening to Mozart, Chopin or Tchaikovsky. I didn't know of any other composers, except my beloved Schubert. Even now I find myself almost weeping when I write his name. I can't explain this.

As for poetry, I was desperately interested in it. But how could I read a volume when a page could make me shake? Poetry is the essence. The world is wise to ignore it, for it could destroy the world. But I got over my schoolboy resistance to Shakespeare and read *Hamlet, Antony and Cleopatra,* and *King Lear.* It was if I had been wandering lost through a trackless desert and had suddenly tripped over a railway-line.

Oddly enough it was my mother, who had no great interest in poetry, who gave me *The Ballad of Reading Gaol* to read. I think my father had met Wilde; if not, I know he admired his work. Reading this poem was a journey. It had more effect on me than traipsing round Africa. And then I came across Wilde's simple little lyric "Requiescat":

> *Tread lightly, she is near*
> *Under the snow.*
> *Speak gently, she can hear*
> *The daisies grow.*
>
> *All her bright golden hair*
> *Tarnished with rust,*
> *She that was young and fair*
> *Fallen to dust.*
>
> *Lily-like, white as snow,*
> *She hardly knew*
> *She was a woman, so*
> *Sweetly she grew.*
>
> *Coffin-board, heavy stone*
> *Lie on her breast,*
> *I vex my heart alone,*
> *She is at rest.*

72

> *Peace, Peace, she cannot hear*
> *Lyre or sonnet,*
> *All my life's buried here,*
> *Heap earth upon it.*

I regretted the "Lily-like, white as snow" and "The daisies." But the delicacy of "She hardly knew She was a woman, so Sweetly she grew" and the simplicity of the last two lines of the poem affected me so deeply that I couldn't read any more poetry for months. I never found much else of value in Wilde's poetry—his plays were another matter.

In flight from the potency of music and poetry, I decided one day to go to the cinema and see a comedy. I could not have chosen worse: I went to see Charlie Chaplin. Here is the quintessence of the pathos I couldn't bear. I ran weeping from the cinema. Chaplin hits the nail again and again. The tramp is a wonderful reduction, symbol of humanity: the tramp who is welcomed and befriended by the drunken millionaire in *City Lights*, but is chucked out again by him when he is sober, is a universal comment.

Having uncovered this soft centre in myself—it was as if I walked through the world naked, with no insulation—I began the laborious farce of finding a camouflage. For a time I became a dandy—or hoped I had that effect. And I posed as a young rake, a sort of embryonic man of the world, going to race-meetings and propping up saloon-bars drinking whiskey which I detested. I sported a rolled umbrella and had my hair cut short. While many of my acquaintances were doing their best to look like artists, I did the opposite.

I had discovered that I was a poet, and to be a poet is not just a concern with words; it is to bleed when you are not wounded; it is to be wounded when you are not hit; it is to enjoy so intensely that enjoyment is unbearable, another kind of pain. The decision to be an artist is not merely the decision to apply yourself to paint, to notes or to words. It is the decision to be conscious, and that is to suffer something like the pains of birth with every moment. It is to be born daily, to die hourly. I had experienced just enough to realise that to be a serious artist is to have responsibility—I mean the ability to respond. You are granted a vision and given nothing but worn-out words or bits of paper or catgut with which to reproduce it. Everything you do is a failure; you know it, even if they don't. The essence of an artist is his internal vision, not his technical skill: many craftsmen acquire that. A vision may be an act of grace, but that grace is heavy, an intolerable burden. To live with it is to be aware that you are Pilate, Peter and Judas to your own Christ. On the level of a puppet or a marionette you have to endure your own parody of the Passion. You feel that you have denied yourself, betrayed yourself and crucified yourself, not gloriously but ridiculously. You wear a paper hat, not a crown of thorns. You are martyred by triviality. Not nails, but drawing-pins—or hat-pins—are driven into your limbs.

Like a cornered rat clawing at a concrete wainscoting I tried to escape from this vocation. I resolved not to read poetry, listen to music, or walk alone. I closed the window so that the wretched birds couldn't fly in. I no longer despised the bowler-hatted brigade, I envied them. I decided to take another look at the City and began to read, though not to fathom, the financial columns of *The Times*.

Naturally my relatives were relieved that I was "coming to my senses," when in fact I was denying all of them. And through them many avenues of escape were instantly provided. My great-aunt promoted me to her bridge-parties. For a time I became her favourite nephew and played the lap-dog three or four days a week at the family mansion in Park Lane.

Aunt Henrietta was a widow. But I doubt if her marriage had ever been consummated by anything but cheque-books. It was certainly childless. The only sign of her late husband, who had had an Australian origin, was a large mascot of a kangaroo on the bonnet of the Rolls. She was a frail-looking woman with a head like a pomaded turkey. She couldn't have weighed more than six stone: beneath her mink was nothing but an inflexible will. She had the manner of Catherine the Great and the manners of a fish-wife. Although she had been born to great wealth she behaved like a *nouveau riche*, showing no consideration to her large retinue of intimidated servants, and enjoying nothing so much as bullying defenceless tradespeople. My great-grandfather had left her an income of £15,000 a year, and her dutiful spouse had expired promptly, and no doubt gratefully, leaving her a similar amount.

With this backing and a good chef she knew everybody who was not worth knowing. Sycophants said she was a woman of culture, but not even her pearls had that attribute; she was more or less illiterate and essentially insensitive. Her sole concern was for her two Pekinese, Snookum and Bebe. While we dined, a footman served them with creamed chicken, which was laid on white napkins on the floor beside her.

Like all the family Aunt Henrietta ran to eccentricity of one sort or another. Hers was the absurd disparity between her extravagance and her meanness. She disliked handling coins—"You never know where they've been"—and most of her transactions were on account, but when she went to a theatre or shopping she would become very cross if she were handed any change. Then as soon as we got home the ceremony would begin. She would ring for a servant who appeared automatically carrying a tray, a bowl of Brasso, some special gloves and various small brushes. This paraphernalia would be set on a table in the green room. Whereupon my aunt would don the gloves, empty the coins from her bag on to the tray and for the next half-hour would be happily employed polishing the offensive pennies and half-crowns. When they were gleaming as though fresh from the mint the servant would be summoned again. This time he carried a collection-box for a charity called the Dockland Settlements, of which one of my uncles was honorary treasurer. The servant would pop the coins in this poor-box and as the last penny went in my aunt would always make the same remark: "And it's a pity the poor aren't as well washed as those coins are."

At this time there were two million unemployed, dole-queues, hunger-marches, and many of my own friends were eking out some sort of existence on thirty shillings a week. But Aunt Henrietta saw nothing incongruous in her feeding her dogs on chocolate, which was always from Charbonnel & Walker. She felt no responsibility at all for the poor; to her they were another breed. And not to be pitied because "if they had any money, they wouldn't know what to do with it," or "poverty is only another word for laziness."

When not dipping pennies in Brasso, my aunt would be busy cutting up used envelopes so that the back of the part which had been addressed could, when clipped together, be used as a note-book. There was a cupboard in the library stacked with these home-made memo-pads, none of which ever carried a note. Or, if not wasting her time this way, "exercising domestic economy" she used to call it, she would be lost in a vast eagle's nest of string. The string from all parcels received was removed and placed in a container: it was a mortal sin to use a pair of scissors. Once a week the tangle of string would be placed before my aunt, who, to set her servants an example, would unravel every knot and wind it all up into a ball. I used to hope that one day she would knit her shroud with it.

She was very proud of her table, but grudgingly admitted that the only other woman in London who equalled it was "that terrible but clever Mrs Simpson." And she was most particular about her melons and candles. She used to maintain, quite erroneously no doubt, that "a really good melon smells a trifle off." Conse-quently one would be dragged round Fortnum's or Jackson's twice a week to smell the melons. This performance was tolerated by both shops, who used to keep a bad melon under the counter, let her or me sniff it, and then deliver edible fruit. When a guest congratulated her on the melon at dinner, and he was never asked again if he forgot this gambit, she would always reply rather pom-pously and ambiguously "I have a nose for melons."

But the candles were a more serious matter. For years my aunt had bought her table-candles from Harrods. They were specially manufactured by a firm called Fields and could always be relied on to burn without producing any surplus wax. But one evening she espied a droplet of wax running down a candle. The footman re-moved the offensive article, and the butler was closely questioned. My aunt suspected some kind of sabotage. The next morning she set off for Harrods, bullied the assistant, and intimidated the manager, who, after a week of trying to placate her, suggested that she should complain to the manufacturers. She regally announced that she would be prepared to visit their factory. For the next few weeks her circle of expectant relatives or hopeful sycophants were informed that she was about to enter Industry to give technical advice. Eventually after months of abortive experiments at the factory and failures at the table, a director of Fields presented himself and sadly confessed that the firm were no longer able to produce this type of candle. They had been hand-made by some old man, who had died, taking his skill or secret with him.

"Very inconsiderate of him," my aunt commented, "and inconvenient too."

From that day she was convinced that England was a power in decline. When we won the Schneider Trophy she invited the winning pilot to dinner merely to inform him that "though we might be able to manufacture aeroplanes that could fly over two hundred miles an hour, yet we couldn't make candles any more that didn't drip and smeech like penny wax-dips."

While I was staying with Aunt Henrietta I observed that the old order was changing. Her butler, Lambourne, had retired and she had had to promote her first footman, Edward, to take his place. He was a man of about thirty-five. One morning while I was sitting with her, Edward came and asked if he might have next Wednesday night off.

"Night? did you say, Edward—why the night?"

"Because, as I have already informed Madam, I am getting married."

"Oh, very well, Edward, then I suppose you must," my aunt said, watching the poor embarrassed creature withdraw.

She at least waited till the door was closed. "But you would think the working class could do that sort of thing during the afternoon, wouldn't you?" she snapped.

With this as part of my background, it was not altogether surprising that I became a socialist at eighteen, a communist at nineteen—to abandon them both at twenty.

Unlike my bird-like aunt, my Granny, who was her elder sister, was fat and gross. She was like a Chinese mandarin and had the most penetrating eyes I have ever seen. My sister and I were summoned to the imperial presence for the first time when I was about twelve. We were dolled up, then waited, made nervous by our mother's sense of the occasion, till the car arrived to convey us from Clapham to my Granny. I asked the chauffeur why he had brought a spare driver with him. Later I learned that no member of the family went out in a motor unless "there was a man on the box."

While we were having tea, my Granny showed me a chess-table which bore the Wittelsbach coat of arms. "You've got Rupprecht's eyes," she said dreamily, "and of course you shall have this and all his other things when I am gone."

She had now moved from Brook Street to 5 Hyde Park Gate, where she lived with two of my father's brothers, who were kept on the lead of her remittances, impatiently waiting for the old harridan to die so that they could receive their part of their grandfather's estate which came to them at their mother's death. It was impossible for me to imagine her Bavarian romance; she was now gross with diabetes and dressed to imitate a tent or a marquee in mourning. But the evidence of her beauty as a young woman still hangs in the Tate Gallery in the portrait by Sargent. Many other family faces make up the Sargent Wertheimer Collection. The Sargent's Mess or "The Chamber of Horrors" my uncles called it.

My two wicked uncles did not however have to poison their mother. All they had to do was indulge her natural greed. One evening when I was sixteen, she died in the family tradition—from a surfeit of oysters, as her two brothers had also done, both on their honeymoon. My mother and I celebrated my Granny's death with unashamed relief. It meant that I now inherited £20,000—or would do so when I reached my majority. Indeed my Granny's death so enriched her children and grand-children that we could all afford the luxury of feigned grief.

Even as the wreaths were being carried on to her hearse, I observed remote cousins unblushingly pocketing silver cigarette-boxes and filling handbags with jade. And before the flowers had a chance to wither the entire house had been ransacked by the black-clothed vultures, with my uncles in the lead running a shuttle-service in taxis to Sotheby's and Christie's. That done they took to bachelor flats, and indulged in their hobbies; one for young waiters and old stamps; the other for waitresses and the making of salmon-flies. There was only Aunt Henrietta left to disturb them.

I had spent a very large part of my time with Uncle Viccy ever since he had returned to England when I was fourteen. He had immediately set up house with my mother's sister. They had been in love before either of them made unhappy marriages and they succeeded in picking up their relationship as if the interval of fourteen years had been merely an unfortunate week-end. I always think of them when people tell me that "breaks are for ever" and "there's no going back again." The answer is it depends on the degree of love.

Since I had no father of my own, Viccy assumed that rôle. It was he who took me off to a doctor for a check-up when he noticed my voice was breaking, it was he to whom I wrote twice a week from school, who told me the facts of life or rather revised them for me. But our relationship was much freer than is usual between father and son. I was fonder of Uncle Viccy than of any man I have ever met.

I think he was the only gentleman I have ever known. His gentleness was as much part of his nature as was his manhood. Prince Victor of Cooch-Behar did nothing that the world remembers, but he was the one great man I knew—and I have known several so-called great men. By great I mean whole. Viccy was a whole man. Whatever his environment, wherever he found himself, he was identified with his surroundings and the people, yet lost nothing of himself. The warmth of his personality needed no social consciousness or religious principles to guide his attitude or dictate his behaviour. He was gentle by nature, generous by impulse. He had a prodigious memory for other people's tastes and birthdays; no memory at all for the innumerable hurts he received. He didn't have to forgive people; it was simply that he had no capacity for resentment. And if somebody happened to steal his watch he would merely ask them the time, quite unaware that the watch had once been his.

By whole I mean he was not a specialist in one part of life and illiterate in another. He could talk about Sanskrit to scholars—he had done considerable research trying to prove that Christ had been in India—and was equally at home in St James's Palace or swopping limericks with barmaids in Maida Vale. He was the sort of man charwomen adore, bus-conductors look for, and of whom bishops disapprove. He was a modest Falstaff, but could have drunk that knight under any table.

Viccy had been to Eton and Cornell and had been A.D.C. to the Duke of Windsor on his tour of India. After his elder brother,

79

Jitendra, had died leaving a son of four, Viccy had been made Regent of Cooch-Behar. He had taken this job seriously and had lived wholly in India until his nephew came to England to go to Harrow.

When he arrived in England he had an income of £400 a month: he and my aunt took a tiny basement-flat in Hyde Park Mansions off the Edgware Road, where the rent was £5 a week. They had one Indian servant, Asraf, a Mohammedan who, with a wife in Bombay, acquired three more up the Edgware Road, and a char. They had no motor. Viccy did most of the cooking. But in spite of this modest way of living compared to his income, within three years he went bankrupt for more than £30,000.

I remember Viccy bundling me into a taxi one day during a holiday from school and handing me a box to look after while the bailiffs were banging at his door. I took the box home, and put it under my bed, never opened it and forgot about it. Weeks later my mother discovered it sweeping. She asked what was in it. We took a look. There was all Viccy's regalia, the diamond tiger he wore in his turban on state occasions, ropes of pearls and jewellery worth a fortune. I shoved the box back under the bed. From time to time the owner would telephone me and ask me to pick out some piece and meet him at Robertson's, the large pawnshop in the Edgware Road. Eventually the box was empty.

Viccy's bankruptcy, the bailiffs and the dunning worried me considerably. I saw him move from one flat to another, descending from the Savoy to the outer reaches of Maida Vale. Little of this failure was his fault, though, because he never disclosed the facts, he was blamed for it. It is true he was generous, especially to children if he was near Hamley's. He delighted in buying toys, and when I was fifteen one day he spent more than £50 on Easter eggs. He was also extravagant in small things such as buying his silk shirts by the dozen from Devereux's. But he could afford that. His bankruptcy was entirely due to his having signed a guarantee to stand surety for his sister, Princess Baby. She was the most beautiful woman I ever saw.

I used to go frequently to their house in Egerton Crescent to play with their daughter Gita. From the nursery we could always hear a wild party going on downstairs. Once our games were heightened by my finding a rolled-up carpet on the floor in the room next to the nursery. Unrolling it I discovered it contained a naked and very drunk Russian cabaret-singer. It was an eccentric house, so close to the respectable umbrella of Harrods. There was always a different "uncle" attached to Auntie Baby; sometimes a night-club pianist, sometimes a French Count.

After his bankruptcy, Viccy took a small office in the City in Basinghall Street. He no longer spent most of his time in the pavilion at Lord's, but used to go to the City every day "to attend to finance." He had got himself involved with some shark who was trying to float a company that was going to fight Viccy's legal claim to the Bijni Raj. The present ruler was insane: Viccy was heir; the constitution of the State stipulated that mental-deficients should abdicate, but the idiot's mother was refusing to have the boy certified. The estate carried an income of £40,000 a year.

While Viccy busied himself drafting a brief in his immaculate hand, preparing the case he intended to bring in the Courts of Delhi, or drinking gallons of brown ale in the Bodega, I was by his side. I also had a desk in his office. We were both "in the City"; he for one reason, I for another. I spent most of my holidays from my crammer's at Cambridge at this charade, busying myself with my invention.

It was a ridiculous idea. But the shark encouraged me so as to keep in with Viccy. We were going to make hundreds, no thousands. The proof of this aberration must still be on the files of the Patent Office. One day I had remarked casually to the shark that it always irritated me when my bicycle-seat at Cambridge got wet and I wondered why somebody didn't market a gadget which could contain an oilskin cover kept in a metal container clipped on the back of the saddle and drawn out on a spring. I was rushed to a patent-agent. Specifications were drawn up. Another prospectus was drafted. This way Viccy gave himself the impression that he was doing something to repair his finances, and I succeeded for a time in not reading anything but the *Financial Times*.

And because I got on with Viccy so well, my essential loneliness was lessened. I clung to my relationship with him, unconsciously aware that my feelings were too vulnerable to withstand the stress of making any other. It was a brief refuge.

Within a few months I became infatuated with one of my sister's girl-friends, who had come to stay at my mother's cottage in Devon. She was called Pic and came from Pontefract. I can't remember much about her. The affair was abortive. But I did at least manage to discover that she was of the opposite sex. It would be unfair to her to call her a sex-teaser. She was only seventeen and had strong pressures from her parents, as I discovered.

When she left Devon, she returned to join her parents in Scarborough. I had an old car which I had bought for £12. I drove straight to London, had a cup of tea and drove another three hundred miles to Scarborough. Arriving somewhat dishevelled, I was introduced to Pic's parents. They disapproved. But I persuaded her to come for a drive. Having just driven five hundred miles, I rushed things but she refused to satisfy me. I drove her back to her hotel and immediately made the return journey to Devon.

But I had no intention of letting the affair end so lamely. Somehow or other I conceived the idea that what I would like to do would be to ride with her from Calais to Constantinople. Alliteration alone I suppose fixed the destination. I immediately made plans. This proved surprisingly easy.

I wrote to Selfridges' Information Bureau saying that I intended to ride from Calais to Constantinople and asking them to give me a list of hotels on the route twenty-five miles apart which could stable horses. I also requested details about visas. Selfridges took this odd request as a challenge. Two people in the bureau were detailed to deal with it. Within a fortnight all the information, complete with maps, was in my hands. I had only to buy a couple of horses. The girl was willing and had promised to come, with or without her parents' permission.

I could think of nothing else. I busied myself with planning the equipment to go into the saddlebags, reducing my girl-friend's needs to masculine austerity, and arranging for currency and bank-credits en route. Busy with these arrangements, my studies at Snelgrove's were completely abandoned. Even when I sat for the Little-go examination I scribbled my answers down hurriedly so that I could get on with my amatory plans. My mathematics papers must have confused the examiners, since between the quadratics they carried a sketch-map of the route from Turin to Belgrade. Despite this confusion they passed me.

But the whole ride collapsed on a detail I had overlooked. I had arranged to meet the girl in London to discuss our final plans and to buy the horses. I caught my bus from Cambridge in a fervour of excitement. When I met Pic, her mother was in attendance. She seemed civil enough but distant.

The girl and I went off to buy some gear. The next day back in Cambridge I received a distraught letter from her saying that her parents, who still knew nothing of our projected ride or elopement, had forbidden her ever to write or see me again. They were sending her abroad. "They have made this decision," the letter went on, "because of your politics." This confused me; I had forgotten I had any politics. I certainly never mentioned my left-wing sympathies to her or her parents. I telephoned to ask her to be more explicit. "It's because you're a fascist," she told me tearfully. I denied the ridiculous accusation, but I could see she was not convinced. There was even less hope of changing her parents' mind. I put the telephone down in bewildered despair. An hour or two later I suddenly realised the cause of their misconception. When I had gone to London the day before, I had been wearing a black rolled-top polo-sweater. I wore it simply because it was a cold day. I had bought a black sweater because it didn't show the dirt. Relieved that I had tumbled on the ridiculous detail that had led up to this misunderstanding I telephoned Yorkshire again. The mother answered; I asked to speak to her daughter and was told that she had left. I began my explanation: my sweater carried no political allegiance—but I was talking to myself. The telephone had been put down. My letters remained unanswered. Returning to my room at Shelford I swept the visas into the waste-paper basket and there and then started to write a narrative poem giving a full and detailed account of our ride from Calais to Constantinople. I had lived every moment of it in my imagination, and I now wrote the memory of what never occurred.

I spent the next three months writing this poem. It ran to over three thousand lines, describing the scenery we passed through, our love-making, our quarrels, accidents to the horses, and even the blacksmiths who shod our mounts. Somehow or other the poem was so detailed, the imagery so concrete, that a publisher offered to print it as an authentic travel-poem. But these arrangements had to be abandoned because I had only one copy of the poem and I sent this to the girl, who never returned it. I have never seen it since.

This abortive romance was commonplace and trivial no doubt. It was painful too, but it had a good effect on me, in so far as it made me realise that any attempt to escape from my internal world was hopeless. The charade in Basinghall Street, at Lord's or on Epsom Downs was abandoned. I knew I had no way out of the prison of myself except by tunnelling my way up through lines of poetry. I didn't realise then that the more I struggled to the surface the deeper I should go, till the prison became a tomb. Art is no way out, it is a way in—to a room spherical in shape, lined with black ebony. There are no windows, no doors. It is completely sound-proof. Nobody enters, you cannot go out. You sit there holding a tedious conversation with your own consciousness, semi-consciousness shall we say.

Anyhow I now went up to Cambridge determined to concentrate wholly on poetry. I decided to read English. I didn't know that those two decisions were incompatible. My father had been at Christ's, but I chose Downing College because Dr F. R. Leavis was the English Supervisor there and I had been impressed with his live interest in contemporary poetry.

I took to Leavis immediately. His passionate interest in literature was apparent. Here was no ordinary don, no mere academic wallower in footnotes and biographical irrelevancies.

At my first supervision, where there were half-a-dozen other undergraduates, he suggested we should read the metaphysical poets—Grierson's edition—and there was an oblique hint that it would be expedient if we became regular readers of *Scrutiny* and occasionally looked at the *Criterion*. Somebody asked him what lectures we should attend. Leavis studied the questioner with a mixture of tolerance and contempt. "I suppose you'd better look in on Dr Richards, and I daresay the Bennetts are still murdering Milton, Potts piffling around on Byron, and then there's old

Henn getting his lecture-notes muddled with his expletives on the towpath. Basil Willey on the Seventeenth Century isn't bad at all. But avoid Q; he's supposed to lecture on Aristotle's *Poetics* but he never gets nearer than his bottle of Cockburn."

With this directive I bought a bicycle, told my bedder to get me up early, and by nine was in the lecture-room with a new notebook, looking as keen and naïve as the girls from Girton beside me. I listened to the urbane dilettantism of Dadie Rylands; I observed Richards doing his Dr Caligari act and impressing a row of assiduous nuns. Dr Tillyard was embalming Milton with the same shroud he had used for the last ten years, and was to use for the next twenty. My interest in Milton had been effectively killed at school; it was not profitable to attend the killing of a corpse. Exactly as Leavis had predicted, Sir Arthur Quiller-Couch tottered into the room at Magdalene puffing a cigar and carrying a decanter of port. He reminded me of one of those china pixies with which people spoil herbaceous borders.

But it was the lecturer on English Satire who broke my patience. He gave the usual facetious asides concerning the poets' lives, listed their well known works and never at any point referred to a text or made a direct comment on any lines they had written.

At the end of this performance, which compared poorly with the English master at school, I cycled straight to Chesterton Hall Crescent to see Leavis.

"What's up?" he asked. I had interrupted his luncheon.

"I've called to tell you I'm sending myself down from the university," I announced.

"What have you been up to—attending lectures?"

I nodded.

"Most of them stick it for a term or two at least," he said; "it's only taken you a week to be disgusted. Very promising. What will you do?"

"I'll stay up on one condition," I offered. "If you give me two one-hour extra supervisions to myself every week."

He agreed. He charged me only 7s. 6d. an hour.

My first solitary supervision was held in the orchard. I noticed that the apples still lay where they had fallen. Leavis's manner was as casual as his clothes; only his speech was meticulous and precise. His comments were always direct and unguarded. The very opposite to his writing, where his sentences were as unwieldy as the later Henry James's, without shape, lamed with parentheses. Straight away he gave me the impression that we were not only colleagues but something more—conspirators, whose aim was to blow up the English Faculty.

Leavis had a striking head; it looked as if it contained a brain, and it did. A high forehead, well defined features. His eyes unflinching, something puritanical about the mouth. And though he was almost bald, he had sufficient hair left to wear it long enough to affront the Fellows. Sideboards added to this Gower Street effect. He never wore a tie even at High Table, and his open-necked collar was, I suspect, maintained by him out of his veneration for D. H. Lawrence.

His first question to me was to the point. Had I read any Pound or Eliot? I had read a little of the latter, nothing of the former. Leavis immediately rectified this by reading "Hugh Selwyn Mauberley" to me as we sat surrounded by fallen apples. He read poetry more sensitively than anybody: far better than Gielgud or Olivier. He read it better because he never missed an ambiguity, a shade of meaning, and finally because he understood the techniques of poetry, realising that it has little to do with a metre and less to do with scansion.

The superb restraint of "Mauberley," its urbane flexibility, the way the verse is handled so that the meaning runs against the verse-structure, impressed me deeply. I had never read anything like this before. All the romantic outpourings seemed tame compared to the tough irony of Pound:

> Knowing my coat has never been
> Of precisely the fashion
> To stimulate, in her,
> A durable passion.

Leavis gave "precisely" and "durable" just the right emphasis by an imperceptible pause before those two words.

The other verse that impaled me as I heard it was:

86

> To Fleet St where
> Dr Johnson flourished;
> Beside this thoroughfare
> The sale of half-hose has
> Long since superseded the cultivation
> Of Pierian roses.

The prose, polish and run of the verse with its important pause after "half-hose has"—and the subtle effect of that half-rhyme— gave poetry a new meaning to me. No longer was it a decoration, it was the window. Leavis told me he thought "Mauberley" was Pound's masterpiece. "Unfortunately Pound has never written anything worth reading since." I wasn't in a position then to question this. I was enormously grateful to Leavis for introducing me to "Mauberley."

At my next supervision he asked what I had read of Hopkins. I hadn't even heard the name. He picked up a book from the floor and read a poem that instantly stayed in my mind entirely, and still does, though I have never looked at it since.

> Márgarét, are you grieving
> Over Goldengrove unleaving?
> Leáves, líke the things of man, you
> With your fresh thoughts care for, can you?
> A'h! ás the heart grows older
> It will come to such sights colder
> By and by, nor spare a sigh
> Though worlds of wanwood leafmeal lie;
> And yet, you wíll weep and know why.
> Now no matter, child, the name:
> Sórrow's spríngs áre the same.
> Nor mouth had, no nor mind, expressed
> What heart heard of, ghost guessed:
> It ís the blight man was born for,
> It is Margaret you mourn for.*

Here was Schubert in words. The same magic. Leavis's sensitive reading brought out the tensions in the poem which are enhanced

* Reprinted by courtesy of the Oxford University Press.

by the pauses caused by the verse-structure. "Unleaving leaves" did not mess either the important effect obtained by having "you" at the end of the third line, and the consequent elision from "man" to "you." Nor the similar run obtained between "care for" and "can you."

When he had read the poem, he put the book down to discuss Hopkins. But he had read the poem too well. There were tears in my eyes. I studied my shoes. Leavis thought I was bored. He tried another poem, a sonnet, which gave the Sonnet back the intensity it had in Donne and never since. Leavis next read "The Wreck of the Deutschland."

This wasn't supervision; this was torture. Great art affects me like great pain. I mumbled some excuse to Leavis and went back to my rooms in College.

I now suffered myself to read Donne, Marvell, Rochester, Pope, Hopkins, Eliot and Pound. (I discovered Samuel Johnson's "London" and "The Vanity of Human Wishes" in Eliot's edition in my room. Clearly I had absent-mindedly picked it up in Heffer's and walked off with it.) These were the poets I could read with difficulty because their work moved me so deeply. But there was no *via media*. I was either intensely interested or completely bored. In the whole of English Literature there are not more than a hundred pages of the first quality: that compares well with other languages.

I now became almost part of the Leavis family. As a household it was in many respects like the Snelgroves'. In it you were consciously apart, part of "minority culture." In intellectual isolation, they had no sense of neighbourliness, no awareness of being a part of a town, a university, or a community.

Queenie Leavis was most articulate: she answered the questions addressed to her husband, on any subject. She was both forthright and aggressive, a militant pacifist, and so imbued with the idea of the equality of the sexes that she made every man feel inferior. This feeling was probably justified as far as she was concerned, because she was a remarkably efficient woman, as able in assisting in the editing of *Scrutiny* as in running the house or bringing up her infant prodigy, Ralph.

This child was undoubtedly remarkable. The Leavises revelled in its remarkableness and were convinced that they had, as a reward for their devotion to literature, hatched a genius themselves. I myself witnessed the child refusing to eat its purée of carrot unless a Beethoven quartet was being played at the same time. I heard it lisping *The Waste Land* before it had heard of Grimm's *Fairy Tales*. It could read French before it could walk; the parents were convinced however that the child's talents were musical.

Leavis had an excellent method of sharpening one's critical awareness. He used to hand me a sheet of paper with two or three brief prose-passages and several isolated verses from various poems. He would then ask you to state their author and their period, and why you had come to your conclusion. If you were not careful you could make some embarrassing gaffes. You might read a paragraph and guess that it was taken from the leading article of the *Daily Mirror*, only to be told by F.R.L. that it was a bit from Thackeray, or you'd be sure a verse was by Pope only to find it was by Shadwell. I enjoyed these tests immensely: not only did this method of teaching reveal one's sensibilities, it faced you with your own tastes. Without knowing who had written this or that you could not trim your reaction to fashion or prejudice. It is not a game to play on your friends if you wish them to remain your friends.

After a few weeks I got to know Leavis very well. In a way this was a pity, because it cut my effective supervision from an hour to little more than ten minutes. The rest of the time he would spend displaying his chronic neurosis to me.

He suffered from an acute persecution-complex; "fond of complaint, and adverse to relief." Though he despised the university and every member of the English Faculty, he would waste half his time and energy gossiping about nonentities and telling you how he had been slighted by them. He would repeat some of these incidents to me even within a week; I used to know them by heart. The poor man was bent with bitterness, convinced that the policy of every literary quarterly was to attack him. If they failed to do so, then the omission was proof of their intention to ignore him.

For hour after hour I would have to sit there listening to the stories of how Tom Eliot (Uncle Tom to Leavis), Pound or Auden had offended him. And what was worse, observe how this personal affront had affected his literary judgment. "Tom Eliot's not written anything since the *Quartets*," he would say; "he's written himself out, sold himself to Anglicanism." "Pound's cantos are unreadable, don't waste your time with them." "I thought Auden had promise, considerable promise but—" "As for Bottrell, I discovered him, printed him, yet do you know . . ." It was endless. Some writers such as Graves, Middleton Murry, Wyndham Lewis, escaped with mere expletives. Lawrence alone had not put a foot wrong, only because they had never met. For Dr Richards he felt a savage resentment. And because the latter's *Principles of Literary Criticism* had been acclaimed because of ideas which Leavis had first articulated, he carried in his pocket a snapshot of Richards leaving what looked like a seaside bungalow. "Dr Caligari leaving the scene of his crime," he would say, putting the photograph back in his pocket again.

After these matters were vented he would pick up a book from the floor and we would go through some poem for the last ten minutes. But I learned more in those ten minutes than any other man at the university could have taught me in as many weeks.

Leavis's great virtue was that he didn't talk "about it and about" but kept his comments to the text. Like a surgeon's his knife would cut into this cliché, that echo or platitude. Emotional falsity, the fake, did not escape his eye; he would pin the derivative down, pointing to this word or that phrase.

Not all his criticism was destructive; with Pope, Marvell, Donne, or Shakespeare in his hand, he would show me how this particular passage was heightened by the use of one word, or how an effect, accent or emphasis was produced by running the sense against the verse-structure. Leavis had a peculiar affinity to Pope. His essay on Pope is probably his best.

But I did not devote myself wholly to literature. My father had coxed the boat for Christ's. To please my mother and to emulate him I had become a cox too, was a member of the Vesta Rowing Club at Putney and used to cox one of their boats occasionally— once sinking in an eight—before I went up to the university.

Though I had a marked aversion to the hearties of the College Boat Club, and they too were very suspicious of having a poet around, two factors weighed in my favour: I knew how to cox, and I weighed only eight stone.

I used to cox every afternoon and quite enjoyed the experience because an eight is so rhythmical and graceful. While my crew of beer-drinking beeves were tearing their guts out I would be sitting comfortably swathed in their sweaters, day-dreaming as they pulled me along beneath the willows. Sometimes I would emerge from my reveries to shout "Easy all," then I infuriated them by scribbling a line or two. At other times I would just curse at them to pull harder if I saw a pretty girl on the tow-path ahead. Not without reason my crew hated me. They used to ask the Club President what they were doing with that bloody intellectual in their boat. I once saw his answer: he just pointed to the scales. There was a sort of colour-bar distinction between us: I did nothing to overcome their prejudice and painted myself a little blacker: they invariably cut me if we met outside the boathouse. When it seemed possible that my weight might win me a Trial Cap or even a Blue, there was nearly a mutiny in my boat. I could hear mutterings up in the bow, where a hulking fellow called Fisher rowed. He also boxed for the university and I had the impression he disliked me particularly. I expected to be thrown in the Cam every time I approached it and was surprised that this ducking never occurred. They had other plans however. One night in College, after a Boat Club dinner, the four crews congregated in force beneath my window. Most were drunk, and those that were not made a noisy show of being so. Their chant was "We're going to drown Duncan. Duncan come out!" This was what I had expected: they were overgrown schoolboys and I knew they were bound to conform to type. I opened the window and peered down at the lynchers, feeling anything but brave. But I thought I might just as well go under with a gesture: I put a Prokofiev record on the gramophone and turned on the volume loud. This flood of "highbrow" music infuriated them further; the poor fellows were now unable to hear their own chant. I heard them stampeding up my staircase like a herd of elk. I locked the door. They started to throw themselves at it. Eventually it caved in. They streamed into my room hiccupping and kicking my records and books to the floor. Five men from the first boat approached me. Then I saw Fisher the heavyweight boxer pushing his way through the pack in the doorway. Was I going to be socked on the jaw before being drowned? Inwardly I said goodbye to my teeth. He came towards me, his fist ready clenched. Then a couple of paces from me he turned. "If anybody touches him I'll knock him straight out," he threatened. The four at my side sidled off.

"But this was your idea," somebody called.

"I know it was," he admitted, "but I'm telling you I'll knock the first bastard out that touches him."

The crews seemed to dissolve. I heard them stumbling down the stairs. Fisher waited till the last had gone, then he picked up my books and put them on the table. I couldn't think of anything to say.

"Sorry about the door," he said, picking that up too. Then I heard him tearing down the stairs to rejoin the others in their celebration. Fisher rowed bow in the boat for the next two years. But he never spoke to me in the boathouse and I only used to swear at him on the river. That was the end of the mutiny. I have no idea what became of this Claggart—but it is clear he did not live in vain.

My other distraction was the Festival Theatre. It no longer exists, but in the thirties it was the most lively theatre in England. The Director, and I believe he also owned the place, used the name Quetzecoatl: he was called Terence Gray. Besides running the best repertory I have ever seen, and staging plays twenty years before they reached Sloane Square, he also knew a great deal about wine, and had a vineyard in France where he grew and bottled his own claret. After Gray retired to France, Joseph Gordon Macleod became the Director for some time. Actors like Robert Donat, Betty Chancellor and Flora Robson were members of the permanent company. Sets and costumes were made on the premises. Toni ran the grill where the food—omelettes and trout were his speciality—was as good as anywhere in the country. Besides excellent productions of the classics, I saw Odets, Cocteau, and

Brecht there almost a generation before they were staged in London.

I had only been up at the university a couple of terms when I met a girl called Laura. It is incredible that I can now write the words "a girl called Laura" with such detachment. Even after thirty years I feel rather amazed. It is clear there is something in the cliché: time heals, that is when you're given enough of it.

Laura nearly got me sent down from the university. Not for anything she did, but for what she didn't do. It was on her account that I considered committing suicide: it was on my own account that I didn't.

I was propping up the Festival bar when I saw her. It wasn't perception, but recognition. Though I hadn't seen her in my life before, her features seemed to be a print of a negative in my mind. She was nineteen. She had jet-black hair, very full almost negroid lips and was petite and slim. Something about her, I think it was the mouth, reminded me vaguely of Tallulah Bankhead, whose photograph I had pinned on the wall of my study at school. Or perhaps it was because her hair reminded me of the present Maharanee of Jaipur, with whom five years earlier I used to spend my Sundays holding hands, while Viccy traipsed us round the Zoo. There must have been some reason why I flung the latchkey to my soul at this girl, and then observed her over three years not bothering to pick it up. Perhaps she attracted me so much because she was the embodiment of the sexual compromise I unconsciously sought. From the waist upwards she was the essence of feminity, but her hips were as slim as a boy's. She had the most passionate mouth I have ever seen: like a poppy stuck in the ivory vase of her neck.

Laura lived in Cambridge with her father, a widower who was in the Admiralty. She had two brothers at the university. The family was well off, in some way connected with a baronetcy.

This wretched girl was so pretty she ought to have been prosecuted for her looks. The University Senate should have had her sent down or put away: to let her loose in a town where there were several thousand randy and unattached young men was irresponsible.

93

As soon as I met her, I observed that my rivals were numerous enough to constitute a college by themselves. Some had sports-cars, some had titles: all had height. I had none of these things and was already lamed with melancholy and a temperament that had no place in the sort of social whirl of tennis-parties and dances to which she was attached.

Expecting her to refuse the invitation—it was intended as an improper suggestion—I asked her almost rudely to come to my rooms for tea. To my astonishment she accepted. A couple of dozen suitors bit the sawdust. They should have celebrated their escape: it was I who had been condemned.

Laura arrived at my staircase carrying a parcel.

"And I've brought some cakes," she said. "Somehow I thought you'd never think of them."

She had been right there: cushions, not cakes, were in my mind. I impatiently watched her nibble her sugared buns. I forgot to make the tea. I let her find the milk. My only impulse was to rape her. I don't know how I restrained it. She stayed a couple of hours and left me still holding an unbitten éclair.

The following day she came to tea again. I hadn't been rash enough to invite her. Not only did she bring her cakes again, but a bunch of flowers for the desk she was to prevent me from ever using. This time I indicated what my impulse was, but she picked up a book, pretending not to hear. It was obvious that she was a virgin—as I was too, though if virginity is a state of mind, I could hardly be described as eligible even then. I realised that she held all the cards and there was no alternative but for me to play her game. I have never liked patience.

Laura now came to my room daily. Indeed she used it as her own. The insolent and unshrewd college porter used to refer not to my rooms but my "married quarters." My bedder made aggravating comments about where I should put the pram.

But every time I went to touch her or reach for that poppy which burned on her mouth and in my brain, she would wrinkle her nose at me, smile and put a record on the gramophone. The pity is she didn't stoop, there was no folly.

I couldn't understand why she kept coming to my rooms: why she asked me to her home for dinner at the week-ends, why she never went to a play or a film unless I took her. In the vac she would write to me every few days, gentle and affectionate little notes telling me family gossip, worrying if I was getting down to some of the reading she never permitted me to do in term. Whenever she was given a small part in one of the Festival productions—she was pretty, but not a good actress—she would insist that I cut even my supervisions with Leavis to attend her dress rehearsal. Unless I was in the wings, she wouldn't dare go on the stage.

But in spite of this constant companionship she remained physically unresponsive. Her proximity slowly drove me mad. It was as if she had every attribute but sex, and had been designed specifically to arouse in those who beheld her the appetite she lacked herself. Ice can be melted: Laura could not. Not only did she escape my bed: she managed to avoid my embrace too, always with enough gentleness to give me the impression that she was merely delaying what she herself did not wish to refuse. It proved a false impression. Naturally I worried why, if I did not attract her physically, she lay around in my rooms, in my punt, and even slid an occasional note from her pocket-money into my wallet. After weeks of maudlin meditation on this problem I came to the bitter conclusion that it was not I who brought Laura daily to my rooms, but Ravel. In those days I had a large collection of Ravel records. We were joined together not by desire but by *Mother Goose* and the *Pavane for a Dead Infanta*.

Deep in the emotional morass to which this girl brought me I started to drink Toni's rough red wine by the crate. I didn't work. I read only Donne: I rediscovered Rochester. I wrote poems and burned them immediately. It was more like blood than poetry. Most of my time was spent attending rehearsals in which I was neither author, producer nor actor. I carried her make-up box. The rest of the company at the theatre openly pitied me. They saw through the relationship and knew I was attached to an impenetrable virgin. They saw I was besotted and shook their heads behind my back.

But the incident that nearly drove me to suicide had a funny side to it. It was in my second year, and Laura was having a birthday party on the stage at the theatre. Most of my set received an invitation. When I found that I had not got one I became suicidal. This was the final humiliation. I drew the curtains in my room, opened another crate of red wine, played my gramophone, and refused to go out. My friends became alarmed. My landlady, a terrible dragon of a woman, complained because of the noise, the dust and the empty bottles. Eventually she stormed in after I had been lying there for about ten days, to announce that she was determined to "clean me up." She started to dust the mantelshelf, moved the clock and said:

"Oh, by the way, this letter came for you. I put it on the top of the clock, but I see it's fallen down behind."

She handed it to me. It was the invitation.

Later I discovered that Laura too had been painfully hurt by my not going to her party. I say this is a funny incident because it seems to me to be so typical of most of our lives. We think we are living it, but it is trivial accidents, like the letter we have forgotten to post, or the telephone-number we have mislaid, that shape the accident we call destiny and the fiasco we misname fate.

I might well have committed suicide during those ten days, and the invitation was behind the clock all the time. I wonder how often this sort of thing has been repeated in my life without somebody coming in to dust?

My infatuation led to my nearly being sent down from the university. Several of my friends were, one or two lodging-house-keepers lost their licences, and the University Film Society was bankrupted and remained defunct for the next ten years. For, in order to keep Laura amused, I decided I would write a film for her. Naturally it was based on Ravel. I took his *Bolero* and wrote a story centred round her. My idea was to cut the film against the rhythm of the music, to produce a new kind of screen intensity. It was a good idea, but the decision to make a full-size sound-picture with such inadequate means and equipment was as foolish as it was magnificent. The University Film Society had in effect nothing but a couple of dozen members: it lacked such essentials as a camera, lights or even a studio. I managed to persuade this Society that unless it made a film it would degenerate into a photographic club. The members supported me and volunteered to act as scene-shifters and lighting-crew. I also found they had got £200 in the bank, and with this I hired an old camera and a furniture-warehouse opposite Magdalene.

A friend of mine, Nigel Spottiswoode, who had a mathematical scholarship from Wellington to Peterhouse, promptly abandoned the probability of becoming a Wrangler and became my cameraman. Alternately he cut the film to my stop-watch timing, in counterpoint to Ravel's rhythm. His reward for doing all this was to fail his Tripos and get sent down.

I called the film *Zanzibar*. It was in 35 mm, lasted half an hour and was in some measure inspired by my own experiences in Zanzibar a couple of years earlier, when I had found myself in the brothel there. Laura with her full poppy-mouth and well covered in Max Factor made an excellent stand-in for the little prostitute who had led me off in Zanzibar. The irony of making my adorable frigidaire play this particular part satisfied my masochism. But the other dancing girls whom I had enlisted or enticed from the Festival Theatre had not her inhibitions. When I told them they were all to appear entirely naked they seemed only the more anxious to try on their costumes. Unhappily the Proctors heard of these rehearsals. I was summoned before them and tried unsuccessfully to convince them that there was a distinction between pornography and obscenity. Finally they decreed that *Zanzibar* could be shot so long as my girls wore "brassières and some form of white knickers." I never understood why the knickers had to be white and suspected the Proctors of some fetish. However, with this generous licence in my pocket, we proceeded to turn the handle, occasionally pocketing the offensive bras for a particular shot.

As soon as a reel was in the can, Spottiswoode and I would bolt to Wardour Street, stay there while it was developed, then see the rushes. Both of us abandoned any other activity and entirely forgot we were members of the university. I also forgot my overdraft and ended by paying for most of the film myself. It cost no more than £500—a trivial sum compared to the usual costing for a half-hour sound-film in 35 mm. True, the cast and technicians were paid nothing. Our only costs were stock, hire of lights, a camera, a studio and the not inconsiderable item of gate-fines.

When the film was complete and the sound-track added we had a private view in Wardour Street, and an afternoon showing at the Academy Cinema. Eventually *Zanzibar* was bought as a curiosity by the Film Society and now reposes, I believe, in its library.

It was when I was returning from one of these dashes to Wardour Street with Laura that an incident occurred which revealed our true affection for each other. We were in the back seat of a car driven by an undergraduate, who had played the part of an old Arab in the film. We were late: the road was wet; the driver took risks. The first thing I knew was the sensation of being upside down. I clambered out of the upturned vehicle and immediately peered into the wreck to see if I could find the copy of *Scrutiny* I had been carrying. Laura, who had emerged at the same time from the other side, was looking for her handbag. Simultaneously we both realised that neither of us had had any thought for the other. We never spoke of this revelation.

Having escaped death that way, I tried a more exhausting method the following morning. It was the Cambridgeshire. I had arranged to meet my mother and sister on Newmarket Heath in time for the race. I decided to ride there and hired a seventeen-hand grey hunter from some riding stables in Trumpington Street. I took the twelve-mile ride there leisurely enough and met my relatives all in one piece. I enjoyed rounding up the bookmakers on my grey and galloping across the Heath to follow the race. The trouble started immediately I set the mare for the ride home. I didn't decide to canter: she did. I didn't want her to gallop, but she would. Urged on by racegoers returning in their cars I sped completely out of control along the grass verge twelve miles back to Cambridge. At every crossroad I shut my eyes while the mad mare galloped across, oblivious of oncoming lorries or such impedimenta as pedestrians and small cars. The faster I went, the more the stupid motorists urged me on, sounding their klaxons at this performance, all unaware that it was involuntary. I stayed on that horse's back for the whole twelve miles only because I lacked the strength to fall off. Even after this escapade, I remember I sat up half the night writing. No excess seemed to tire me. I had too much energy, which lack of food or sleep did nothing to diminish. (At forty-seven I suffer from the same ailment. And I am writing this at six o'clock in the morning, impatient with a city that has to snore around me. I shall have written a couple of thousand words before breakfast, then the whole day will yawn before me. No wonder I get up to mischief.)

In spite of the tangle of frantic distractions which I erected round myself, so that my rooms were turned into something between a film-studio, a builder's yard and the dressing or undressing room at the Windmill Theatre, I could find no escape: I still ached with loneliness, though never alone. The self is a prison, we are the jailer, mine merciless; the sentence without remission.

I felt that I was pursued; and I was quite conscious of what it was that hunted me down: it was a pair of eyes, bruised with sadness, not weeping, for they had already spent their tears. Like a Dorian Gray, but the portrait I kept in my attic was not of a young man growing old, but of an old man never young.

When I was with Laura, making the film, coxing on the river, I was aware that I was only playing at these things: the essential me, "coffee, muddle and misery," could not belong, was not identified, and the more I laughed, the sadder his eyes grew.

Stevenson made a simplification when he divided a personality into Dr Jekyll and Mr Hyde. I had to contend with not another single person but an entire crew—"they climb on board and few obey the Captain." But behind this motley gang, the various parts I would try to play, these eyes would look. Sometimes I would see them in the mirror and go unshaven for days. And about this time he or it or whatever began to whisper to me. I was not suffering from the hallucination of voices. There was nothing psychic in the experience, nothing supernatural (how can nature, if it contains the whole, have something which is "super" to it?).

I did not "hear" messages, nor abstruse directions to do anything. I just heard words or phrases of unwritten music. Generally they were single words: and I would suddenly find myself saying the word aloud without relevance to anything. I can remember riding my bicycle down Petty Cury one day and nearly falling off with wonder at the utter beauty of the word "alleviate." For days

I found myself repeating this word, just as some people find themselves whistling a melody that has got on their mind. There were many such words—"Lebanon" was another. I could never remember two lines of poetry together. I never bothered to try. It was not the *sense* of words that captivated me, but their sound. Sometimes I found myself seduced by a word when I had no idea of its meaning, or even when it was in a foreign language.

And just as some words were like melodies to me, so others hurt my ear. I still have a feeling of physical revulsion when I hear certain words: "plate" is one, "knickerbocker" another. There are dozens which, with their awkward consonants, make my flesh creep. It is not because I have any psychological associations with these words: it is that the value of their syllables offends my inner ear. Words I have never heard before can, and often do, produce an almost physical reaction from me. Only the other day I found it difficult to listen to the News although immensely excited about the astronauts, because I could hardly bear to hear the ugly word "orbit" constantly repeated. By ugly I don't mean to infer that I won't use these words. There is a place for ugliness. Ugliness doesn't exist.

But we are a long way from that. We are at Peterhouse. I spent most of my time in Spottiswoode's rooms in Peterhouse rather than in my own at Downing. This for several reasons. Spottiswoode was sympathetic to me for the way Laura treated me, or at least he endured my moan; he also had a collection of Beethoven and Mozart records, was the cameraman on *Zanzibar*, and last but not least the chef at Peterhouse was the best in Cambridge. His *crème brulée* was unsurpassed, his *pommes frites* and mushroom omelette never equalled. This man ought to have been given a Ph.D.

Incredible as it may seem, I was nearly twenty before I heard a Beethoven symphony. I had run into Schubert as a child. I had also heard *Tosca*, *La Bohème*, *Cav* and *Pag* and *The Tales of Hoffmann*. Those and a dozen Schubert songs were the extent of my musical acquaintance. May all the schools and tutors I had before I reached twenty disappear to eternal deafness. To leave a boy as I was left without giving him Beethoven, Mozart, Verdi and a dozen more is to starve him, leave him without bread. This is what I call cruelty to children. The N.S.P.C.C. should acquire an ear-trumpet. Music is an element: how can people live without it? If I had to grade the necessities of life I should put them in this order: the sun, for without that we are dead; horses, for without them to look at we are blind; music, for otherwise we are deaf.

The effect on me at twenty of hearing Beethoven (particularly the Seventh and Eighth Symphonies—Schiller's words in the Ninth never pleased me) and Mozart, Bach and Stravinsky was as though I had previously lived all my life in a tube-station and had one day emerged to be introduced for the first time to the sky. I no longer felt anything like so much alone: though I could not be with people, I could be with music. I bought a huge bust of Beethoven; it went everywhere with me, then somebody stole it from my rooms.

With so much music to hear, I hardly read at all. And while I listened, especially to Mozart, herds of unshepherded words would crowd into my mind. They milled, they had no context or syntax, no dog barked them into meaning, they were just words strung together, sometimes to, sometimes against, always related to, the rhythm of the music.

Though twenty-four mile rides on runaway horses failed to tire me, music did. Lying on the floor listening to Beethoven, Bach or Stravinsky would exhaust me so that I could hardly get up.

Sadly I realised I had been deprived of the one language I needed. For I could not write or read music. I decided—the worst and most stupid mistake of my life—that it was too late to learn. I could never compose, even though the music was in my head. This realisation was like being told I was going blind.

Using the hint of Hopkins's sprung-rhythm, I started to experiment in writing poetry to obtain some of the effects I found in music. I wanted to avoid the rhythm or voice being terminated or dropped by the terrible dead wall of full-stops. I tried to invent a new kind of punctuation to indicate where I required a "carry over," the verse-equivalent of ⌢. These experiments absorbed me. At the time of writing a few of the poems seemed to achieve some of the effects I sought. Effects of these rhythmic experiments, including the excessive use of the colon, were carried over and used in my first full-length play *The Unburied Dead*, which I wrote two years later. But for the most part I abandoned it all, partially in revulsion against the "stream of consciousness" diarrhoea of James Joyce and Henry Miller. Faced with their incoherence I reverted to clarity and order. I destroyed all the poems I had written in this phase. There were about a hundred.

It is disturbing to think how we sometimes affect other people's lives when they have no impact on us. This was the case with E. Dighton-Power. I had forgotten his existence. Even writing this didn't remind me until today. I first met him when I was at school in Yorkshire. In my last term when as a prefect I had gone into the town to have a meal in a café, a man of about thirty got into conversation with me, and as we left the restaurant he bought me a packet of cigarettes. I thought nothing of this, nor did I question his generosity when on several other occasions I found him in the café. Each time he paid the bill and gave me some cigarettes or something to cook for my supper in my study. I gathered he was a bank-clerk and I thought that he gave me these presents because he had been to school himself and knew how one's pocket-money ran out in the first month of term. I never had any reason to think he had any other motive.

After I left school, I thought it a coincidence that his bank should have moved him to London. He suggested we should meet and he used to give me supper at the Popular Restaurant in Piccadilly. No longer did I eat beans on toast. E. Dighton-Power pressed whitebait and oysters on me. His presents became more generous—a Dunhill petrol-lighter, boxes of Rothman's cigarettes. I took this as my due, thinking that I was, after all, giving my time to somebody who was lonely and who didn't interest me at all. He was to me one of those bores who become as burdensome as a conscience. He was also a tedious snob, but there was nothing vicious about him. He was simply pathetic.

On my return from Africa, when I went up to Cambridge, I found him one day standing outside the College gates. He told me that his bank had transferred him to Cambridge. I was annoyed at the prospect of many tedious meals, but saw nothing sinister in the fact that his bank seemed to transfer him wherever I went. For weeks at a time I never saw him. Then I would have a twinge of conscience and dine with him. He always paid the bill. The meals became more lavish, the presents more generous.

During my second year at the university I was so involved in making *Zanzibar* that a whole term passed without my wondering why I had not had an invitation to dine with Mr Dighton-Power. Curiosity eventually took me to his bank, where I discovered that he had been sent to jail for embezzlement.

I should have realised that the presents were beyond his means. It all seemed so pointless. He had worked for fifteen years in the bank. I told my friends what had happened. They all assumed, probably correctly, that he had some homosexual attachment to me. He had not shewn it. It had never crossed my mind. I prefer to believe that he simply enjoyed my company: he was lonely.

I decided I would try to trace him when he got out of prison, to see if I could help him in some way. But what happened? I forgot his existence entirely until I came to write this page. Now the guilt of this omission is alleviated only by the thought that the poor man probably died in the war. And I always thought of myself as a kind person with a gift for friendship. But I see I can even kill off a friend by supposing him dead to lessen my sense of obligation. It seems our capacity for friendship is in proportion to our needs. I required nothing from Mr Dighton-Power.

All this time I continued to see Leavis for two or three hours' supervision each week. One day I arrived early while he had still got people with him downstairs in his study. Queenie suggested I went to a small room upstairs. Sitting there I noticed some verses on the floor in Leavis's handwriting. I read one or two and couldn't place the author—were they examples he'd taken for an essay in *Scrutiny*, excerpts to see if his pupils could place them, or were they poems he had written himself? I never asked him. I do not know. But the suspicion that he was perhaps "poet too" encouraged me to show him some poems I had written. I remember the moment vividly. Even before I had handed the poems to him, he looked as if I had betrayed him. I was bewildered: I could sense that our close relationship had been broken. I did not understand why. He read the poems very carefully once, twice, and then a third time, without any comment. One contained about eight verses. I had worked hard on them. The others were songs. I waited fearful. Leavis put the typed pages down and looked into the fire. He never spoke. It was as if my poems had carried news which gave him unspeakable grief. Then Queenie came into the room to say lunch was ready and suggested I should stay and join them. Leavis ate his meal in silence. I was utterly miserable. Were my poems so bad that he could not comment on them? Had I made him feel that all his work, his tuition, was entirely wasted? I did not know. I left the house after the meal utterly dejected. On the way to my rooms I put the poems in a litter-basket. I didn't write another line for six months. During that time I felt a difference in Leavis's attitude to me. We were no longer close conspirators: I had somehow gone over to the enemy. I sought every means to make him feel that this wasn't so. When he complained that he could never afford to leave Cambridge, I promptly wrote and offered him our cottage in Devon. He refused. My invitation had been a mistake too. Leavis resented being deprived of his complaints.

I had to wait three terms before Leavis made any kind of reference to the poems I had shown him. And then, when he did so, it was as an aside. We had been going through *Ash Wednesday* together, a poem Leavis admired considerably.

"Of course Uncle Tom has a considerable lyrical gift," he said, and then, almost vindictively, "but he can't write anything that sings, like you can." That was all he did say. I found it incredible that he should have been silent for so long about something he must have known concerned me deeply. Such insensitivity shocked me. If he had not liked my poems, then saying nothing about them might well have been a kind of gentleness. But to have admired them and let me feel they were only fit for the litter-basket was hardly an act of an integrated sensibility of "awareness," to use the word always on Leavis's own lips.

For the rest of the time at the university I sensed a growing resentment in Leavis towards me. Gradually I came to the conclusion that, like many critics, Leavis hated creative artists. Apart from his veneration of, almost his crush on, D. H. Lawrence, he resented anyone who could make what he could only criticise.

This was a pity, for apart from Pound he had a better ear for poetry, its intricacies, balance and subtlety than anybody I know. But when he came to write himself, as any *Scrutiny* essay shows, he became almost inarticulate and his sentences sprawled tortuously.

For my last year at Cambridge I managed to persuade Dadie Rylands, the Dean of Kings, to let me move into a house in Newnham Terrace. Ravel records, bust of Beethoven and Laura moved with me. I decided to write and direct a documentary film on Psychology. This was a ridiculously ambitious project. The university bent over backwards to stretch its regulations to accommodate me: I was allowed to use the Mond Lab as a studio, since I was captivated by the shape of the staircase: Professor Cockcroft and Dr N. Feather (whose fag I had been at school) interrupted their experiments trying to split the atom to come and hold lighting-equipment, elderly dons tripped over cables and turned a blind eye to the equipment I borrowed from the Cavendish.

One day Feather asked me if I'd like to look at a little film he'd just made. I went into a studio in the Mond and he showed me a film of nuclei bombarding an atom.

"Will you smash it?" I asked him.

"Eventually," he replied, as though the experiment had no implications outside his lab.

Psychology proved much more expensive both in time and money than *Zanzibar*, but there was no particular event or technical interest in the film. The picture was made up of bits and pieces from my own personal case-book. One sequence depicted a hand-washing phobia and was entirely drawn from my own experience. A professional film-star called Moira Reed, whom I had met through my sister, played the mother in this scene and of course received no payment. I believe I did offer to take her to Belgium for a week-end but she refused. I suppose she felt she had already devoted enough of herself to my napkins.

The maximum chaos was achieved when I came to shoot the dream-sequence. I myself played the dreamer: Laura the object of the dream. In this sequence the dreamer looked out of a top-storey room and saw a close-up figure of a girl standing in the garden beneath him. He then ran down a corkscrew stair (I played this on the staircase at the Mond Laboratory, shooting it in slow motion, then alternately speeded up). As he descended, the dreamer looked out from a window at the girl in the garden, and the lower he went the more distant she seemed; the dreamer became frantic, and jumped whole flights of stairs, till he eventually reached the garden to find the vision he sought entirely disappeared.

In spite of this message, this public statement of my obsession, in 35 mm, did not have even a microscopic effect on Laura. She remained my sisterly shadow; always available, never anything but platonic. When I tried to embrace her or revealed the tension she induced, she would assure me I'd be all right if I had some coffee or a cigarette or went for a walk. She treated these passionate outbursts in precisely the same way as she reacted when I said I had a headache, sympathetically running to a chemist to assure me I would soon recover. Some men get knighted for climbing a mountain, some are canonised for suffering torture and being burnt at a stake, but their courage and endurance are no greater than mine who for three years did nothing more heroic than butter her muffins and find her lipstick.

I was obsessed, repressed, depressed and confused. My friends advised one course; her friends another. There was little to choose between their advice, except I observed that women had less tolerance of her than men. Naturally I was asked whether I endured this suffering because I enjoyed the pain. But that wasn't the reason. I suppose the answer is I endured it for three years because I believed it would end every day.

I once met a man who had been living seven years with his wife without a word crossing her lips. She had sent him to Coventry one day because he had complained that she had not darned his socks. The complaint developed into a row. He went out and got drunk. The next day he apologised, but she would not forgive. I asked this poor creature how he had endured seven years of silence in his own home? He replied.

"You see, every meal I hope she's going to say something to me."

"Seven years is a long time," I remarked, thinking of my own

106

experience. "Don't you find chastity a bit of a strain—or have you got a girl-friend?"

"No, I haven't," he said emphatically, shocked at my last suggestion. "I am faithful to my wife."

"But I thought you said you haven't even spoken a word for seven years?"

"Sexual intercourse," he replied primly, "is hardly the time for conversation."

He was a nice little man. An engraver.

By my last term at Cambridge I had been reduced to emotional pulp. I had read little; what I had written I had destroyed. There were two films to my credit, but my bank had a different opinion. I had been rowed several hundred miles over the Cam. I had stage-managed a Footlights revue, but that too was a distraction rather than an achievement.

As the Tripos approached I began to feel reckless. I had only a hazy idea what the papers were. The recklessness carried over into my attitude to Laura.

One sunny afternoon when she was sprawled in my punt after gorging herself happily on cold salmon and hock—she was a girl with a healthy appetite in one direction—I tried to kiss her. Her reaction was similar to any normal person's if approached by a hypodermic needle filled with yellow fever. As I have indicated, I have a great deal of patience with people, none with things. But I now succeeded in losing my temper, or at least made some show of doing so. I don't raise my voice when I am angry; I almost whisper.

"You can't over the last three years have been entirely unaware that I am physically attracted to you?"

"What did you say?" she asked, trailing her hand in the water.

I regained my temper sufficiently to raise my voice.

"You know bloody well I want you," I said.

"Yes, you made that clear within a minute of meeting me three years ago."

"Well? But you're not attracted to me?" I said, wondering why if that were the case she was usually not only beside me but as now frequently half-clothed and on her back too.

Her reply astounded me. I don't think anything I have heard ever surprised me as much.

"I know what you've suffered; I have too; I'm pretty certain I'm more attracted to you than you are to me. That's why I've had to be so controlled."

I looked at her. She was not lying.

"Then for Christ's sake let's go to bed," I said pushing off and paddling as hard as I could.

I noticed she was weeping. I mistook the cause: I thought it was tension, not sorrow.

"Let me off here," she sobbed as we approached a landing-stage. I stopped. I didn't believe she would get out. But she did. And she walked off without looking round. Her tears were from sorrow. I didn't see her again for a week and then observed, what my friends had been quick to tell me, that she was now the constant companion of a man called Edwards. She no longer came to my rooms. I felt as if I had been divorced. That our marriage had not been consummated made no difference. I telephoned; she was never in. She was invariably with this man called Edwards.

Bewildered by this turn of events, especially her confession which had precipitated it, I confided in a friend.

"You're incredibly stupid about people," he told me. "Didn't you realise Laura was determined to marry you. She didn't want to be the poet's mistress, but his wife. That's why she's kept you at a distance."

"But why did she walk off immediately after admitting she wanted me too?"

"Because she knew she'd played her last trump. And still that didn't make you propose to her. So she threw in her hand. You know what a good card-player she is—and a good Catholic!"

This is the problem I pondered while I sat staring at my Tripos questions. No wonder I discovered one day when I got back to my rooms that I had stupidly given in the question-paper and still had my answers, such as they were, in my pocket.

But Laura didn't look back. I have often noticed that women have an ability to hold obstinately to the wrong decisions. She continued to keep company, as they say, with this man called

Edwards. I knew him; he was everything that I was not: tall, handsome, gay, a good tennis-player and dancer. What's more he was rich. I had been to his parents' flat in St James's. Edwards was destined for the Diplomatic Corps. I began to see Laura's progress leading inevitably to an Embassy. But this didn't happen. I don't know what happened to her relationship with Edwards. But I did discover what had occurred to him.

It was more than fifteen years later when one of Edwards's sisters came round to see me after the first night of one of my plays. I asked her casually what had happened to her brother, quite expecting her to tell me that he had married Laura and was First Secretary somewhere.

"Haven't you heard?" she asked.

"No. I'm sorry. The war, I suppose?"

"No, he's not dead, exactly."

From her tone I could only conclude that he had had some terrible accident. I remembered his bad taste for fast cars.

"We don't know what happened to him," his sister went on. "As far as we can discover nothing did. He just changed completely. Perhaps you remember he was the sort of person who enjoyed life and was very good at it—he came down from Cambridge and was supposed to go into the Diplomatic."

"Yes, I remember."

"But one day he just went out and disappeared. After about three months we found him. He had taken a dingy bed-sitting-room off Clapham Common. He was quite well when we found him. He was lying in bed reading the Sunday papers. That's what he's been doing ever since."

"Reading the Sunday papers?" I asked facetiously.

"Precisely that," she replied solemnly. "For the last fifteen years he has done absolutely nothing but live in his bed-sitting-room, reading the Sunday papers. He only gets out of bed to wander to the pub at the corner and have one pint of beer and buy some cigarettes, then he goes back to his room, gets into bed again and reads the papers for the umpteenth time. He has no friends, he hasn't married or got a girl-friend. He goes nowhere, writes to nobody. He seems perfectly fit and quite content. There doesn't seem to be anything in his life but this absurdly ugly room and the litter of the Sunday papers. I visit him once or twice a year, but he doesn't even bother to give me a cup of tea. He's quite well off. But he doesn't spend anything except the money he gives his landlady."

"And the cost of the Sunday papers?"

"And the cost of the Sunday papers."

Our conversation was interrupted. I've often wondered what part Laura played in causing this psychological débâcle? Probably I shall never know. It occurred to me that I might masquerade as Fate, find Laura, abduct her, take her to the bed-sitting-room at Clapham and leave her in bed with Edwards while he continued to read the Sunday papers.

Pessimist that I was, I couldn't have foreseen any of this when I came down from Cambridge. A few weeks later I was informed that the Examiners had been generous enough to award me a Third Class. Appropriately I arranged for the College porter to attend the Senate, or whatever the drill is, and take the degree on my behalf.

In those days there were over two million unemployed. It was a period in which everybody was busy reforming everything but themselves.

During my last week at Cambridge a deputation of friends called on me. They had come to redeem me. They regarded me as degenerate, a reactionary, aloof from their concern.

"If you'd only take part in the struggle," they said, "you'd soon be as popular a poet as Auden."

"What struggle?"

They told me that the unemployed miners of the Rhondda Valley had decided to march to London as a protest.

"Now's your opportunity," they urged. "Will you write them a March?"

"Wouldn't it be more helpful if I paid their fare?" But I was ultimately persuaded; and when I had written the lyrics for which Alan Bush composed the music, I found myself respectfully addressed as Comrade. Many of my friends decided to accompany the miners all the way from Wales as a gesture of what they called "solidarity." I thought this was a little excessive and said I would meet them in London.

Several days later they all shuffled into Whitehall like an army of undernourished ghosts. They were far too tired to sing. I found myself deeply moved.

I immediately decided that I would live as the miners had to live. I thought that it would be good to see what the so-called progressive theories, which my friends believed in, looked like from the point of view of the person who was to be improved. I did not examine my motives any further; perhaps it was merely that I wanted adventure.

Within a few days of coming down from Cambridge and, somewhat to my own surprise and my relatives' dismay, I left London and proceeded to the Yorkshire coalfields. I planned to live as a miner, and not merely with them as a social worker. Realising that this would entail some alteration in my appearance, I got out of the train at Sheffield and registered at a small temperance hotel, where I was given a very sordid room that was all bed to no purpose.

The next morning I began my masquerade. First I had my hair cut short. Then I went to a pawnshop and bought a second-hand coat and trousers, adding a slouch cap. I put these on in the shop and pawned my own suit as the best means of hiding it. A critical inspection of myself in the pawnshop mirror revealed, however, that there was something wrong with my costume, for I was still wearing my own tie and shirt; so I promptly pawned these too and bought an uncomfortable woollen shirt which I left collarless and completed with a brass stud and a garish muffler.

I paid my bill and put the rest of my money in an envelope and posted it home. Now quite penniless, I left the temperance hotel, aware that any change in my abode could only be for the better.

I went to Chesterfield and from there tramped across slag-heaps to the small mining village of Holmwood. As I walked down the street I felt the inhabitants' eyes like corkscrews in my back. At the first colliery I came to, I asked for a job in the pit. The manager first asked me where I had got my sunburn. For a second I thought he had penetrated my disguise. Promptly I told him I had been doing some odd jobs on a farm, for it was haymaking time.

"Know anything about horses?" he asked.

"I once worked in a circus." My interviews with my house-master now stood me in good stead: I lied to perfection.

He promptly signed me on to look after thirty-five pit-ponies at the bottom of the shaft.

"Be at the pithead at 6.30. Your wage will be £3.15s., less stoppages."

The awful interview was over; I left the office elated. I was now a miner.

I then walked up the street, looking for a room. I knocked at one of these tombstones; a plump, cheerful woman opened the door. I asked if she took lodgers. She hesitated. I was about to turn away.

"I could do with some luck," she said. "You can have board and lodging for twenty-five shillings a week."

As she showed me up the stairs to the back room, I pondered how my presence could possibly bring her luck.

"When you've had a cup of tea, perhaps you'll tell my fortune?" she pleaded.

I realised that my disguise as a miner had failed, but I had suc-ceeded in passing myself off as a gipsy. It was the second time that day that my sunburn had come to my rescue.

A high tea was being prepared in front of the range, which burned gaily with the best coal.

The woman, Mrs Smithson, began to ply me with questions. I told her I should want calling at 5.30 a.m.

"You've got a job in the pit?"

I told her I was to look after the ponies. This confirmed her suspicion as to my race; and she quickly drank her tea and passed me her empty cup.

Like a fool I automatically filled it.

"Wasn't there enough grouts in it?" she asked, drinking quickly.

"The leaves from the first can describe your past," I said, "and the leaves from the second foretell your future."

She was most impressed and passed me her empty cup.

I glared into it. The woman folded her hands as if at a confessional or before an oracle. My mind was a blank. The only thing I could observe was that, in her excitement, she had forgotten to stir her tea. The sugar looked like pack-ice; the leaves like logs in a Canadian river. This wasn't very helpful.

"Won't you tell my future?" the woman said pathetically.

I continued to stare at the crystals of sugar—that sunny dome! Those caves of ice! Then, almost absent-mindedly, I began to mumble Coleridge's poem about the Abyssinian "damsel with a dulcimer."

> That sunny dome! those caves of ice!
> And all who heard should see them there,
> And all should cry, Beware! Beware!
> His flashing eyes, his floating hair!

I looked up. The woman was almost in a trance. Tears streamed down her face. I made a strategic withdrawal, feeling like a cross between Don Juan and Aimee MacPherson.

The next morning I was called at 5.30. I tumbled out into the indifferent dawn, feeling cold and as miserable as a new boy at school. The boots tramped ahead of me; not a man spoke. I followed them through the colliery gates and joined a long queue in front of a small window where a man passed out lamps as the men mumbled their numbers. When my turn came, the lamp-man stared at my face.

"New?" he asked. "Your number's on the lamp."

The flame was no brighter than a nightlight. And it was heavy. I followed the others' example and hooked it on to my belt so that it hung between my legs. Then I joined another queue at the pit-head and waited for the lift.

The miners glared at me through their red-rimmed eyes.

"You the gipsy at No. 10?" one asked. "Pinched old Williams's job, he has."

The lift rose to my rescue; about a dozen of us were bundled in. As it dropped, so did my courage. At the bottom I stood knee-deep in a pool of fear. I glanced up the shaft: the light, like a little saucer, lay at the top of it.

A foreman led me up one of the burrows till we came to a great wooden door. I quite expected a thousand long-tailed fiends to spring out at me. I began to suffer; not so much from my actual situation as from my imagination, which had given my companion the identity of Virgil.

We entered the stable. It was as long as a London tube-station. Thirty-five ponies were tethered to their stalls in a long line. Behind them was a mountain of dung. Virgil turned into King Augeas and handed me a fork and a birch-broom to get moving on his well-known stables.

"Where do I put it?" I asked him.

He showed me an iron truck which ran on rails now hidden beneath the dung. Augeas now left me. I pushed the truck up till it was behind the first pony and began to load it. After I had cleaned the first three stalls I made the terrible discovery that the stable ran up-hill at an imperceptible gradient. The truck was already heavy. I could not begin at the top and load it down-hill, since the dung had to go up in the lift.

It was a relief when I heard the great door open and King Augeas return to give me my next job. This consisted in mixing up a truckload of chopped straw and bran and feeding each of the ponies. They were stocky animals of about thirteen hands, well-groomed and in excellent condition. Augeas told me that many of them had been down the pit for over fifteen years. A little board above each stall was inscribed with its inmate's name. I noticed two newcomers at the end had blank boards, and christened one Beatrice and the other Eurydice.

After I had fed them I was put on to grooming: by midday I was too exhausted to stand. I curled up in one of the mangers to eat my snap. At the moment all the lights went out. The ponies became restive: several began to whinny madly and one of the newcomers, Eurydice, broke her halter and began to gallop in the darkness. I went off in pursuit.

As I groped my way for my lamp, it alone could convince me that I was alive. As I reached for it the lights came on again. I was not dead; somebody had mended the fuse.

Almost immediately a dozen helmeted, black-faced boys came into the stables. They harnessed their ponies to lead them towards the coalface to draw the loaded butts back to the lift at the bottom of the shaft. I persuaded one of these boys to stay in my place and I led Beatrice off and followed the others into the darkness. It was like walking through black velvet: the air was so laden with dust that it was as if one were breathing warm sand.

The pony knew its way and led me through a labyrinth of tunnels. After about a mile we came to a place where a conveyor-belt tipped the coal from the face into the tubs. The roof was too low to walk any further. While I waited for a loaded tub I crawled up through a maze of pit-props to the workings. The road here was only four feet high; as I edged along I could hear the pit-props talking to each other as they took the strain of the earth settling above them, after a charge had been fired at the face.

The face itself was only three feet high. Men lay on their sides, stripped to the waist, hacking at the wall with a pick-axe. Their mates, kneeling beside them, loaded the stint on to the conveyor-belt, which, like an endless crocodile, clawed its way through the workings. I was terrified: each stroke of the pick-axe brought down part of the wall. It looked like energetic suicide, a desperate effort to bury oneself alive. But these matchstick pit-props held the roof of slate and, as soon as the coal was cleared, the miner placed another prop in position and rammed a wedge home with a sledge-hammer. All this time they were oblivious of danger, and spoke only of the relative merits of football players.

As I lay there a miner suddenly began to bash the wedges from the pit-props that supported the roof behind us. I assumed that he had gone mad, and made a gesture to stop him. A row of white teeth grinned at my alarm. It was not mass-suicide, but their usual method of closing the face behind them after they had removed the coal. When half a dozen pit-props had been removed, the roof collapsed, closing its jaws only a few yards from us. I felt rather like a rasher of bacon in a gigantic sandwich of slate. I elbowed my way back to the pony and led the truck to the shaft, reaching it just as the morning shift finished. Once more I shuffled into the cage with my black-faced companions.

Going up in the lift was like being born again. I knew of the miracle that is light, the mercy that is air, and for an hour was content to sit enjoying the security of the sky that could not fall on me.

The next day was the same day: the same trudge to the pit-lift: the same mountain of dung, loads of chop and the deadly echoes of shots being fired at the face. A man called Mancroft who had been stable-lad before me was sent in by a deputy to inspect my work. He examined the feed I had given the ponies.

"It's quite Friday," he announced enigmatically and disappeared.

Another day he returned to help me whitewash the feeding-bin. When he discovered that the nozzle of the spraying machine was blocked, he said.

"The bloody thing is all Monday."

Gradually I cottoned on to the fact that Friday, being pay-day, was for the miners synonymous with good. Monday was the opposite.

After a few days it got around the pit that a Monday gypsy had got Mancroft's Friday job. Then I had one or two visitors. The colliers used to come into the stables and send me off on the maddest errands. I fell for each leg-pull. The first occurred on my fourth day, when an old miner told me to go off down to the engineer's shop and see if the window was shut, and if it were to open the Monday thing. I hastily obeyed, dropping my broom and scuttled off down an unlit tunnel with nothing but my lamp to guide me. I suppose I went half a mile before it dawned on this recent graduate that there were no Monday windows in any Monday coalmine.

On another occasion I told a collier that I was thirsty. Both our bottles of boiled water were empty.

"If you go along to the deputy's office at pit-bottom," he told me, "you'll find he keeps a crate of oranges there. Ask him for one."

Off I went and tapped on this tyrant's door.

"What the bloody hell are you doing here?" he bellowed. "What do you want?"

"An orange?"

"A what?"

"Somebody told me you kept a crate of oranges here."

"Did they? Well I don't. No, don't go away, come in. Perhaps you'd like a glass of iced beer instead?"

116

"Thank you," I said suspiciously, then watched him take a tumbler from the cupboard behind him. In a perfectly elaborate mime, he took the top off a non-existent bottle, slowly pouring the imaginary beer down the side of the glass. Then he handed it to me. I continued the mime, drinking it with relish, wiping my mouth and handing him back the glass.

"That was delicious."

"If I see you in here again you'll get your effing cards," he said, angry at my impudence.

At the end of a week I received my first pay-packet. It worked out at only 7s. 6d. a shift: I had hoped for 9s. 6d., but there were many stoppages or deductions. I paid Mrs Smithson my board of 25s. This left me 10s. pocket money for the week. But worse was to come: that evening a notice outside the Manager's Office stated casually that there would be no work till the following Wednesday. I discovered to my relief and horror that this excluded me; the horses had to be fed; the daily shift carried down only maintenance men who worked the pumps.

This lay-off was due to the quota-system which the Government had introduced. To keep the price of coal up, pits were allowed to produce only so much coal a year. The whole village apathetically attached itself to the dole-queue, from which the allowance was 2s. 7d. per day.

Like a live lobster being boiled, I felt myself going redder every day. After a few more weeks of this I realised I would be not a communist, but probably a full-time assassin.

I was angry; exhausted with a feeling of impotence. What was most frustrating was the placid way the colliers and their wives accepted the conditions of work, of living. If you mentioned the matter or suggested some improvement, they thought you were "a bit daft."

But the village stopped talking dog-racing for forty-eight hours when one morning, about a month after I'd been there, seventy colliers received their cards in one day. Some of these men had been working for twenty years in the pit. They were left without even their chains. They could do no other job; there was no other job. Their future was embodied in the slag-heap that overhung the village like a mountain, its ash blowing into everything.

I began to understand my friends at Cambridge who had called me degenerate and asked me to write a march for the Welsh miners. But I realised there was little point in writing marches.

After three weeks I realised that I had eaten fish and chips at 10 p.m. for twenty-one nights in succession. The "fish" was served in a sort of felt glove. They called it batter. The chips were flabby. You smothered this food with some sauce from a bottle, so that you couldn't taste the fish. And in order not to taste the sauce either you swilled the lot down quickly with very sweet, strong tea. I became obsessed with the desire for oranges. I even dreamt of them. I dreamt of a girl with a necklace of breasts, and each of her breasts was an orange.

One evening after I had scraped off the grime, Mr Smithson, my landlord, said he could put me in the way of earning a few bob. He was obviously doing me a favour, giving me the opportunity before his own son. Outside the house I asked him what the work entailed.

"Nothing to it," he said; "you get 3s. 6d. and all you've got to do is box the cinema-manager."

"I can't box," I replied.

"Don't worry, he's dead."

The idea of scrapping with his corpse appealed even less to me—in spite of the programme I'd seen last Saturday. I turned to go.

"All you've got to do, chum, is help lift the bloke into his coffin and screw down the lid. The undertaker asked me if I knew of anybody, so of course I thought of you."

"Why?"

"Don't you want to get on?"

"No, I want to get off."

Shrugging his shoulders he led me into the local pub. After he'd drunk five pints and four double whiskeys he began to confide in me.

He started by asking me if I wondered how he could put a £5 note down on the bar when he only had a job as a lamp-checker drawing £4. 10s. a week? As the question was obviously rhetorical I said nothing. I knew he gave Mrs Smithson a housekeeping allowance of £3 a week, because she used to tell me that my board

118

and lodging at 25s. and her son's contribution of 15s. made the total to £5.

To impress me Mr Smithson produced three fivers from his pocket. There was a man in the village whose hobby was coining two-shilling pieces—I had bought several for a shilling each and passed them off at the cinema, and I wondered whether this fellow had extended his operations to printing.

"They're genuine," said Mr Smithson, reading my thoughts. "Fact is I run a book on the Q.T. It's a poor week if I don't show £40 on the right side."

"And you still give your wife only £3?"

"Sure. You see, chum, I've got a girl in Sheffield. I'd like you to meet her."

"Why?"

"Because I guess you can pick em! Yes," he said now quite maudlin, "I'm taking her to Brighton for a fortnight. Missus thinks I'm going into hospital. Yes, I've seen life."

He rambled on and then suggested that he should write up his life as he called it and I should get it published. This suggestion alarmed me. Drunk as he was it was apparent that he had seen through my disguise.

"Why do you think I could help?"

"I've been a bookie twenty years," he leered, "so I know a toff. They smell different-like. And let me give you some other advice. If you want to pass yourself off as a working man, don't stand up when my wife comes into the room, don't put your sauce on the side of the plate but sprinkle it all over your food, don't wait till you've swallowed your grub before you drink—we drink to wash it down; and don't look so bloody sad—try and look vacant."

"All my race look sad. And I picked up some habits when I was a waiter."

"Where?"

"Epsom," I said quickly, fishing a fag-end out of my pocket and wiping my nose with the back of my hand.

"Like hell you did! I tell you a bookie can smell out a toff, same as a dog does a bitch."

As I walked him down the street I made a bargain with him.

"I'll keep your secrets if you forget the idea that there's any mystery attached to me."

We were by his front door. Mrs Smithson was waiting up. The threat was opportune, the blackmail successful.

After a few weeks in the stables I began to get on top of the work. It would take me from 6.30 till 9 a.m. to muck out, forking the dung into the truck and pushing the load to the pit-bottom. Then I would have my snap of cheese-sandwiches, an apple and boiled water. I could never spend long on this break because the longing for a cigarette became insufferable. From 9.15 to 11.15 I fed the ponies, mixing their bran and chop and watering them. Then it took me an hour or two to groom and do some odd job such as whitewashing a stall or fixing a halter. But generally I was through about 1 o'clock and could then lie on the straw in one of the empty stalls. My thoughts would then exhaust me more than the work had done. Manual labour, even a miner's, was comparatively relaxing. Sometimes I would just sleep, sometimes I'd lie there worrying, not at the conditions in the village, but about the people themselves. At other times I would scribble on the whitewashed walls. These poems got covered up in a day or two and I never bothered to take copies. In them I was trying to forge a new style by abandoning the tired formula of saying that something was like something. I wanted to force the attribute into an adjective or an adverb. As for instance "pneumatic lorry relief"; "poster-plastered day"; and thus concentrate the image. My ultimate aim was to do the same for verbs. I remember writing the lines:

> In the forest of my dreams
> My fierce desire
> Stalks her movements
> Like a tiger.

Disgusted with this cliché-style I kicked the whitewash with my boot till it flaked off, then I rewrote:

> In the forest of my dreams
> My fierce desire
> Tigers her movements.

There is a difference.

Then the siren would go and I'd pick up my lamp, bottle and snap-bag, walk along the track to pit-bottom and wait for my turn for the cage.

This lift was a daily gift of the miracle that is light. With the red-rimmed eyes of the colliers packed beside me, my lamp hanging heavily on my belt, the steel door would slam and up we'd go. Sometimes I could see rivulets of grime running down the shaft. But whatever the weather, when we jolted to the platform on the surface, it was light. Every day I experienced birth this way. And because I felt such gratitude for light—gratitude for my eyes—everything else, such as politics or resentment about the conditions of the work, seemed trivial to me. Concern with politics or social questions is a luxury which exists only when life itself is secure. And life is light. The paradox is that we can fully enjoy only what we have been deprived of for a time. Sailors rescued from a submarine worship the solidity of land; astronauts know earth-sickness as we can only experience home-sickness; but most of us, like the colliers beside me, who trudged from the lift to hand their lamps in, were so used to the daily miracle that they did not notice it. But an accident down the pit can bring those rescued quickly to their knees. For gratitude is a prayer. This experience taught me that life can be enjoyed—that is, lived—only when we are insecure. The pity is that everything now moves towards giving us security, comfort, and when we have been given all that, life itself will be stolen from us. True luxury, real affluence of living, can be obtained only if we are blind so as know the gift of sight; hungry to realise the grace of food, and sick enough to apprehend this miracle that is life. Material well-being can only make us spiritually undernourished. We are deprived of the basic, fundamental gratitudes (beatitudes) of being. What is the point of giving men security of living and stealing from them the insecurity that alone can give them the experience of life? How poor is a man unless he has wept for joy because he can see? How starved, unless he has clapped his hands and danced just because it is raining and the rain will, he knows, make his potatoes grow? We say that we are striving to give every man a full life, but he has, I suspect, not begun to live unless he has lain sometime or other on his back in a field and clutched at the earth beneath

121

him and cried with pleasure just because the sky was above him.

Such were my incoherent thoughts as I stumbled out of the pit-yard every day, dragging my heavy hob-nail boots, swopping poor jokes with my mates, and cadging a fag off them, with hardly enough strength to walk up the street to my lodgings.

On my way I used to pass a great slag-heap with a foul pond beside it. The water was yellow with sulphur. Not a shrub grew on the slag; not a weed stood beside the water. For me this pond was utterly beautiful. Coming up from that velvet void of blackness anything was beautiful, could give pleasure to the eyes. Standing there then I realised forcibly that ugliness doesn't exist. Any *thing* is beautiful: its very existence makes it so. I used to imagine what my reactions would be if I were sealed in a black sound-proof ebony sphere for a week, unable to see, to hear, or to touch. I realised that in such a state one would find any sound music; any shape exquisite; any article precious. These musings made me certain that objective criticism couldn't exist. Beauty is a question of vitality; the only ugly thing is death.

Then I would remember I was famished and filthy and go on up the street where my dinner, loaded high on a plate, would be already waiting in the kitchen oven. Mrs Smithson would be standing there by the stove, the extravagant fire always glowing brightly, the big kettle always on the boil and a large teapot ready. She would take my empty water-bottle and sandwich-tin, help me off with my dust-caked boots, then pour water into a tin bath, turning back to help pull my shirt off. I have never found anything quite so luxurious as these baths in the back scullery. I remember the moment I looked forward to most; it was a simple one, the pleasure of blowing my nose and freeing my nostrils of the loathsome cake of coal-dust. But though I would wash hard, not all the grime would come away; by sweating in the pit, the dust got into the pores of the skin. But that was no hardship.

Then I would wolf my dinner; meat, a mountain of potatoes and Yorkshire pudding, all soused in thick gravy, shovelling it in and washing it down with sweet tea, the local newspaper propped up on the teapot.

Then Frank Smithson would come in. He worked on top at

the pit. Being a white-collar worker, he didn't get the same consideration as I did from his mother. And after the meal we would go to the billiard hall or catch a bus to the next village, where Frank had a girl-friend, Angela.

She was a dark, petite creature who served in a shop in Chesterfield. Her hair was attractive but she was far from pretty. There was an understanding, but no enthusiasm, between them. They had £40 saved, and planned to get married when it reached £100. I observed that as they approached this target Angela became increasingly extravagant on little things.

Frank thought his fiancée was beautiful: I found it difficult to understand this opinion. So did he too, poor fellow, when one day he had the misfortune to get his eyes tested. I remember the disappointment he expressed on the bus home the day he first saw her through a pair of spectacles. From that day I realised that both needed rescuing before their savings mounted to entomb them in each other. But I could do nothing except teach Angela to smoke and persuade Frank to risk an occasional half-crown on the dogs. But he was an unlucky man and even dogs he backed won at long odds.

For a few days, as Angela saw their savings mount, she started to flirt hopelessly with me as a forlorn means of escape. Frank, observing this, only encouraged her. I decided that to avoid further envelopment in this direction I would, in future, leave them to themselves and spend my time on these evenings with Angela's girl-friend, Maureen, who lived a few doors away in the same street. She was a dull-looking girl of about twenty with large eyes, large breasts and a listless air of unwanted virginity about her. We also had something else in common: her tuneless upright piano which was in the front parlour with teams of relatives' photographs on it.

She played her piano to me the first day we met. This was quite an achievement on her part, for her parents considered themselves a cut above colliers, and when her mother heard I "worked down t'pit" she looked down the promontory of her nose and indicated that I might dirty her parlour. But Maureen insisted, and in a few moments was banging out some terrible musical-comedy tunes. Bored, I picked up some old Grade II music-book containing "gems from the classics." I asked her to try something from this. She played badly, but the piano was so out of tune it was difficult to know whether her finger or the note was at fault.

For half an hour I fidgeted by the window, enduring emeralds from Brahms and sapphires from Schumann. Then suddenly I heard a melody I had never heard before. It was so beautiful I had to rush from the room, from the house, before the girl or the mother could see my tears. Years later I heard the melody again. Of course it was Schubert—"The Shepherd on the Rock."

My precipitate exit proved most unfortunate. Nothing I could have done could have intrigued Maureen more. She came from a world of painful politeness and precise conventions: my rudeness was a new experience for her. From that day she flung her cap at me: her listlessness disappeared. She became as energetic and determined as any woman about to devour a male.

Perceiving her intentions, I decided to avoid her front parlour at all costs. And the next day when we met I refused her invitation to go home with her, and then, seeing her disappointment, foolishly suggested that we went for a walk instead. This cheered her up.

"Where to?" she asked.

"Down through the woods," I replied casually.

At this suggestion her eyes glistened predatorily. We walked in silence, Maureen a pace ahead. She knew, she said, of a place where some foxgloves grew. The trees were mostly silver-birch, smutty with soot, the ground between them soiled with litter and the occasional insoluble contraceptive. But Maureen pressed on till she found her dozen lanky foxgloves, which did give me a momentary yearning for Devon. Mistaking my nostalgic expression for something to do with her, she sat on a tree-trunk and handed me a sandwich of silence. Having been to the cinema often too, I dimly perceived that the setting was appropriate for an embrace. But being cruel, I paused to examine my feelings; a casual scrutiny revealed I had none. Then from mistaken kindness I took the girl's hand.

This was fatal. If I had, I later discovered, tried to tumble her there, my act would have meant that I was just like the others. But by just taking her hand I was "showing respect," "being serious."

124

Having made this mistake, I withdrew from one error only to make another. I suggested that we should walk over to Hardwicke Hall. I was feeling tired, but preferred to move rather than sit there holding this wedge of silence beneath her articulate eyes.

"It's getting dark," she said modestly; "they'll wonder where we are."

"Let them," I replied, helping her up from the tree-trunk.

"Are you sure you want to go for a walk?" she asked ominously.

"Yes."

Her response was to squeeze my hand. Almost immediately she began to tell me of her ambition to live on a farm. I listened vaguely, unaware that she was planning our future together.

"You're so good with horses," she said eventually; "I daresay you'd be good with cows too."

I walked on, too tired to listen to her schemes. But the further we went the more confident and voluble she became. Two hours later we entered her house. Both parents were waiting up—in the front parlour.

I expected disapproval. But Ma beamed at me and, to my surprise, Dad offered me a cigarette. Mother and daughter disappeared into the kitchen to make some tea. Meanwhile Dad asked me a few leading questions: I discovered that my intentions towards his daughter were now taken for granted. I was bewildered and felt I was reading the end of a bad novel, having missed out a key-chapter or two. When the two women returned from their natter in the kitchen, the mother started off by calling me "Ron." By the second cup I realised that I was now accepted as part of the family. Somehow or other they assumed that Maureen and I were unofficially engaged.

In a panic I made my get-away and hurried down the street to find Frank, who was sitting in the kitchen making toast with Angela. I dragged him off, and on the bus told him of my predicament.

"You asked for it, chum!" he said. "In these parts if a man takes a girl for a walk through the woods *after dark* it means they're going to get married."

"Why?"

"Or will have to, same thing."

"But I never touched her."

"Only you know that," he said.

I discovered that protocol in a coalmining village is more rigid than in an Embassy. And the next day, when I braved Maureen's house to make it clear that my intentions were that I had no intentions, I found I had walked into a *fait accompli*. Ma invited me to call her Mother; Dad addressed me as "Son"; and Maureen was playing *The Lily of Laguna* as though it were the praying mantis's triumphal war-cry.

Not a word had been said, not a kiss exchanged. She knew that I knew I had, as it were, been bowled a fast one. And I suppose she realised that she had better play fair.

"Let's go for a walk," she said.

"I don't feel like walking."

"Then we can lie down, can't we?" she replied suggestively.

It was clear that, having sold me the house, she was now prepared to let me view the premises. With security in her pocket, her brazenness was almost clinical. But I was not angry with her: she was playing the game as she had been taught it.

"No, I don't feel like a walk," I repeated dimly; "besides, it looks like rain."

"Then we can stay here," she said, getting up to shut the front parlour door.

" Ma's out," she added, flinging herself on the sofa.

I was still not angry, but nauseated by the whoredom of matrimony. It was as if I now held a receipt.

"I want you," I said, and then paused cruelly—"to play the piano to me."

She got up sulkily.

"Chopin," I said, handing her the Grade II music-book.

And while she played the wrong notes, I tiptoed unobtrusively from the room. I never saw her again.

The next afternoon I didn't change, and I told Frank that I would give our daily visit to the neighbouring village a miss. He went off disappointed. It was clear he preferred my company to his fiancée's. When I had seen him off on the bus, I wandered across some fields and lay down in the sun. I must have dozed off, for when I opened my eyes, two policemen stood above me.

126

"Get up," one of them commanded, taking me by the collar. I didn't move.

"Where did you sleep last night?" the other bobby asked, yanking me up. "You'd better come along with us."

"What for?" I demanded.

"Vagrancy," the first policeman said.

"I've got a job here," I replied.

"Sure you have!" the second man commented, bending down and holding my legs while the other examined the turn-ups of my trousers.

"You can't fool us, gipsy," he said, pointing out the grass-seed lodged in the creases of the cloth; "you've been sleeping out, haven't you?"

"The grass-seeds could have got there by walking through grass."

"Don't give lip," he said; "either you get going, or you come along with Constable Mancroft to the station."

"Mancroft?" I repeated remembering that was the name of the man I had replaced in the stables down the pit. It was on the tip of my tongue to give Mrs Smithson's name to prove that I was not a vagrant, but instead I produced my union-card as proof.

The bobby examined it, and put it in his pocket.

"You'd better get going," he said.

"Give me my card back."

"What card? I haven't seen any union-card, have you?" he said, winking at the constable. "We'll give you half an hour," he added, "before we pick you up."

With that the law walked off. I pondered whether to ring my solicitors, and stay and fight the matter. Instead I went to see the manager of the pit. He listened, then told me he could do nothing and it was no use my going to the pit next day without a card.

I walked past the pond for the last time, then caught a bus to Sheffield. I had nothing to pack. I decided to write my goodbyes. An hour later, still wearing my pit-clothes, I caught a train to London.

After leaving the coalmine I took a small flat in Brixton, which I shared with two friends from Cambridge. We paid 30s.

127

a week and lived on herrings and stew. I used to make this on Monday morning, and it invariably went bad by Thursday. The two friends were Asquith and Spottiswoode. Asquith was a mathematician who had been at school and Cambridge with me. Spottiswoode was now an electrical engineer. He had invented an electronic movie-camera and together we formed a company called Electro-Optical Industries. All my allowance was spent in buying valves and condensers. I used to busy myself writing pamphlets and poems. My sister acted as typist and char to the three of us.

I now became involved in politics; a typical 1930's figure, dining at the Café Royal and worrying abstractedly about the working class. But I could find no point of sympathy with the Communist Party and its violence, or the Socialist Party and its Victorian ideology. I wanted revolution: I shrank from violence. Democracy struck me as the rule of the lowest common denominator.

Every day the dole-queues lengthened and the armaments piled up. War seemed inevitable. I joined the Peace Pledge Union and wrote a pamphlet for it called *The Complete Pacifist*. In this I explored the use of non-violence in industrial strikes. The first edition of the pamphlet—it was the first thing I had written which had got into print—was well received by people like Aldous Huxley, Eric Gill and the Rev. Dick Sheppard. This "flat ephemeral pamphlet" became an official publication of the Peace Pledge Movement and was reprinted by the Bodley Head. Spottiswoode and I now stalked the countryside addressing Peace Pledge Union meetings, holding forth on non-violence and drinking gallons of tepid coffee on behalf of the cause. At this time I was persuading hundreds of people to refuse their call-up when it came for conscription and was directly responsible for many of those people going to gaol. It was embarrassing that I never went myself.

About this time there was a "stay-in" strike in the Rhondda Valley. Some twenty or thirty miners had decided to stay at the bottom of the pit-shaft until their demands were met. I immediately left for Wales when I heard that the miners were thinking of smashing some of the machinery underground if the management didn't meet their claims. The pit was at the top of the hill outside the village. When I arrived there I was looked on with considerable suspicion. I was not a welfare officer, I didn't look like a reporter, I wasn't a clergyman, and I certainly wasn't a Welshman. I walked up the hill towards the pit-head, and about a dozen women, wives of the men who had been underground for four or five days, accompanied me. They didn't know what I was going to do; I didn't either. Eventually I sat on the ground by the pit-shaft and tried to explain to these women that if their men started to smash up the machinery the public would lose sympathy with their cause and they would play into the management's hands. To my surprise the women saw my point immediately: they wished I could go down to make the men understand. I could not do that, but, when the time came for the women to send down a basket of sandwiches, I smuggled a letter to the strike-leader and I also sent down some tobacco for the men to chew. When I walked down the hill the women were friendly to me, but I noticed that the police were following me.

I went into the Union office to see if I could see the local secretary. He was a Communist and wanted to know what the bloody hell I was doing poking my nose into their affairs. It was clear to me that he was directing the strike and wanted it to become as violent as possible. He was hoping to get the other miners to come out, and was quite indifferent to how much suffering was caused in the Valley. I left his office, went for a long walk, deciding to stay on and see the thing through. But, while I walked, the Communist had not been idle. Returning to the village, I decided to take a room. I had to go from pub to pub only to be turned away. Each one told me that they had no accommodation. After I had been to six pubs I started to go to ordinary houses to try to get a room. An old woman eventually agreed to take me in, but after she had shown me to a room and I had nipped out to get some cigarettes, I suppose she had a visitor; at any rate she changed her mind and said that her husband had not agreed to her letting the room after all. I went down the street and succeeded in taking another room. Two hours later the landlady gave me the same story. I could see she was lying. It was now dark. I had no alternative but to walk the village, banging on doors, to no avail. About midnight I found a coke-brazier in the street where the road was up, the night watchman's hut by it. It was frosty, but quite warm beside the fire. I curled up on the pavement, utterly exhausted, and had just managed to doze off when the police came along and arrested me for vagrancy. ¡This was precisely what the Communist Secretary had intended. He knew that by persuading pubs and boarding houses to refuse to take me in and tipping my condition off to the police they would have no other alternative. The police admitted their predicament to me when they had taken me to the police station.

"Your best plan, chum, is to make your way out of here," a friendly sergeant told me. "You'll never get anybody to give you a bed if Wilfred Jones decides you aren't to have one."

They let me sleep in the cell and treated me civilly enough once I had decided to catch the train in the morning. Indeed one of the policemen brought me a cup of tea to my cell in the morning and accompanied me down to the railway station.

But I had other people to see me off. Somehow the women whom I had spoken to on the hill also knew of my predicament. I was extremely touched when I saw them turn up on the platform with a little packet of sandwiches for my journey.

"Your letter down the pit has done some good," they said. "Our men aren't going to break anything up. Madge has had a note up to say so."

I left feeling that I had not completely wasted my time. And I had taken another measure of Communist methods.

Some time after this, Dick Sheppard died and Spottiswoode, who was now working permanently at the Peace Pledge Union, decided to organise a memorial concert at the Queen's Hall. He suggested that I should write something. His idea was to get a performance of Stravinsky's new work *Jeu de Cartes*, and it was suggested that I should write the words for a cantata especially for the occasion. Spottiswoode had been working at times with the G.P.O. Film Unit at Blackheath, as a cutter. He had told me before that there was a promising young composer there who had been writing music for a documentary film on the Post Office which had words by Auden. His name was Benjamin Britten. Spottiswoode thought he might be a person I could work with, and arranged a meeting.

Britten and I met at the Mainly Musicians Club in a basement behind Oxford Circus. We immediately planned our cantata. It was going to be a very ambitious piece, full symphony orchestra, soloists and choir. I promised Britten the libretto within a few days. We now met frequently, either at the Mainly Musicians Club or at his home in Finchley, where he lived with his two sisters and his mother, above a grocer's shop. His mother was a birdlike woman, very possessive and very proud of "Benjy." I used to go to this flat a good deal to work with Britten. Our *Pacifist March* soon took shape. Britten composed it in a month. I remember the music was slightly derivative from Mozart's *Turkish March*. Britten was aware of this. He orchestrated the piece, writing the score out in a large red leather-bound manuscript-book. It was a very ambitious piece, almost Berliozian in conception. Two or three people heard Britten play it over. They were very impressed. The work was never performed; the orchestral score has disappeared. Britten says he gave it to Stuart Morris, who was the new secretary of the Peace Pledge Union. I myself suspect that Britten himself has locked it up in his trunk which contains an oratorio with an aria sung by God and various other ambitious and youthful works which he does not wish anybody to see. I also—but not for the same reasons— lost my copy of the libretto.

I had now started a correspondence with Ezra Pound. I had sent out a number of copies of my pacificist pamphlet, including one to him and one to Gandhi. Pound's comments on my pamphlet were not very complimentary. As was to be expected, he pointed out that I had failed to give due importance to economics. Owing to the prim prejudices that had been inculcated into me by Leavis, I myself looked upon Pound at this time as a renegade poet who had become a Fascist. Accordingly I wrote back a rude postcard in verse mourning the black-shirted poet and pointing out that the black shirt was probably because he was mourning for the talent he had lost since writing "Mauberley." This piece of incredible insolence only produced more letters from Pound, who approved of my rude verses and urged me to start a poetry magazine.

I continued to meet Britten and a friend of his, also a

131

composer, called Henry Boys, and we would sit for hours discussing the composers whose reputations we intended to deflate in this new magazine. I remember that Britten was most emphatic that Delius deserved mowing down. Brahms was another of his *bêtes noires*. At this time he believed only in Berg, Mahler and Stravinsky. The name of Puccini made him feel sick. I could never agree. Boys, whose taste was more eclectic, had more intelligence than Britten and I put together. He had a kind of Buddha-like appearance and used to get lost in Kensington, where he attended Ouspensky's lectures.

Britten and I were now constant companions. He used to play Schubert to me. I had been looking for Britten for ten years. Sometimes he would play Chopin, but it was Schubert that I would make him play over and over again. We used to sit for hours discussing operas that we were going to write, or ballets in which I would write verse-commentaries and he would be delegated to making a few noises off.

And besides these interests we shared other problems. Both of us were without a father; both of us were hopelessly tied to our mother; both of us had a sister. Sex was another problem we shared. I recall one very dark November evening, having sat with another friend in a forlorn café, and both of us shuffling down Wardour Street to look for an "experience." We stood in a doorway, watching the prostitutes pass, my friend fearful that I would make a move, I terrified that he might, but more confident that he wouldn't. I remember his immense relief when I suggested that we went back to the café and had another coffee. Anything better than those hags. He agreed. It was a very sad evening. There were many like them.

One morning at this time I received, to my surprise, a reply from Gandhi, to whom I had sent one of my pamphlets. He wrote saying he was very interested, made some criticism of it and suggested I should read *The Gita*. I immediately sent him a cable suggesting that we should meet. He replied also by cable giving a date and the place: Wardha. I hurriedly looked at a map and saw that Wardha was in the centre of India. I noticed from the calendar that Gandhi's date was little more than three weeks away. I immediately booked my passage to India and telephoned Britten to tell him what I had decided to do. He was very alarmed, fearful that I was never going to appear again.

"I cannot come to India," he said, "because I can't afford the fare, but I will come as far as Paris to see you on your way."

Henry Boys also agreed to do this and, by the week-end, the three of us left Victoria. This was the first time Britten had been out of England, but I had been to Paris once before when I was at school. I led my friends straight to the hotel where I had stayed then; it was called the Hôtel Indo-Hollandais, a dingy little place in the Rue d'Hauteville, off the Boulevard Haussmann, but cheap. We decided to spend five or six days there before I had to go down to Marseilles to catch the boat to Bombay.

We slept in one room, or rather shared one room and never slept. We talked most of the night. I had bought a copy of *Ulysses* and used to read it aloud; Britten had a score of *Le Sacre du Printemps*; while Boys was usually reading Berg. This visit was an adventure. The three of us were extremely happy, experimenting with food, buying books and rushing round Paris in taxis. I took them along to Shakespeare & Co and introduced them to Sylvia Beach. We went to *Fidelio*. I got the false impression that Britten did not admire the work, when it was the performance he had reservations about. After the opera we walked to Notre Dame; Britten was impressed by the stained-glass rose-window, I by the gargoyles. The next day we went to the Folies-Bergère. A commissionaire at the theatre suggested that we should visit a brothel before the performance. I remember we were led upstairs to a sort of Empire drawing-room. We were urged to buy a bottle of pink champagne. Then a dozen or so girls came in and stripped in front of us. I had a distinct feeling that I was about to give them a medical examination. Britten was blinking in terror. I regarded these females with strange aversion.

"I don't know what you think," I said, turning to him, "but to me they're all like boiled potatoes."

We scuttled out, leaving the champagne undrunk and immensely relieved to get into the street again.

We hurried off without discussing where we were going. For the next hour we walked round and round Notre Dame.

133

I left Paris a day or two later, and Britten and Boys came to the station to see me off. Britten seemed extremely oppressed, saddened beyond his understanding. I asked him on the platform what was wrong and I remember he said:

"I know that my life will change from today. I have a sense of doom. I can't understand it, but it oppresses me."

I dislike ships, or rather the gin-fizz life on them. But on my journey from Marseilles to Bombay I was relieved of this kind of enforced social pressure by being entirely ostracised by my fellow-passengers soon after we sailed. I achieved this distinction on the first evening out when I discovered I had been placed at the Captain's table. After a course had been served, I happened to notice that all the Indians, even though they were first-class passengers, had been segregated to separate tables for Asiatics at the end of the dining saloon. This shocked me. I immediately stood up and asked the Captain to excuse me, left his table and seated myself with the Indians. As a consequence the whites cut me for the rest of the voyage—all except one elderly Scotsman who seemed determined to fumigate me with his pipe and frequently drew up a chair beside me on deck.

The ship called at Genoa, Port Said and Aden. The only excitement I found at these places was a letter from Pound at each begging me to read Villon, questioning my enthusiasm for Hopkins, and again urging me to return via Rapallo so that we could join forces and start a literary magazine. I didn't answer these letters. At this time I was feeling so incensed at the human squalor I had seen in the mine at Holmwood and at Rhondda, at the lengthening dole-queues and mounting armaments, that I could think only about politics. Poetry seemed an indulgence: like St Jerome I almost vowed not to read any more. Of course this negation had an inverse effect. Poetry perched on my consciousness as soon as I woke up. But I tried to ignore the whisper: and if I caught myself writing a few lines I would throw such "subjective hosannahs" overboard. I tried pathetically hard to read Karl Marx. But the false simplifications on every page used to make me throw the book at the wall. Then I would swallow my spleen and try again. But the more I read of economics, the more certain I became that neither Marx's capitalism nor Pound's usury were root-causes of the squalor, but were in fact themselves manifestations of the spiritual bog. My mind was confused. But what I did perceive was that materialism was not enough. I didn't know what I meant precisely by spiritual values; my religious beliefs were hopelessly incoherent and I was still suffering from the nausea and hangover caused by the slush of school chapel. I had no truths in my pocket. I only had a few certainties: Schubert, Donne, and Schubert. But as I waded through the turgid Victoriana of *Das Kapital*, and those great bores the Webbs, I knew the Communists and Socialists were right enough, only to be terribly and dangerously wrong. And as a compass, a remark of Aldous Huxley's kept coming to my mind. "You can't mend a wrist-watch with a hammer." I believe the image was originally Gerald Heard's and appears in one of his books. At any rate it helped me to counter in my own mind the temptation of falling for easy solutions which are only bedevilments. Gradually I saw that if people confined themselves to materialism, to things, they would become things too.

I was so worried by all this, so sick at the sores which are called the romantic East, that I hardly noticed the fact that I was in Coventry on the ship or that it had reached Bombay.

Here I refused to go to the hideous and vulgar De Luxe Hotel and booked in at a hotel for Indians. I regretted this: the sanitation there stank more than colour-prejudice. But I was rather touched to observe that my ubiquitous Scotsman with the pipe had been sufficiently influenced by my ideals to book in at the same hotel.

A day or two later I took a train to Wardha—and was more than surprised to find both Scotsman and pipe, not only on the train but in a reserved seat next to mine. I remarked on the extraordinary coincidence.

"It almost looks as if you're following me," I said.

"I am," he replied, "and I wish you'd stay at a better class of hotel in future."

He told me that my cables and letters to Gandhi had been intercepted and he had been detailed to see that "I didn't get up to mischief or throw any bombs." I promised to keep him informed of my movements, and after that we played poker in trains all over the continent.

I reached Wardha on January 23. At the station I looked for a taxi. There was none. I was persuaded to hire a primitive vehicle called a tonga. It resembled Boadicea's chariot, having wooden wheels without any kind of rims or tyres; three hand-sawn planks constituted the body and they were nailed direct on to the axle. The emaciated driver sat on the shaft and steered the lean bullock by twisting its bony tail. There were no reins, no springs and no road. It was all ruts and bumps. I do not know how far Gandhi's *Ashram* was from Wardha station. I shall always believe it was too far. After half an hour of bumping across an arid, infertile scrubland I could do no more than cling on, for I lacked the strength to fling myself off.

Suddenly the sadistic and reckless driver pointed out a figure walking towards us; I was too shaken to be interested. But the driver pulled up and there was Gandhi smiling mischievously above me. He had walked three miles to meet me. I crawled off my tonga, quite expecting him to congratulate me on my survival, or at least make some comment on my arrival, for I had travelled several thousand miles to keep this appointment.

"As I was saying in my last letter," he began before I had time to dust the tonga off my back, "means must determine ends, and indeed it's questionable in human affairs whether there is an end. The best we can do is to make sure of the method and examine our motives."

Whereupon we began to walk across this desert scrub, continuing our discussion as though neither time nor place had interrupted our correspondence. I noted that Gandhi never referred to my arrival—which I suppose was one way of making me feel at home and saved us from wasting time by discussing something of no consequence.

For the rest of our walk he continued to discuss the ethics of action and explained what he meant by "selfless action." "I will give you a *Gita* as soon as we get in." He also asked me about the pacifist organisation in England.

I told him that one of their difficulties was the expense of propaganda. He smiled ruefully at this.

136

"The right action contains its own propaganda and needs no other," he said. "It's the same with all these movements, societies, or sects; they waste their time and energies saying what everybody ought to do, but if they themselves were to act up to their own principles, that would be sufficient and arresting propaganda. Truth needs no publicity other than itself and, like a small stone thrown into a pond, its ripples will in time inevitably reach the circumference. The only thing to consider is the solidity and the weight of the stone."

Eventually we reached Gandhi's *Ashram* and he immediately showed me round. He called it *Segoan* and had settled there some years before, when he announced his intention of withdrawing from Congress and devoting his life to the betterment of the Indian villages.

I think he had chosen this site for two reasons—first because the neighbouring village was one of the most backward in the country; and secondly because the natural conditions could not have been more difficult. It looked like a desert; indeed it was one, except where Gandhi's efforts had produced this small oasis of fertility around his *Ashram*.

This tiny settlement built of adobe had now become the political and spiritual centre of India. It consisted of a simple one-roomed house with verandahs on two sides. We ate our meals on one and I kept my belongings on the other. There was no furniture or decoration of any kind. The walls were of mud or adobe: the floor was swept earth, trodden hard. This was Gandhi's workroom. There was a rug and a spinning-wheel on the floor, and in front of this a soap-box which served as his desk. I observed that it was inscribed with the word "Lifebuoy." Yet it contained his library; there were five books; I noticed one was by Tolstoy.

Adjoining Gandhi's cell were several others, in which Miss Slade and the other members of the *Ashram* lived. Here too they used to teach the village children.

These buildings were enclosed by a bamboo stockade, in one corner of which three or four villagers were pressing sugar-cane, and in another a great draught-bullock trod an endless journey drawing water from a well to irrigate the extensive kitchen-garden.

Outside the stockade Gandhi showed me his idea of a lavatory. It consisted of a narrow hand-dug trench with a portable shelter.

"You've no idea how difficult it is to persuade the villagers to bury their excreta," he told me.

The kitchen consisted of a pump and a fire, both in the open. On the verandah opposite sat a middle-aged woman shelling peas with remarkable dexterity. Gandhi introduced me to her. She was his wife, Kasturbai. She seemed very shy and could not speak English. As soon as we had moved away he told me that twenty years ago he had undertaken a vow of chastity. And with the amazing frankness which later I was to take for granted, he said that he had married at an early age. He paused. "I was only thirteen." He told me how Hindu parents waste so much time and money over the marriage-celebrations of their children, who are themselves often unaware of their betrothal. And how his father and mother had decided to stage one extravagant celebration and marry him and his two brothers off in a grand triple wedding. Only when he was measured for new clothes did he realise that his wife had been chosen. He told me, too, of the shyness and the agony of intimacy he and his wife felt when thrust into this premature wedlock.

I formed the impression that Gandhi, the reformer, was born on his own wedding night.

"The marriage was unhappy at the start owing to my jealousy, and I have never forgiven myself for all the sensualism I indulged in, which left me no time to teach my wife. She remains almost illiterate. As you notice, she cannot speak English."

For my part I had thought no less of her for this lack; her homeliness attracted me as a relief from Gandhi's own intellectualism. I was unable to understand his sense of guilt in this respect, nor could I appreciate his concern that Kasturbai could speak only Gujarati. After all, I thought, she can shell peas.

But even so I realised then that Gandhi's child-marriage had left him with a deep sense of shame, which nobody could remove. He told me that in his sixteenth year his father was bedridden, suffering from a fistula. He had to do duty as nurse. "Every night I massaged his legs and retired only when he asked me to do so or after he had fallen asleep. All the time at my disposal, after the performance of the daily duties, was divided between schools and attending on my father. I would only go out for an evening walk either when he permitted me or when he was feeling well.

"This was also the time when my wife was expecting a baby—a circumstance which, as I can see today, meant a double shame for me. For one thing I did not restrain myself, as I should have done, while I was still a student. And secondly, this carnal lust got the better of what I regarded as my duty to study, and of what was even a greater duty, my devotion to my parents, *Shraven* having been my ideal since childhood. Every night while my hands were busy massaging my father's legs, my mind was hovering about the bedroom—and that too at a time when religion, medical science, and common sense alike forbade sexual intercourse. I was always glad to be relieved from my duty, and went straight to the bedroom after doing obeisance to my father.

"The dreadful night came. My uncle was then in Rajkot. The brothers were deeply attached to each other. My uncle would sit near my father's bed the whole day, and would insist on sleeping by his bedside after sending us all to sleep. No one had dreamt that this was to be the fateful night. The danger of course was there.

"It was 10.30 or 11 p.m. I was giving the massage. My uncle offered to relieve me. I was glad and went straight to the bedroom. My wife, poor thing, was fast asleep. But how could she sleep when I was there? I woke her up. In five or six minutes, however, the servant knocked at the door. I started with alarm. 'Get up,' he said, 'Father is very ill.' I knew of course that he was very ill, and so I guessed what 'very ill' meant at that moment. I sprang out of bed.

"'What is the matter? Do tell me.'

"'Father is no more.'

"So all was over. I felt deeply ashamed and miserable. I ran to my father's room. I saw that, if animal passion had not blinded me, I should have been spared the torture of separation from my father during his last moments. I should have been massaging him and he would have died in my arms. But now it was my uncle who had had this privilege. He was so deeply devoted to his elder brother that he had earned the honour of doing him the last services. My father had forebodings of the coming event. He had

139

made a sign for pen and paper and written: 'Prepare for the last rites.' He had then snapped the amulet off his arm, and also his gold necklace of tulasi-beads, and flung them aside. A moment after this he was no more.

"The shame, to which I have referred in my autobiography, was this shame of my carnal desire even at the critical hour of my father's death, which demanded wakeful service. It is a blot I have never been able to efface or forget, and I have always thought that, although my devotion to my parents knew no bounds and I would have given up anything for it, yet it was weighed and found unpardonably wanting because my mind was at the same moment in the grip of lust. I have therefore always regarded myself as a lustful, though a faithful, husband. It took me long to get free from the shackles of lust, and I had to pass through many ordeals before I could overcome it."

Gandhi then went on to speak about the necessity of continence and chastity in the pursuit of *Brahmacharya*. I felt that our respective ages gave him a natural advantage in the discussion.

After he had shown me round the rest of his *Ashram*, he introduced me to Miss Slade, or Mira Ben, to use the Indian name she adopted when she became a devoted follower of the Mahatma. She wore a plain white Indian costume, not a sari, but such as the Untouchable beggars wear. Her grey hair was entirely shaven. This forbidding appearance did nothing to conceal the kindness of the woman. Often I used to go to her bare little cell and watch her teaching the village children to spin cotton or attending to their filthy sores, and I was always struck by the essentially English thoroughness of her work. No shaven head or loin-cloth of coarse linen could hide those qualities. I formed the impression that she was a character as courageous and as resolute as Florence Nightingale.

I also met Rakumari Amrit Kaur, an Indian princess who had given away her estate and joined the community. She was a very beautiful woman.

Others in the *Ashram* included Gandhi's two pretty granddaughters who were devoted to him, and a young man called Pyaralel who had abandoned a promising university career for a religious life. He acted as Gandhi's amanuensis.

I was then told the discipline which the *Ashram* followed. "We rise at 4 a.m. for communal prayers," Gandhi said shyly, "but I shall not expect you to attend. After which we do our toilet, breakfast, and then work."

He suggested that I should talk with him alone for two hours every morning and then accompany him on his walk. He outlined the rest of the day. Every moment was devoted to service to the neighbouring village, except for those times which were given to regular prayer and meditation.

I had brought a bed-roll with me and the first night I slept on this on the verandah. I was wakened by the sound of a chant; its rhythm was the most complex I have ever heard. The stars were still shining; it was 4 a.m. All the members of the *Ashram* were sitting in a circle round a log-fire in the open. Gandhi was reading the Vedas, and after each *sloka* the others chanted the responses. I did not understand a single word but the rhythm was articulate by itself.

After this service we used to wash and breakfast on figs and the green loose-skinned Nagpuri oranges. Then everybody would go to their tasks just as it became light. The *Ashram* was veterinary college, dispensary, hospital and school to the village, to which the peasants used to come with their ailing animals, and children for free medical service, and instruction in husbandry and rural crafts.

"Patient example is the only possible method to effect a reform," Gandhi told me as we walked through the sugar-cane plantations, towards the little village which was a mere collection of fly-blown and squalid shacks, an eyrie for well-fed vultures.

"This is the real India," said the voice beside me; "it is one which visitors to the Taj Mahal seldom see."

The hovels were improvised, not built. Their walls were of mud, their roofs of flattened petrol-cans, tattered mats in place of doors; and none of them could boast a window. But it was not the extreme poverty and filth of the place that appalled me most, but the complete inertia of the derelict inhabitants. They were too emaciated for work, too apathetic for hope. There they sat in front of their homes without even the energy to remove the flies settling on their sores. I tried to compare this sight before me with the slums of the Rhondda Valley, but there was no point of comparison. The dour streets of inhabited tombstones in which the colliers lived were gay and neat cottages compared to this.

Gandhi let me absorb the scene. "Hardly the brightest jewel, is it?" he said. "There are tens of millions living like this; usury has brought them to it—they are mortgaged three generations ahead, and what they sow the moneylender and the tax-collector harvest." He told me of the injustice of a fixed charge, that is to say, taxes which are not computed on the yield of the harvest, but a relentless burden when drought produces insufficient even for next year's seed.

As we stood there I noticed four or five men who were squatting in front of us. They were relieving themselves. I glanced around me: what I had taken to be the droppings of dogs were, I realised, all human excreta. They were outside the hovels, beside the only well. No wonder the people were ridden by disease and the children poxed with sores.

Gandhi stood silent. A look of intense pity and sorrow came into his face. There was no anger. He did not step forward and give them a lecture on hygiene or modern sanitation. He did not plead, cajole or reprimand. But with the same expression of abject humility, as though he himself was personally to blame for all this suffering and filth, he began to scavenge the excrement and bury it with his own hands. I helped him. As we did this together, the villagers at first stood by and watched. Then the example of their beloved Mahatma worked upon them. He was clearing their filth away without a look or a word of complaint. Within a few minutes the villagers began to follow his example. Gandhi's act of selfless action, of service, had achieved in a moment what coercion or teaching could not have done in a century.

Here was an example of practical politics, of applied religion, an excellent introduction to philosophy. I had gone to India to talk to Gandhi, but this incident taught me more than all the discussions we had.

When we had finished cleaning round the well, Gandhi took me into one of the "houses." It was dark, entirely unfurnished, a sort of noisy grave with tubercular children in fly-blown corners. The smell made me feel sick. To my surprise I saw that his face was now radiant with pleasure. I looked for the cause. In a corner of the room sat a woman using a *charka*, or home-made spinning-wheel. Another example of his had been followed.

As we walked home, he told me something of the economics of rural India and how many of the village crafts had been so discouraged and neglected as to be forgotten.

"For instance, they go without sugar, though these palms above them will yield it if only they are tapped in the proper manner. And the Government has, by taxing Indian cloth to encourage Lancashire exports, left us almost naked, though cotton will grow here and used to be spun in the homes."

He explained his *Khadi* Movement, and how he had made a vow many years ago to spin so many yards of yarn every day. The result was that cheap Indian cloth could now be bought in many villages. And that evening he gave me a portable spinning-wheel which was fitted into a little case, and a blue rug made from cloth he himself had spun. I still have them.

"The spinning-wheel is not only the very symbol of passive resistance," he said; "it is also a means of meditation. And so long as the peasants spin they have their self-respect and a measure of independence."

I began to understand what he meant by the relation of religion to politics. "Every act," he would repeat daily to me, "has its spiritual, economic and social implications. The spirit is not separate. It cannot be." This point of view was, I think, his most important contribution to twentieth-century thought. It was the basis of all his activities. Those people who ask whether Gandhi was a saint or a statesman do not begin to understand him or his achievement. He was one because he was the other; in him they were identified, and this was the secret of his success as a politician and of his integrity as a religious man.

The midday meal at the *Ashram* was taken squatting on the verandah. I used to sit next to Gandhi, for he was most concerned that I should eat enough. The food was vegetarian and quite delicious. I was particularly fond of the hand-ground bread with white butter. The only condiment allowed was salt, as Gandhi disapproved of all seasoning and would not permit Indian curry to be served, as he maintained that such seasoning not only ruined the palate but was bad for the health and aggravated the senses. He said curries were aphrodisiacs.

He told me that though he had been born into a religious sect which practised strict vegetarianism, he had once tried eating meat. Apparently when he was at school the doggerel rhyme:

> Behold the mighty Englishman
> He rules the Indian small
> Because he is a meat-eater
> And is five cubits tall

had persuaded him to change his diet. This step meant breaking with the habits of his parents and the strict rules of his religion and had to be done in secret. But he told me, "Since I wanted to be strong and daring and to free my country from the English, I decided on the experiment." He and a friend went to a lonely spot by a river and there ate some goat's flesh. That night he had a nightmare and dreamed that a live goat was bleating inside him. He persisted in these surreptitious feasts for a time but eventually returned to the diet of his forefathers.

Such detailed principles of diet and behaviour did not make Gandhi a prig or deprive him of his sense of humour. One day I noticed that, whereas I and other members of the *Ashram* ate off brass plates, Gandhi used an old battered tin bowl. I asked him why he preferred it.

"It was given to me when I first went to prison, and as I'm always ready to go back there it's only right that I should continue to use the bowl."

He spoke of his prison days with joy and with genuine gratitude to those who had detained him. You cannot punish a man who is grateful for the punishment and insists on regarding his jailer as his host. Every privation only enriched him. His dignity lay in the acceptance of every humiliation.

Yet in counterpoint to these qualities he had a wry and mischievous side to him. I was never sure when he was not teasing me. And when people began to praise him to excess or almost deify him, as some of his followers did, his defence was to turn imp.

One day he asked me to accompany him to Wardha, where he had promised to attend a conference of Anglican bishops in India.

We did not travel by tonga; an open car called for us. As we drove into the town, the car was pelted with flowers and surrounded. One earnest devotee, a girl of about twenty, jumped on the running-board in order to touch the Mahatma's garment. As she leaned over to do so, Gandhi broke the spell by boyishly pulling her nose.

"I am not a god," he used to complain to me; "if the truth were known I am tempted more than most men, but perhaps less than those who are sinners." In that distinction was all tolerance.

Another time I myself had been asking him earnest questions about his "fast unto death," for there is no doubt that he would have died voluntarily on that occasion if the Government had not been persuaded by public opinion to act at the last moment.

"Do you know what I did on the first day of that fast?" he asked me. "I got the prison dentist in to measure me for this set of false teeth."

Whether he meant by this that he had had no intention of fasting to death, or that he had ordered the teeth as an act of faith that the Government would recognise the righteousness of his cause, he didn't say. But in fact I discovered that the latter was his reason, though Gandhi told me the story in order to suggest the former out of modesty, and to make me believe that his will-power was not as great as his reputation.

To say the least, I was most ill-prepared for the religious discipline and austerity of Gandhi's *Ashram*. I had come merely to talk—there is nothing so comfortable as a discussion on remote ideals—but Gandhi would always take my theory gently by the scruff of its neck and rub my nose in the practical and personal implications. It was a useful but painful lesson. In this connection, one day he interrupted one of my more abstract dissertations with a little story from the life of Buddha, which I suspect I have not remembered correctly, but it is probably well known.

"The Buddha had a young disciple," Gandhi told me, "whom the Master left in the desert promising to return to him in three years to see how he had progressed. During this time the disciple built a house, which he proudly showed the Buddha when he returned. The Master examined it and then told the disciple to take the house to pieces and erect it again a few paces farther away, promising to return in another three years. The disciple did as he was instructed. The Master returned, examined the house again, but told the young man that he must now abandon it altogether and sit by the river and meditate, promising to return again at the end of another three years. The disciple did as he was instructed. When the Master at last returned he asked the disciple what he had done with his time. 'I can now walk across on the surface of the river without getting my feet wet,' the young man boasted. 'Then you have wasted your time,' said Buddha, 'for there is a ferry just round the corner.'"

The implication of this parable was not entirely lost on me. Gandhi was the most practical man I have ever met.

When I arrived at the *Ashram* I was a heavy smoker, and of course nobody there ever indulged in that habit. I used to steal off somewhat furtively into a field of sugar-cane, where I had first to overcome my horror of snakes before hiding in the crop to light a cigarette. But Gandhi was not to be deceived. He took my addiction very seriously, and in order to help me break it he told me how he and a friend had once become fond of smoking and used as children to pick up the ends of cigarettes which his uncle threw away. "They were not very satisfactory, and so we began to steal the servants' pocket-money in order to buy cigarettes. But even so we found it intolerable to have to smoke in secret, and eventually we became so disgusted with these parental restrictions that we decided to commit suicide. We stole off into the jungle and tried to poison ourselves with some seeds, but we were so frightened of dying that we only took sufficient to give us stomach-ache. However, it cured me of smoking—but not of thieving. I once stole some gold out of my brother's armlet, and was then so overcome with remorse that I wrote out a full confession and gave it to my father. He read it. He said nothing. He only wept. This was for me an important object-lesson in *ahimsa*—in love."

As Gandhi told me this incident, I was again made aware of how most of his convictions sprang from his experiences as a child. His love for his parents, and the fact that they were both deeply religious people, could not be under-estimated in assessing the growth of his character.

His concern about my smoking became of great importance to

146

him. Urgent matters of political moment, such as correspondence with the Viceroy, were all put aside to keep me provided with toffee made of palm-sugar as a substitute for cigarettes.

"If you can't master yourself in this," Gandhi used to say, "how can you hope to do anything else?" And he would then quote the *Gita* and tell me that detachment from the senses was the first step in the ladder, without which there was nothing.

After lunch it was the custom for the members of the *Ashram* to retire and meditate. I soon realised that a voyage up the unexplored regions of the Amazon would be an easy expedition compared with a journey into my own mind. It is an extremely embarrassing experience to discover the shallowness of one's own thought and one's complete inability to concentrate.

"Meditation is not for him who eats too much, nor for him who eats not at all, nor for him who is over-addicted to sleep, nor for him who is always awake."

After a few days Gandhi took me for a long walk till we came to a little hut in a clearing. The occupant had put himself under Gandhi's teaching. He was what is termed a Yogi; and had been in this place for over a year. The hut was no more than a summer-house and contained no furniture except a table and a chair. There were no papers or books. I commented on this. "The sacrifice of wisdom is superior to any material sacrifice; for, O Arjuna, the climax of action is always realisation," he murmured. I stayed talking to him for several hours. This man had the physique of a boxer and the poise of a dancer. There was about him a lake of calmness; being with him was a kind of solitude. He emitted peace in the same way as a heater radiates warmth.

When I got up to go I noticed there was a chill in the evening air. I glanced round his bare hut. "Don't you ever catch colds?" I asked him.

"No," he said with a simplicity which was without a trace of pride; "I do not allow them."

So that night I foolishly abandoned the luxury of my bed-roll on the verandah and followed Gandhi out into the open where he used to sleep on the damp ground. I awoke with a heavy dew on me and a severe chill. However, I persisted in sleeping in the open till the chill got steadily worse. Gandhi was sympathetic but in no way alarmed at my sneezes. I also had a temperature and the discomfort of a stiff neck. Eventually, when leaving the *Ashram* to visit a colony of Untouchables, he sent me to an osteopath.

As I had daily conversations with Gandhi, I had a unique opportunity to study both the man and his ideas. But I was too young to appreciate much at the time.

There is no need to describe his appearance: his features were photographed. But I shall always remember the anachronism of the large cheap watch which dangled on a safety-pin attached to his loin-cloth: worn this way, time itself appeared to be a toy, an invention of the Western mind.

His face was too animated to give the impression of serenity; his mind too active to suggest repose. Though his dress was almost comical in its simplicity, with his shaven head, steel-rimmed glasses and single tooth, yet one was unaware of his appearance, and only impressed by his extraordinary strength of will. His humility was so complete as to be the very essence of dignity. His hands, like all Indians', were extremely beautiful, with thousands of years of craft in his long supple fingers, by comparison with which any Western hand is a clumsy paw.

During these discussions he never raised his voice above a whisper, and the spinning-wheel was never still.

I told him of my experience of the stay-in strike in the coal-mine at the Rhondda Valley, and asked him what training was required for passive resistance. His answer was naturally such as to leave English politics far behind. "There is no short cut," he told me, "but the way of the spirit, which is one of detachment, of self-abnegation, of being unattached to all desires. If such truth resides in one man, all follows inevitably from that. But without that essence, nothing."

All conversations, whatever their point of departure, returned to the teachings of the *Gita*, the gospel of selfless action. And there was always the insistence that there was no life but a spiritual life.

There was no need for me to ask him why he concerned himself with politics, for I had seen him clean round the village well. To him it was all service, selfless action, action that is a prayer.

"I do not believe that the spiritual law works on a plane of its own," he used to say, and he had no patience with what he called "the futility of mere religious knowledge." To Gandhi the whole of life resided in every part. He did not allow the distinctions— religion, culture, politics or art. His insistence on the necessity of being unattached to the senses reminded me of my own Jerome-like vow not to read poetry. I could not understand him when he used to tell me that all sensual gratification is sin. And I used to disagree. I remember that I argued on the lines that it did not matter what one loved but how; the object being un-important, the quality, the purity of love, being all important. To my mind the legend of *Le Jongleur de Notre Dame* is an example of this.

Gandhi saw sin in every sensual pleasure. It seemed to amount to a nausea with life itself. I was at times reminded of the petti-ness of English Puritanism, and I suggested that perhaps the most perverse sensual gratification was to be obtained not by satisfying one's senses, but by denying them satisfaction. Gandhi smiled at this. "That is also a danger," he said, "but there is no point in renouncing an object that one still desires."

With infinite patience and good humour he tried to make me understand the difference between what I called Puritanism and what he referred to as Brahmacharya. "What you are talking about amounts to a mere negation of this life, but what I am talk-ing about is a means to an everlasting life. There is a difference between renouncing an object and relinquishing it." As usual he quoted the *Gita*. "The sages say that renunciation means forgoing an action which springs from desire, and relinquishing means the surrender of its fruit." This last phrase "the surrender of its fruit" was always on Gandhi's lips. It was the key to the philosophy of selfless action.

But in spite of his endless patience with me in these discussions, I refused to understand, for at that age I was determined not to do so. In retrospect I realise that I did, but would not admit it. And to preserve my own tastes and habits I subconsciously began to seek points of disagreement, with all the desperation of a goldfish clinging to the little bowl I knew in preference to the lake I did not dare to experience.

One day during a walk he defined sin to me as "being acted

upon by the senses." I remember I instantly asked him if he considered listening to Mozart a sin. The question was all-important to me.

"All attachment to the senses is death," he replied. It may seem strange but I used Gandhi's light dismissal of Mozart as the reason for refusing his invitation, which he later made to me, to return to India and live with him for a year.

We were, of course, often talking at different levels, yet I was reminded that most of his early influence had been Western in origin. It was Ruskin's *Unto this Last*, Carlyle's *Heroes and Hero-Worship*, Tolstoy, and even Mrs Besant and the literature of the Theosophical Society in Bayswater, which had influenced Gandhi as a young man. But these writers only awakened a spiritual strength that was already there.

I discovered that most of his ideas concerning self-sufficiency, rural crafts and vegetarianism were derived from Tolstoy. But the derivation is unimportant. The essential contribution Gandhi made to twentieth-century thought was his insistence on the need for a lower standard of living, in opposition to the Western notion that progress lies in an accumulation of material prosperity. He maintained that the essence of civilisation consists not in the multiplication of wants but in their deliberate and voluntary renunciation.

He preached a higher standard of spiritual living, and maintained that a lower level of material well-being was a necessary prerequisite. His ideas were the very antithesis of both Marx and Ford. This being so, can his importance to contemporary thought be over-estimated?

I do not think it can. I believe that Gandhi's teaching is of permanent value, especially to the West, which is so bemused with the experiments of science that it is completely blind to the potentialities of the spirit. Gandhi's political efforts were entirely without "concern for the fruit."

While I was at his *Ashram* he asked me if I would lecture to his school for Untouchables which he had founded a few miles off. I did this several times, and the last time I went there one of the men came up to my desk and presented me with a pair of wooden sandals.

"We've made these for you," he said, "so that you can forever walk on us."

There was no intended ambiguity or bitterness in his remark. It was genuine affection and humility.

This gift of plain wooden sandals amused Gandhi immensely. For only the evening before I had blotted my copy-book in his eyes. I had gone into Wardha and, on an impulse, had bought a pair of expensive sandals covered in gold braid for his pretty granddaughter. Everyone could see that I couldn't keep my eyes off her, and I believe she was only about sixteen. She moved so gracefully, a flower with feet. And the feet were delighted with my sandals, but they did look very incongruous in the surroundings. Gandhi didn't seem to mind my making the gift, but only the amount of money I had spent on it.

"You ought to have carved some out of wood," he teased.

"Too uncomfortable," I replied, little realising that I would soon have experience to back that opinion. And there was no possibility of wearing the Untouchables' sandals out. I could see I would have to walk on them for ever.

When I decided to leave the *Ashram*, Gandhi gave me a portrait of himself which the poet Tagore had painted on a piece of sandalwood. Mahedev Desai wrote out the *slokas* from the *Gita*, which we used to recite at morning prayers, on the back of it. And he also gave me letters to his friends in Benares, Agra, Bombay and Calcutta. I had already arranged to stay with his son Devadas, who was editor of the *Hindustan Times*, in Delhi.

But first I went to Calcutta. No city in the world degrades humanity as Calcutta does. It reduces the human being to the rank of a blow-fly on a carcass. Nobody has seen filth, poverty or degradation until they have been there. Rhondda is a garden city by comparison. My Scotsman was pleased that I couldn't get a room in anything but the Grand Hotel.

As soon as I arrived there, a friend of Gandhi's who was a doctor called on me to ask how my chill and stiff neck were. There was no need for me to reply. My symptoms of flu were horribly apparent. My throat was sore, my nose congested, my head ached.

"Come out to my surgery," he said, "and I will cure your cold in three seconds."

I accompanied him to the suburbs. He gave me breakfast. Then he strapped me into what appeared to be a vertical iron camp-bed, which lacked a mattress. When I was secure and rigid he went to the side of the room and pulled a lever. My iron support crashed horizontally down, jolting every bone in my body. Then he unstrapped me. I was silent with indignation.

"That's put an end to your cold," he said, as I staggered to my feet.

I snorted—through clear nostrils. I shook my head, but it no longer ached. Not a symptom, no trace of my cold remained.

I left Calcutta on a long train-journey to Santinikaten. This was where Rabindranath Tagore lived, surrounded by a sort of Indian Dartington Hall. Gandhi had urged me to go and see him. "You two poets ought to meet," he said, and I carried a letter of introduction. I was not particularly excited at the prospect. I had tried to read Tagore, and found it was like the early plays of Yeats. Perhaps the trouble was in the translation. I had been told by Viccy that he had a genuine lyrical gift, and could detect some of this when the poems were spoken to me in Bengali, which I couldn't understand. But Tagore had other aspirations: he wanted to be regarded as a great mystic.

He sent a car to meet me at the station. A servant took me to a guest-house and I was shown over the community, where I was particularly interested in Bose's sculpture. I could see the great seer sitting on a verandah as though in a trance. He had a white beard and looked like Father Time. Eventually I was summoned to his presence. He had forgotten my letter of introduction from Gandhi, and mistook me for an American journalist who was trying to get an interview. I disillusioned him about this, and he fell into another "trance." We couldn't have impressed each other less. The next morning I caught a train to Agra, hoping that the monument there wouldn't disappoint me too.

From Agra I went to Bombay, where Gandhi had given me an introduction to several members of Congress who entertained me. It was there that I received a letter from him suggesting that I should return to England to tidy up my affairs then come back to his *Ashram* to live a further year with him. By the same post he sent me a parcel of toffee to prevent me from smoking. When I reached Port Sudan a letter in his own hand begged me not to smoke, and in London another parcel of toffee was awaiting me.

PART THREE

The Birth of Being

W HEN I reached Port Said I decided to hire a car and drive across
the desert to Cairo. I had had enough of the sea; even waves of
sand were an improvement on the waves of the sea to me. We had
gone about thirty miles when the car started to boil. While the
driver was trying to fix the fan-belt, I produced some letters which
I had picked up at the port and had not opened. One was from my
friend Spottiswoode. It said: "I have met a very beautiful girl,
alpha-plus. Can't wait to introduce you. Am very much in love
with her."

I rejoined the boat; got off at Marseilles and took a train straight
to Rapallo. I arrived there about 2 a.m. and, realising that the
hour was slightly unsuitable for calling at Ezra Pound's flat, I
approached a porter at the station and asked him to direct me to
an hotel. He pointed to a light about a couple of hundred yards
away. Feeling very tired after a long train-journey, I went straight
to this place and asked for a room. An old crone led me upstairs.
I thought she was asking me if I wanted to be called in the morning; I replied that I did. My Italian has never been very good.
The proprietress lit a small lamp; I surveyed an enormous bed and
was soon fast asleep.

But after a few minutes I was awakened by the noise of the door
opening. A girl stood there. I immediately assumed that the old
crone had mistaken the hour at which I had asked to be called, so I
simply turned over and tried to sleep again. As I was dozing off I
recalled how inadequately the maid who had just woken me had
been dressed. No doubt, I thought, she has now gone back to bed,
too. I suppose I slept for another hour, and then I had a strange
dream. The room now seemed full of some half-dozen almost
naked women who stood round in the most grotesque attitudes. But
eventually these phantoms disappeared after lolling about my bed.

When I awoke—without being called at all—I remembered the fantastic figures of the night and dismissed my dream as beneath contempt. I hurried round to Pound's flat and, after a suitable time had elapsed, summoned up the courage to ask him if he could lend me the money to pay my hotel-bill.

"Where did you stay?" he asked. "I'll send the money round."

"At some small hotel near the station," I replied, "but I can't remember its name."

"There isn't an hotel near there," he said, "so there's nothing for it but for you to take me to it."

We walked round there.

"This is the place," I said, recognising the door. Pound raised his eyebrows imperceptibly, stalked in and paid the bill. I remained outside.

"Do you always put up at brothels?" he asked, giving me the change. Then I realised that the only curious thing about my dream was that it had not been a dream at all.

Ezra taught me more in one day than I had learned in a year at Cambridge. The practice of apprenticeship should be revived. He began by reading to me one of Guido Cavalcanti's *canzone*, and then gave me the book as a present. There was I with an honours degree in English literature and I'd never even heard of Cavalcanti, let alone become aware of the form of a *canzone*. And, like many other student graduates at Rapallo, I continued to have, as it were, a post-graduate course by postcard from the Chancellor.

Only last week one arrived. It read: "Tell the young to read Goodwin's Greek Grammar, chapter on prosody." (Incidentally, it is an excellent beginning for those interested in how poetry is made; and one calculated to discourage many aspirants who are convinced that the writing of poetry is merely a matter of having a bright idea or an emotional puff.)

Pound was then a burly leonine figure; his hair and beard still had traces of red in them; he dressed carelessly and casually: an open-necked shirt with a Byronic collar, a thick white sweater, and a leather belt keeping his slacks up from his tennis-shoes. He looked and moved very much like a lumberman who had just come in from taking a swipe at the undergrowth. Which is in fact what he had been doing, only his pen was his axe—or rather his type-writer was, for I saw that he worked at a huge old machine on a tiny untidy desk and even banged out his first drafts of poems on it.

His flat was tiny, at the top of a building above a restaurant where his phallic-looking head by Gaudier Brzeska stood among the café-tables. And there were several other Gaudier carvings which immediately took my eye in his study. I had never heard of Gaudier: Pound remarked that I looked very much like him; he showed me a photograph of the sculptor to prove it, and then by some miracle managed to find what he was looking for among the chaos of paper in his cubicle-sized room. It was a packet of post-cards which Gaudier had written to Pound from the trenches in France, and also his trench-notebook, a small autograph album, in which the artist had made sketches, notes and drawings of animals. I was immensely impressed by every page. Gaudier's single line had that certainty about it which, to my eye, is the hall-mark of a great draughtsman. Only Matisse could equal it: but there is something feminine in Matisse: Gaudier is essentially masculine—a distinction which it would not be wise to press. Pound showed me other drawings and paintings by Max Ernst, Picasso, Dali, Wyndham Lewis and Modigliani. But none of these impressed me as much as the Gaudier.

I suggested to him that the Gaudier notebook ought to be published exactly as it was. He was enthusiastic.

"Take it," he said impetuously. "See if you can persuade Possum to do that."

"Possum?"

"My nickname for Tom Eliot."

While Pound excitedly barged about, stacking me with papers and books, his wife Dorothy sat demurely in the next room. She was an extremely handsome woman with one of those well-boned faces which age can write over but never erase. There was something cold, tentative and withdrawn about her. She served China tea from a silver pot. I looked for the cucumber sandwiches. Even at my first meeting I was struck by something which was more worrying than the apparent incongruity of their personalities. Dorothy was pure Kensington: and with Ezra in tow it was as odd as if she had wandered into Harrods with a buffalo on a lead instead of a poodle.

After fidgeting with small buns on small plates, Pound suggested that he and I should go for a walk along the front. He stuck a black sombrero on his head, a great yellow scarf round his neck, and grabbed a cane. I found it difficult to keep up with him as he strode from idea to idea without any apparent connection.

"You must read Dante," he said, "and take a look at Vivaldi too. Of course Edgar Wallace knew a thing or two about flow. Don't under-estimate writers who've got flow." Then he was off on Frobenius or economics.

When I could get a word in edgeways, above the gale blowing across the deserted sea-front, I asked him why he didn't write more in the style of "Hugh Selwyn Mauberley."

"You write it," he replied rudely and justifiably. It was a very silly question.

But when we got back to his flat he answered my question in another way, reading chunks of his Cantos to me—or rather chanting them. I was so surprised at his artificial style of reading that I could hardly listen to the lines themselves.

We dined downstairs, sitting at a table beside the Gaudier, and while we ate planned a new onslaught against the Philistines which was to do for the thirties what *Blast* had achieved twenty years before, Pound scribbling out lists of people whom he thought I should meet, know, and perhaps persuade to contribute to the magazine.

"Print yourself and this fellow Britten," he said, "and I'll jab around here and there in the background and twist a few tails. Here's your first subscription."

When eventually I decided to go, Pound had again to accompany me to the station. He had given me so many books that somebody had to carry them.

He urged me to go straight to Paris and gave me notes of introduction to Brancusi, Cocteau, Stravinsky, Léger, Max Jacob, Hilary Hiller, and a man in London called William Joyce of whom I had never heard.

But I went to Cotignac instead, as I had promised to visit Miss Russell, a composer. (I had met her in Devon where she too had a cottage.) I went for a walk with her and came across a very attractive old mill with a few fig and almond trees around it. It was empty. I asked if it was to let and found the farmer who owned it. I offered to rent it, when I understood him to say that the rent was thirty shillings a week. He scribbled out an agreement. I signed. It was only when I got back to Miss Russell's cottage and looked at it that I saw that the rent was not thirty shillings a week, but thirty shillings a year. I immediately gave instructions for windows and a bathroom to be installed and persuaded Miss Russell to find me some furniture. I had no idea what I intended to do with the place, but I was attracted to it. Naturally it had a stream by the door.

She saw me off at the station and gave me a picnic to eat on the train, a bottle of wine and some cold artichokes. I don't know whether it was because I was now on my way home, or because I had just acquired this cottage—La Basse Combe—but I shall never forget the typhoon of ecstasy I felt standing on the station. I think it was called Carnoulles. I found myself recalling the third movement of the Seventh Symphony of Beethoven, despite Britten's influence, and to each note there was a word. Unconsciously I had written a poem to fit the music. I don't know when I had done this, but the whole thing was there. I wrote it down in the train on the way to Paris. I suppose I left the manuscript in the compartment.

This kind of unconscious literary composition to music occurred frequently now. Sometimes I would write a poem and find that the music was in my head as I wrote it. But to my grief I could not write a note of it down. Once, a few years later, when I was walking down a hideous street in Sheffield, I was overwhelmed with the music that was rushing into my head. I could hear every instrument. It was not that I was writing it, but it was writing me. I could not write a note down. I was terrified that I should forget the themes. I telephoned to my sister in London and hummed the melodies to her, but she could not put them down either. I never told Britten of these experiences.

At this time I felt an energy in me which I could not understand or contain. The only image that I can liken it to is that of a blowlamp. I was frequently elated, sometimes depressed, but I had some energy which I could not contain. I used to wake up in the morning sometimes with whole poems in my head which I had dreamed. All I had to do was to write them down. And I could never write fast enough.

At this time I wrote my first play. It was called *Birth* and was immediately produced at a little theatre behind Charing Cross Station. Auden's poem *Spain* was given after it. The audience could hardly hear my play because there was a thunderstorm going on outside. I never bothered to take a copy. It didn't seem important, when I could write another one on the bus going home. It was not a very good play. I am glad that it can't be found.

A day or two after I reached London, Spottiswoode asked me if I would meet this girl about whom he had written to me so enthusiastically. He was proud of his discovery, very much in love, wanting to show her off to me. I was too busy for the next few days, trying to get my magazine started, but eventually I agreed to meet them for lunch at a vegetarian restaurant in Leicester Square. Her name was Rose Marie. Spottiswoode introduced us. We did not notice him leave or pay the bill. I took her to a gramophone shop to listen to the Unfinished Symphony: even at that moment I couldn't forget Schubert. Then I asked her if she would do some research for me at the British Museum. She looked the very opposite of a blue-stocking, but I had told her I was starting a magazine and she had offered to help. The British Museum wasn't the right place to send her, but it was better than not sending her anywhere, or rejecting her offer of help altogether. I always made use of everybody on the basis that I was doing them a favour. I had to telephone to Spottiswoode next day to ask her name. He told me it was Hansom—a descendant of the famous architect who also invented the Hansom cab—and that she was a Goldsmith's Scholar at the Royal Academy of Music.

"I'm sorry you are in love with her," I said. "I am too."

She said she wanted a grand piano. But I didn't realise that she wasn't serious. I immediately rang up Britten and told him to meet us. He was the obvious person to choose the piano. We went round Chappell's, Britten playing every piano in the store, until he found one he approved of.

ROSE MARIE

My attachment to Rose Marie was complicated by the fact that my best friend was in a similar predicament with her. She seemed to have innumerable boy-friends besides us two. That gave us some bond. Another disadvantage with which I had to contend was the fact that her brother took a strong dislike to me, and I had the feeling that her other relatives would have a similar feeling when I met them. Rose Marie was training to be an actress. She had had a film test with Antony Asquith and was being considered for a part in a film. To tease her, I went into her agent's in Wardour Street and asked if I could go on their list. The man who interviewed me noticed that I was sunburnt from being in India. He asked if I could ride a horse. This was the one thing I could do. Before I had left the office he had offered to sign me on for a small part in a film with Marlene Dietrich. I did not accept, but Rose Marie never fully forgave me for getting this offer so easily.

Then Spottiswoode proposed that I should accompany him and Rose Marie for a few days to the country, and suggested that we might go down to Devon for Whitsun. We were close friends, but not that close: there was nothing perverse in our relationship. I saw clearly that he was including me in the week-end only because she was unlikely to agree to the idea of going with him alone. In spite of being a film starlet, she had only recently left the convent, and a third party, even this one, for the week-end lent cover to convention, or at least camouflaged his intentions. I agreed with alacrity, but reminded him that I was very attracted to the girl and, in these matters, counted myself sufficiently a man to be no gentleman. But this warning only amused him: he had known her for weeks longer than I had and was quite confident that I should prove an amenable gooseberry. He took my only too apparent attraction to her as a proof of his own good taste; and my commendation, as it were, only served to make him value his prize the more. Another reason was that I had immediate access to a Devon cottage on the coast and was therefore worth taking along as ballast.

Rose Marie agreed to this week-end, but said she didn't want to come between Spottiswoode and me. "You couldn't," he told her, making the challenge as clear to me as it was to her.

Accordingly, with all our intentions clear to ourselves if not to our companions, we set off for Devon. I recall that on the train, while Spottiswoode read, Rose Marie sat fascinated by all the lies I told her about my adventures in India. She was incredibly credulous. Seeing that I carried a leather-covered riding-stick which contained a sword that I had bought in India, she asked me if I had ever killed anybody with it. I told her I had, but not many. To my confusion I saw she believed me. Clearly Spottiswoode had painted his friend in primary colours—both Pacifist and Brigand. No wonder she was intrigued, making me take the sword repeatedly from its sheath and drive it in to the crop again. Freud would have been interested in her fearful fascination with this stick: I should have been cheered too if I had been able to fathom its significance.

I had rented an old mill on the coast for the occasion. It was about the most remote cottage in the county. I had known it since I was a child, and it had always attracted me; I swear I had not realised it had only one bed.

Spottiswoode was not amused when we made this discovery.

"I hope you don't mind sleeping in that wicker chair in the kitchen," he said smugly, thinking of the large double bed in the small single bedroom.

After a meal that I had concocted, since neither of my companions could cook, Rose Marie said, "I'm going to bed. I hope you two sleep well in that chair." Off she went. Spottiswoode's smug smile slipped. For the next two hours we smoked, and I commiserated without feeling sympathetic. His predicament more than halved my own.

About three o'clock in the morning we each threw cushions on the floor and pretended we were asleep. After half an hour, to the accompaniment of my feigned snores, he creaked his way up the stairs to Rose Marie. I sat up and lit a cigarette and to my considerable relief I heard her getting out of bed before he had opened the door.

"We can't sleep," he said lamely but truthfully.

Her response was to come downstairs. We brewed some tea.

"I do see how difficult it is for you two to sleep here," she said,

164

smiling in the direction of the single easy chair. "You'd both better come upstairs."

"Both?" Spottiswoode murmured.

"Both!" she repeated emphatically. "I promised my mother I wouldn't sleep with either of you, but I never said anything about sleeping with you both. There's safety in numbers, they say. Anyhow you can both come to bed or both sit there and smoke all night—whichever you prefer."

She went, leaving us to look sourly at each other.

"You'd better come too," Spottiswoode said eventually, "and I hope you die in your sleep."

"Don't worry, I shan't sleep," I said, following him up the stairs.

"One each side of me," Rose Marie murmured sleepily.

We undressed and glanced across at each other. Spottiswoode had put his pyjamas on. I could not emulate him that far. I had no pyjamas. It was, and is, against my principles to buy unnecessary things. Wearing pyjamas is to me like using a rain-coat when you go bathing. Spottiswoode glared; he perceived this gave me some sort of an advantage. If looks could kill, both would have dropped dead. As it was, we slid grudgingly into bed.

The situation was comic, but at the time I didn't see the humour. I was a virgin. It did not amuse me particularly to find that the first time I found myself in bed with a woman, another man should be lying on the other side of her. My feelings were not confused: I had fallen in love with Rose Marie the moment I met her three weeks before. She was one of those women whom even women call beautiful.

My head touched the pillow: there wasn't the slightest chance of sleep. I closed my eyes and kept both ears open. The slightest move or rustle from Spottiswoode would have been his last. He too knew enough about me not to trust me in any matter of real importance. Like two Beasts we lay, guard-dogs to one another, each side of Beauty, who, either from innocence or from wicked calculation of the full security of her situation, slept genuinely.

I was like an iron filing lying within a field of force. The urge to turn towards her was such that I had to grip the iron rail of the springs at the side of the bed beneath me to prevent Faraday's Law about Unlike Forces being put into effect. I felt what the tide feels as it is turned about and dragged in or out by a moon beyond a pillow of clouds.

The hours passed. Then as I lay there, against all the laws of nature, I felt her stir sleepily beside me, then her naked leg moved and fell across my thigh. Aware of what had happened, Spottiswoode coughed from the sideline. I took his vocal intrusion as a generous gesture of protest—that some mercy should be shown to me. But it was in vain; women, I discovered, have even less mercy asleep than they have awake. The sleeping magnet now moved even closer towards me. Spottiswoode coughed again: a less considerate tone behind it. Still asleep the vice of leg withdrew. For the next half-hour she lay isolated from us both, fast asleep. Then suddenly I felt her hand moving towards mine: I gripped it and beneath the covers of the bed I allowed my fingers to show her fingers all the passion that my body felt for her body. Her hand responded to every pressure from mine. Let Spottiswoode lie there, I thought, no matter so long as our hands promised and rehearsed what with time and opportunity we would perform. For the next ten minutes I was, if not satisfied, at least assuaged.

Then suddenly Rose Marie sat up, and got out of bed to go to the bathroom. As she moved to the door it suddenly seemed to me rather odd that I should still be able to hold her hand while she had moved three yards away. A similar revelation must have crossed Spottiswoode's mind: we looked at each other, loathing in our eyes, releasing each other's hand instantly as though we held a poisonous crab. Then we began to laugh. Rolling helplessly about the bed, contorted with hysterical laughter. Then Beauty returned, but the Beasts were too suffused with hilarity to let her into the joke. Sulking a little she got into bed again. We let her sleep, dressed and went for a walk to the cliff.

It didn't escape me however that destiny in that department of my life had a perverse sense of humour: when I had tried to sleep with the girl in Johannesburg, I had clutched a sponge mistaking it in the dark for her breast; and now I had been thwarted again fondling my rival's hand as I lay beside the object of my desire.

166

This set-up did not endure very long. I had too many advantages, too few scruples. Spottiswoode had to work for his living, whereas when Rose Marie returned to her parents' home in Sheffield, a week after leaving Devon, I was able to nip on a train and follow her there. She met me at the station, confused, not knowing how she could explain my presence or my appearance to her very conventional parents. They asked me what I was doing in Sheffield and I said pursuing their daughter. This did not go down so well, and her father, finding a cricket-bag in which to put a pair of pyjamas—for I had come precipitously without any luggage at all, walked me off to lodge at a terrible temperance hotel. However, next day Rose Marie borrowed her parents' car and we drove over the Yorkshire moors. Like any girl in this situation she enjoyed the fact that both Spottiswoode and I were in love with her at the same time, especially as we were the closest of friends.

I was doing my best to forget the fact that Spottiswoode had given me a letter to give to the girl. I was tempted not to hand it over, but knowing that he had made the tactical mistake of expressing his resentment, I did eventually give the letter to her. She wrote a reply, which I thought far too conciliatory. When I returned to London he asked me if I had delivered his note.

"Yes," I replied, "but she didn't answer it."

I watched him take her photograph down and put it in a drawer. I suppose I should be ashamed about this. I am not, because I know it would have made no difference. There are times when we are justified in expediting destiny, or at least giving it a bit of a shove.

During the winter my sister finally persuaded my mother to give up the house in South London where so many of her relatives lived, as it were, on her. She resisted the change; to precipitate it I myself moved out of the house, taking a furnished room in Pembridge Square in Bayswater. The only article that accompanied me was my large bust of Beethoven. I chose Bayswater because Rose Marie lived in that district. She shared a flat with her brother. I decided to lay siege.

For the next few weeks I spent my time in my Bayswater cell, proceeding with my siege operations. It was not easy: Rose Marie had many boy-friends, stage-impresarios, film-producers, all with means beyond mine, and she was a girl who wanted to get on. It was like standing in a queue. But I was never despondent, though my sister was. She said I was not writing and she resented Rose Marie for distracting me and wasting my time. She had met her only once and looked upon her as a blonde epidemic to which poets are prone in their twenties. When she realised that she could not dissuade me from this persistency, or lessen the infatuation or the distress she thought it was causing me, she decided to intervene and to assist me, in the belief that the sooner I achieved my ends the quicker I would recuperate and finish the poems on her desk. Accordingly she lent me her new car on Coronation Day, so that I could drive Rose Marie out into the country to pick bluebells. This was generous of her: she was proud of her first car and knew only too well that lending it to me for a day was a risk; she had no reason to fear I would smash it, but she was certain I would scratch it and splash it with coffee and cigarette-ash. When this sacrifice didn't cure me, and she saw that the day in the country had only made my attachment worse, she telephoned Rose Marie at my instigation and told her shortly that it was her duty to abandon her resistance and go to bed with me. This intrusion did not help and of course had the opposite effect.

"Your mother and sister are so obsessed with you," she said, "I doubt if there's room in your life for another woman." She was wrong in this estimate by at least two women. After staying in my Bayswater room for a month, I decided to change my tactics, leave London for Devon and start writing a play about coalminers. All I had was the title *The Unburied Dead*, but there was a great deal turning over in my head: in particular I wanted to try and write lines of which the actor could not drop the last word on the floor. I was still messing about with all sorts of musical notations to help add to poetic rhythms, and I was fascinated too with the possi- bilities of avoiding conventional metaphor—"so-and-so like so- and-so"—and was trying to drive the comparison into the adjective itself.

About this time I received a note from T. S. Eliot suggesting that I go to see him with a view to contributing something to the *Criterion*. I was delighted at the prospect of meeting him, but was not very enthusiastic about writing for his magazine, which, with my youthful arrogance, I then dismissed as academic and stuffy. Like Eliot's prose-style, I thought it was too cautious, a collection of parentheses. Obviously Pound had written to Eliot and made the suggestion that we should meet.

We had tea in his tiny room at Faber's. He already had the habit, I suppose because his room was so small, of littering the floor with books, which he would occasionally consult while they were still in that position. I think it was this method of reading that gave him his stoop.

He suggested that I review a book for the *Criterion*. I said I would like to review some new poetry.

"No," he said; "that wouldn't do you any good. Don't read any modern verse; it will only distract you from your own. I'd like you to review this book on India."

He handed me a dull-looking tome and generously suggested that I should send him some of my play when I got down to writing it. This remark made me decide to return to Devon.

Not wishing to go alone to West Mill I asked a young Canadian, called John Reid, to accompany me. He had come over to Europe to write and to see Ezra Pound. Pound had sent him to Eliot, and Eliot had sent him on to me. He was writing a novel, which never appeared. After a week of work I became restless and, without changing my riding clothes, took a train to London. I went round to Rose Marie's flat in Garway Road. One of her brother's friends informed me that she had been seeing a great deal of an American film producer and that she was now at the Dorchester with him. I saw that my evasive tactics had been a mistake. I was plunged in depression. The friend offered to distract me by taking me to a party. Still wearing my riding boots, I sulked by sitting on the stairs. Eventually I stomped off about midnight and returned to Rose Marie's flat. She was still not there. Maybe she was sleeping with this tycoon? As far as she knew, I was safely buried in Devon. I decided on an impulse to make my presence and position embarrassingly clear. I broke into the flat, placed my two knee-length riding boots outside her bedroom door, knowing that she and her film producer would see them when they came back, and got into her bed.

After a couple of hours I heard the taxi, heard her ask him in for a drink, heard his muttered comment as he passed my conspicuous boots outside her door. It was a quick drink. I clapped my hands with glee and waited. It was worth waiting for. But about five she woke me up to say I had better get out of her room before her brother spotted me. This entailed retrieving my boots and holding them in my mouth while I climbed through the window. Her room was in the basement. I emerged to street-level to find I had walked into the arms of a policeman.

"This will take some explaining," he said. "You had better come along to the station."

Breaking and entering, he called it. I thought there was some ambiguity in that, but tried to point out to him that I knew the people in the flat.

"I'll knock 'em up and see if that's true," he said.

"No, no, don't do that," I urged; "far better put me in gaol."

I walked down Westbourne Avenue in my stockinged feet. I took a long chance and decided to tell the policeman the truth. He listened with a grin on his face. If he did not believe me, it was clear he wanted to. He helped me put my boots on and saw me on my way home.

I often forget events, never feelings. And my feelings the day after I had made love to Rose Marie for the first time were such that I wanted to be with them alone. I did not even wish to be with her. I knew the sensation was too precious to risk any distraction from it. I felt I had come home. I had discovered what it was women had for me: and I liked it.

> The child in the womb
> Is at one with the world,
> And the man hurries back
> To the womb's oneness,

I said to myself. I remember walking up the Bayswater Road feeling such gratitude for life that every footstep was a sort of inarticulate prayer. It was not the sensation of now belonging to this woman, but of belonging to all women. I was grateful for the gift of the opposite sex. She had given me so much more than herself. I felt connected, connected to her, to those on the pavement, to those in their graves and those in the cradle. I realised that if sex does not give this kind of religious experience it is empty, meaningless and, in being meaningless, obscene. I pondered the connection between sex and religion. Then realised the verbal fact: sex connects; the word *religio* in Latin means to connect. These thoughts were not without dangerous implications of which I was aware. But to feel my thoughts out, or rather think my feelings through, I left the pavement and walked in the park. I did this because, though I was released, I was not relaxed. I had the sensation of such energy inside me that I felt compelled to have space about me, for fear that I might ignite or singe anybody who came near me. I am not blind to the danger that all this must sound ludicrous, religiose and highly suspect. But let me be honest and you be derisive: the facts were that I felt I was wrapped round an energy, contained an energy, that could play marbles with the stars. Even then I looked at this ecstasy objectively: and though I derided it, it was there. And I felt a still joy in it and then a deep fear of it. The sensation became an experience: the experience was of an energy that was not derived but seemingly self-creative. It was not merely that I apprehended the nature of divinity; I was for a moment of that divinity: it was not that I was near to God; I was God. And what the devil do I mean by that? I mean: I felt at the centre of being. I mean: I felt such life in me that there could be no death of me. I mean: I was. You must believe, if you cannot understand. Then, as it thundered at my first birth, so it appropriately began to thunder at this birth of being too. I was grateful for the thunder. Then it began to rain: there was no shelter: I was grateful for the rain. An hour or two later I woke up, as they say, or to be more accurate went to sleep in everydayness. I record this not to give the impression that I am unique: on the contrary, I believe this is what many experience.

The next day I took Rose Marie to meet Viccy. This was the natural thing for me to do: to introduce the girl I loved to the man I loved. I knew how much they would like each other. We arrived at his flat in Sussex Gardens on our way to a lunch appointment. Asraf, the Indian servant, let us in and said that His Highness was still in the bath. I left Rose Marie in the sitting-room and went to the bathroom to urge Viccy to hurry up and come and meet her. Normally he would have just picked up a bath-towel and a bottle of champagne. But he shook his head:

"I can't meet her," he said. "I haven't shaved."

That much was obvious and quite irrelevant. But I could see he was strangely depressed and didn't press him. He saw my disappointment.

"Bring her to dinner tomorrow," he said. "I'll be all right then."

"She's going away."

"As soon as she comes back then."

But he never met her. Viccy was killed by a car as he was crossing the Great West Road to watch a cricket match at Osterley Park, a couple of weeks later.

His was the first death I experienced. I was immensely fond of this unknown great man. He was great in heart.

At this time Rose Marie used to go to Bunbury, telling her brother that she was spending the night with a mythical girl-friend. We used to make love all night. It seemed natural to repeat what gave pleasure. But because we were both so inexperienced we saw nothing abnormal in that, after which we would sleep soundly. But then we were able to sleep together only two or three times a week. These nights used to end with our getting up in time for lunch, after which we invariably squabbled about my refusal to marry her.

"But I want you to be the mother of my children," I said, to prove my affections were serious.

This made her even crosser with me. She left my room in a pet. I climbed happily out on to the window-ledge and sat there with a box of white-heart cherries, squirting the stones at her receding form. Everything repeats itself. But as her figure disappeared round the corner, I felt remorseful and scribbled,

> *Our solution lies*
> *In the ease of each other's eyes.*
> *All our distress starts*
> *Soon as we talk,*
> *Walk away from our hearts.*

> *Your tongue's acrobatics*
> *Cannot cure my blood's bewilderment,*
> *Nor your lips alleviate or budge*
> *Limpet:my love.*

on a postcard and, with that posted, I knew our quarrel was over till matrimony was mentioned again.

Only three months ago I had been spending my time talking about the virtues of chastity with Gandhi. The chastity was his, I said to myself, the virtue is mine—for doesn't virtue derive from vir: a man?

But life was not easy for us. I could not sleep in her flat, and she could not sleep in my room, which was in a very respectable boarding-house, although many years later a man called Heath murdered somebody in the very room I had rented. However, I got over this difficulty by hiding her in the cupboard when I ordered my breakfast—two pots of coffee and two poached eggs.

Now history suddenly repeated itself in a most sinister way. Rose Marie had a friend who was also on the stage, and my relatives, including my mother and sister, thought I was having an affair with her. They did not approve. Incredible that the stage should carry such connotations. Even my mother was apprehensive. My great-aunt began to employ a London taxi-man, who trailed me and made a weekly report to her. She enjoyed asking me when I dined alone with her what I had done the night before, and, when I lied, contradicting me.

"If you don't give up this girl," she said eventually, "I shall cut you off without a penny."

She did this frequently. Whenever I met my uncles we used to discuss who was in and who was out. We all lived in terror, believing that she had over half a million to dispense among us.

When my sister came of age, we observed that our own funds were invested in companies which were profiting from the armaments race. We insisted that the trustees should sell these shares, and with considerable reluctance they ultimately agreed to re-invest the monies in land. My sister and I then bought some

173

farms. One of these was Mead in Welcombe: it adjoined West Mill.

My plans for the quarterly magazine which I called *Townsman* slowly took shape: there was constant correspondence with Rapallo. I decided to go to Paris to use the various introductions Pound had given me, and to get contributions for the first number. But Rose Marie had become my first interest: I postponed the visit several times. Eventually one morning I decided I had better go. It was November, extremely cold with an east wind. Having recently returned from India, I felt the cold even more than usual: and to to add my discomfort I had lost my overcoat—or rather done what I usually do; taken it to be cleaned, lost the ticket and forgotten to which shop I had taken it. I solved this sartorial problem by wearing Rose Marie's black satin pyjamas under my suit. Thus sensibly attired I crossed the Channel and called on Stravinsky.

He was living in the Faubourg St Honoré, in a very elegant apartment. He was spruce and gnome-like, immaculately dressed, and looking more like a business executive than a composer. But this impression changed as we sat talking: he was precisely like a cricket wearing spats. Just as a cricket will stay immobile, then suddenly bound into the air with a spring of compressed energy, so I had the feeling that Stravinsky might bound through the ceiling at any moment. He looked so alert, nervous though not neurotic, as though he had just emerged from one of those baths where you are rubbed with ice and beaten with birch-twigs. We talked for some time about the magazine, he offered to contribute to it, and introduced me to his son, Soulima, who he suggested might write something too. His wife was in the flat but in the background. Suddenly in the middle of talking about some aspect of *Townsman*, the cricket sprang.

"I want to show you something," he said, and led me into his study.

It was a small room, clinically tidy with an upright piano. Stravinsky went straight across the room to a shelf beside his piano and took down a portrait which he gave me to hold.

"You are exactly like this man," he said.

I held the portrait I did not recognise, and Stravinsky stood beside me as though he was observing a two minutes' silence.

"Webern is the greatest composer of this century," he said finally, and took his portrait from me and put it back on the shelf.

From that moment our relationship was less formal. He told me he always composed at the piano: he had to hear the note to be absolutely certain it was precisely the sound he wanted. Dozens of kinds of pencils, paper-clips, contraptions for punching papers and threading them together littered a side-table. The room was full of gadgets or desk-toys which he believed made him more efficient.

Stravinsky was almost pathetically pleased that I had called on him. He feared that my generation "had got lost in Sibelius and had never heard of his music." I told him how much I admired *Symphony of Psalms* and his *Symphonies of Wind Instruments*—especially, I said, the very last part of it. He picked up a score and went to the piano.

"You mean from here?" he asked.

"Precisely."

"Yes," he said, "I joined that bit on. I wrote it originally as an epitaph for Debussy."

I tried to interest him in Britten, but he was too self-absorbed to be aware of anybody else's work. He did not refer to Pound. He was interested only in Webern, somebody he could use. I mean nothing derogatory in that.

Using another of Pound's postcard introductions, I called on Brancusi. His studio was difficult to find. He was already old, very much the recluse, looking more monk than sculptor, wearing a long smock and a smoking-cap. He gave me the impression that I was the first visitor he had had for months, and that the outside world had ceased to exist some time ago. I don't think I have ever met a man more completely self-absorbed in his own world. He was entirely dedicated to shape and, like a small child, switched on the little electric motors which turned his carvings round very slowly. He looked at them with innocent admiration, as though they were nothing to do with him, but were new creations that had suddenly appeared. Here was a man who looked eighty but was six. His only other enthusiasm was for cooking.

Brancusi did all the shopping himself. His household consisted only of his sculpture. One could not imagine him living with anybody; they would have been an intrusion. He gave me a large number of photographs of his work. I was entirely captivated by it and said I would try to persuade a gallery in London to give an exhibition. He was interested but not optimistic. I am sure he put it out of his mind. Before I left I promised to go back to sample one of his dishes.

I found Cocteau eventually, living in a small hotel in the Rue Cambon, called the Hotel de Castille. For some unknown reason I had had the impression that Cocteau was dead. When Pound had said I should try and get him to contribute to *Townsman* I had been surprised. But when Pound assured me that Cocteau was still alive I had then assumed that, if he wasn't dead, he must be a very old man. I don't know why I associated Cocteau with a venerable figure with a white beard. At any rate I was quite unable to hide my surprise when a very sprightly fop teetered into the room. Fortunately Cocteau mistook my surprise for elation at the sight of him. He was as vain as a *jeune premier*. For the first ten minutes of our meeting we discussed neckties, and his in particular. He then talked about his enthusiasm for Charlie Chaplin and Marlene Dietrich: we had something in common. Then other celebrities were drawn into his conversation and I felt that I had interrupted somebody who was snatching a moment to talk shop between rushing to fifteen pressing parties. I felt a long way from the *Ashram* at Wardha. Cocteau promised to send me poems and some criticism. I never reminded him.

Max Jacob was not to be found. I missed Hiller too. But I found Léger at work in his enormous studio. He went straight to the point: his work. He was, he said, experimenting with underwater forms and trying to get their plastic shapes into his canvases. He showed me about fifty, all of seaweed forms. I was interested but could see that it would be too expensive to reproduce them in colour. He was anxious to get them shown somehow and said he wouldn't mind if they were printed in black and white. He gave me what photographs he had. His work seemed only decorative, not basically creative like Brancusi's.

I left Léger's studio intending to go to see Sylvia Beach at the

Shakespeare bookshop to make arrangements with her to sell *Townsman*. But on my way there I suddenly felt something stronger than home-sickness; it was a sense of insecurity amounting to panic. My impulse was to fly back immediately: and that is exactly what I did, without even going to my hotel to pay my bill or collect my suitcase. On the way to Le Bourget I stopped the taxi, rushed into a dress-shop and bought a blue silk blouse for Rose Marie. Hating the idea of having to pay customs on it, and lacking any luggage to conceal the gift in, I decided to wear it myself. I peeled off my coat and pocketed my tie. As I slipped the blouse on, I noticed that the shop assistant was looking intrigued. I had forgotten that I was already wearing Rose Marie's pyjamas. The girl was convinced I was a transvestist. However I was too excited to bother about her reactions and rushed out to my taxi. At the next street we stopped for the traffic outside a pastry shop. In the window there was an enormous open flan filled with fresh wood-strawberries. In case she didn't like the blouse: I would take this too. I bounded out of the taxi again, bought the flan, which measured nearly two feet across, and then discovered that the shop hadn't a box large enough to contain it. It was not my fault that I eventually arrived at the airport holding this enormous cake, nor that the pastry broke and the silk blouse got covered in jam. In this sticky but happy condition I reached Croydon, and then rushed to London to replace the two presents I had spoiled on my journey. In my excitement it never occurred to me that any present would have been acceptable: I set off for Rumplemayer's to buy a strawberry flan, and then to the Galleries Lafayette for a blue silk blouse. With these two articles in two separate boxes I took a taxi to Rose Marie's flat in Bayswater. On the way I realised I was still wearing the blouse stained with jam. I peeled it off, stuffed it down the seat of the taxi, and put the new one on, forgetting I had no longer any customs to evade—such was my excitement to see her.

After a few more weeks in London Rose Marie herself urged me to return to Devon to get on with my play, and I now felt secure enough to go. The condition was that I telephoned to her twice a day.

I endured a few weeks, then, hearing that she was pregnant, I dashed off to London again. It was a false alarm, but I had no intention of persisting in this kind of existence. I hired a large American car and went round to her flat about midnight. It took me till four o'clock in the morning to persuade her to elope. She took no luggage, and left a note for her brother to say that she had gone off to stay the week-end with a girl-friend. It was a week-end that lasted half a lifetime.

We lived very happily for a time in a rented bungalow at Welcombe which had hardly any furniture in it. My mother took a full twenty-four hours to forgive me for eloping with Rose Marie, whom she had not met, and for living in sin on her doorstep. But within a short time she was lending Rose Marie sheets, pots and pans, and advising her about her shopping. The only furniture we had was a primus stove and an Arab horse. Our being so impractical made my mother feel useful. If Rose Marie and I had been capable and independent, the rifts might have remained. But once women lend each other sheets, they are friends. A wise man keeps them short of linen.

West Mill was not available. The locals were outwardly shocked about my living in sin, but extremely curious to get a glimpse of it. We got very irritated at their peering over the hedge and prying, as country people do. One evening when it was dark I heard footsteps on the gravel outside and saw the shadow of a Peeping Tom pass the window. Neither of us could cook. Our main dish was porridge. There was a large saucepan of it, now cold and congealed, on a primus stove on the table. I told Rose Marie that the next time the nocturnal visitor showed himself he would get the full contents of the saucepan in his prying face. I stood to the side holding the saucepan ready. I saw the beady eyes and flung the full contents at them. Unfortunately I had not taken the precaution of opening the window and, as a consequence, the porridge rebounded on me. It was hilarious, and for a fortnight we lived with few other possessions than the Arab horse which I had persuaded my trustees to buy me.

Unfortunately the primus was nearly our undoing. While I was out one day Rose Marie upset a saucepan of boiling water over her foot. When I returned I discovered that she had burnt herself

178

almost to the bone. In ignorance we bandaged it and within a few days the foot was septic. For a time we did not know whether she would have to have it amputated.

The "week-end with a girl-friend" had now become extended to a fortnight. I decided to try to get a lease of West Mill.

I do not know why I had always wanted to live in this place. Perhaps I mistook its loneliness for solitude; or, a greater error, assumed its solitude would mean serenity. At any rate, as soon as I heard that the Mill was vacant, I went down the steep cart-track with the old miller, who still owned the place. I noticed that his legs were bandy, like two barrel-staves, and that his enormous shoulders were bent as from a life spent in carrying great weights, but, as he was a miller, this did not surprise me.

The cottage looked rather like a drunken charwoman; its thatch had slipped over its eaves; the untidy ivy hung like wisps of hair over its blowsy walls.

"It's got great character, this house has," said the miller, trying to impress me. He was right; this cottage had character, but of what kind was another matter.

"And it's as old as these hills themselves," the miller added, in the vague hope that its vice might have decreased with its age.

We went inside. There were, as I knew, only three rooms. And, if one excluded the large open fire-place from the sitting-room, then one could say there were only two.

The cottage was unfurnished, but full: full of clutter. In the barn Rose Marie and I had to stand on each other's feet, for the floor was covered with the queerest assortment of rubbish that I had ever seen. Bits of cork, coils of rope, slabs of grease, lumps of brass and planks of every length. Five ships' doors now lay across the bed where we had slept à trois.

"I'll clear this stuff out," the miller offered, trying to make the deal.

"What about water?" I asked him.

"There's a well."

"A lavatory?"

"There's a bucket."

"You only need some nails and you could be a fakir," Rose Marie suggested to me.

"With inconveniences like these," I retorted, pointing to the pump without a handle, "none of our friends will ever visit us. This is just the place we're looking for."

I was trying to settle down to write a play. I was fleeing from London distractions. And, mistaking discomfort for simplicity, I bought the cottage there and then.

"What are we going to do about furniture?" my incredibly tolerant girl asked.

The miller offered to sell us a single bed, a card-table and a rocking-chair.

"As for the rest, you'll soon pick that up," he said with a tired sort of resignation which I didn't notice at the time.

Having removed his pile of doors from the bed, he puffed his way up the hill again.

Rose Marie surveyed her home.

"It won't take you long to dust it," I consoled her, "once he's cleaned this stuff out." Then I took my turn in our only chair as she went along to explore the cupboards.

"This is just the place to write in," I mused. And, as a gesture, I began absent-mindedly to sharpen a pencil. And that was as near as I got to my play; for, at that moment, there was a cry of excited delight coming from the depths of the cupboard underneath the stairs. Rose Marie had found an old rusty kettle, two cups and a knife.

"If you were to stop wasting your time, sharpening a pencil," she said as she emerged, covered in cobwebs, "and were to go and find some firewood, we could boil this kettle and have some tea."

"If we had any tea," I replied, bluntly puncturing her domestic fantasy.

"Anyhow, if you got some firewood, we could sit by the fire— or, at least, one of us could."

I put my pencil down. It was a full year before I picked it up again.

It now seemed necessary for Rose Marie to inform her family where she was and what her plans were. She wrote to her mother saying that she was living with me. Her mother had already met me in Sheffield and had formed the opinion that I was dark enough to be oriental. She arrived within twelve hours and said that I had probably drugged her daughter and that she was taking her away. To confirm her suspicion that I was an Indian, she demanded to see the whites of my finger-nails. She was disappointed that they did not confirm her suspicion. But the poor woman's anger was justifiable, since I was at this time making no move to marry her daughter. In fact I articulated the principle that I did not believe in marriage, and that the only contract was between two pairs of eyes. She stayed two or three days. We detested each other. As I see it now, the right was on her side. When she left, Rose Marie remained. It was an act of extraordinary loyalty to me. I didn't value it at the time. I took it as a matter of course.

I now had a home, a place and a person to be with. I was no longer lonely, though I was now able to be alone, that is to say, I could sit on the beach knowing that she was in the cottage; and if I was homesick it was because I had a home. I had only to go away for a week-end to find that I would return in less than a day. I suppose I did everything possible to strain Rose Marie. I refused to marry her. She was referred to by the locals as "Mr Duncan's lady" and, not only did I load her with this obloquy, but made her domestic life as difficult as possible, also as a matter of principle. In those days I bristled with principles and was a prig. I believed in the simple life, and it has always been necessary for me to act out my beliefs. Consequently we lived in this cottage without any of the amenities or conveniences. We had no bathroom, a bucket for a lavatory, no taps. She had to take a pail to the well. Having been a coalminer I did not think it right for people to use coal unless they were prepared to be coalminers. So the poor girl had to cook on bits of gorse or driftwood that I dragged up from the beach or she clawed out from the hill. On no account would I allow any tinned food in the house. This was because I believed that economic self-sufficiency was the only guarantee for political freedom. I was determined to crack the round of serfdom where the people are dependent on wages, and their living expenses barely cover their wage. I became an enthusiastic and efficient gardener. We grew not only our own vegetables, but our own tobacco. I kept goats for milk, hens, ducks, and turned my starlet into an Irish peasant. She played along with me all the way, even to the extent of taking up weaving, potting, and rearing chicks. This activity led to many tragedies.

I started off by buying fifteen White Leghorn pullets, fully grown. They were beautiful birds and arrived in crates from Norfolk. With great excitement we undid the crates and to our astonishment the Leghorns flew to the roof of the cottage. Unlike other breeds of poultry they will do this. But we didn't know it. We went into the house for an evening meal and when we came out the birds had disappeared. We were both distraught; our first animals had been lost within half-an-hour. We went back to the house and went upstairs to bed. It was dark: we had no electric light. I lit a candle. The fifteen leghorns were all perched on the bed.

My sister had given Rose Marie and me a present of a double bed for Christmas. One night, a few weeks after we had received this pneumatic raft, I was lying in it half-awake just as it was getting light. It was my routine to get up at dawn so as to be the first on the beach to pick up any wreck. That particular morning I lay there waiting for it to get light, wondering what the tide had washed in, when I had the distinct impression that I had seen a maggot on Rose Marie's forehead as she slept beside me. I turned away chiding myself at the fact that my habitual morbidity was getting out of hand. It is one thing, I thought, to see the skull beneath the skin, but quite another to see a fat maggot on the brow. I turned towards the lovely face on the pillow beside me to reassure myself. But to my horror I now saw at least a dozen maggots on her brow and cheek.

I wondered whether I ought to get a doctor to deal with my hallucinations. Pensively I got out of bed to dress in order to get down to the beach. Rose Marie woke and sat up in bed; she noticed that I was looking distressed. I told her that I had imagined her face covered in maggots and she held out her arms to me. While we embraced, these lines came into my head,

I pressed my lips on Helen's mouth
And kissed a skeleton.

182

Then another maggot miraculously appeared on her cheek. I withdrew, it fell to the pillow, she screamed and jumped out of bed. We stood each side of our luxurious raft and stared down at my morbid mirage which had already multiplied. Can hallucinations be contagious? I asked. She had no need to answer: for we both observed that a rain of maggots were coming from a crack in the floor-boards of the ceiling above the bed. Relieved that I only had reality to contend with, I raced up into the rafters of the thatched roof of the cottage.

"It's nothing," I shouted down. "It's only a dead rat!"

"Only?"

"Only!"

She did not know my fears.

In February 1938, after a hard winter at West Mill, Rose Marie and I left our Noah's Ark collection of livestock in the care of my sister and went to Paris, and then to Rapallo on our way to La Basse Combe, the cottage I had rented but never visited, at Cotignac. It was her first journey abroad.

At Rapallo Ezra put us in an hotel adjoining his flat in the Via Marsala. Our arrival at the hotel was not without immediate incident. While Rose Marie was unpacking, I threw a cigarette out of the window which set fire to the large sun-canopy over the restaurant beneath. When the fire had been put out and the panic had subsided, Rose Marie decided to take a bath. Soon screams emerged from the bathroom. Apparently as she lay in the bath she had noticed a pair of eyes prying at her through the ceiling. I called for the proprietor. He couldn't be discovered. Eventually we heard him tip-toeing downstairs. He promised to catch the Peeping Tom, his indignation confirming that he was the culprit. Years later I had a similar experience in Spain under even more embarrassing circumstances, when I saw the eyes of a picture above a bed move.

Although we were living next door to Ezra he constantly bombarded me with notes during the day, even though we met for lunch and for dinner. We used to lunch beside Gaudier's bust with Ezra and Dorothy, and then dine at our hotel with Ezra and Olga.

Olga Rudge had been Pound's mistress for many years. She was an American by birth, but very much a European in manner. I believe they had met in Paris. She was a violinist who earned her living as music-librarian to Count Chigi at Siena. When I first met her she was a very handsome woman of about forty. She had a tiny flat in a villa at San Ambrogio, overlooking Rapallo. It was reached by climbing innumerable wooden steps. I suppose it was these steps which kept Ezra so fit. He used to spend his evenings with Olga, his days with Dorothy. It was apparent that he had a deep affection for both, but neither ever referred to the existence of the other. This omission gave the situation an atmosphere of Jamesian unreality: but it appeared sophisticated and civilised on the surface. Rose Marie and I tried to remain on that surface, though we lunched with Dorothy and dined with Olga.

A day or two after our arrival I was sitting with Ezra at his desk. He had been reading the first two acts of the play *The Unburied Dead* which I had written before setting up house with Rose Marie. And when Dorothy went into the kitchen he furtively took a small snapshot from a wallet in his desk and passed it to me, his face beaming with pleasure. It was of a fair-haired girl of about six.

"That's Mary," he said proudly. "My daughter: Olga's daughter."

He took the snap from me and studied it, affection in every pore of his face.

"Your best piece of poetry?"

"Just so."

There was a noise off. Ezra hastily stuffed the photograph into his desk, locked it and began talking in a loud voice about Baudelaire as Dorothy entered with a tray of coffee and *panetone*.

Perhaps she had been listening. At any rate I remember she immediately began talking about their son, Omar, who was at a prepschool in England.

The next day Ezra took Rose Marie and me to have a meal with his parents, who had also settled in Rapallo. I can recall nothing about them except that his father was called Homer, and that his mother, a frail bird-like little woman, gave me a cake that had a cherry on the top of it. There are times when I am as unaware as a

184

stone and remember nothing of an event or a meeting except some detail which is wholly unimportant.

The only other incident that I can recall of this visit is the occasion when I indulged, as usual, in my obsession for fishing—or, to be more accurate, dangling a line optimistically and fruitlessly from the stern of a small boat. Ezra had tried to dissuade me, without any apparent reason. So Rose Marie and I hired a tiny dinghy, borrowed a line and some bait, and off we went. I rowed out into the bay, began to fish and then observed that the sea was getting choppy. The whole bay suddenly raced with white horses. There was Ezra pacing up and down the front, furious with anxiety.

"You may be the reincarnation of Shelley," he bellowed, "but I'm damned if I want to be Trelawny."

At Cotignac Rose Marie had to make a home from scratch —her third essay at this within six months. While she collected bits of furniture and pots and pans from the village, I sat supposedly writing the review for Eliot's *Criterion*, but putting my pen down every ten minutes, bored with criticism, and picking up my axe instead. The cottage had a small number of very ancient olive-trees surrounding it and they needed pruning from the suckers growing round the trunks. I also had to saw vine-roots or gather fir-cones for the open fire. But in spite of these absorbing distractions I persisted with the review, trying to hammer out a telegraphic style. My aim was to pack as much meaning into as few words as possible, dispensing with any word that could be taken for granted. The first draft of the article ran to fifteen hundred words, but by pruning out the dead and unnecessary words I reduced it eventually to three hundred without any sacrifice of meaning. I kept remembering T. E. Hulme's dictum "No man has more to say than will go on a postcard."

Eventually I posted the review to Eliot. He sent me thirty shillings, the first money I ever earned as a writer. I was thrilled with the cheque. I would have had to spend nearly a whole week down the pit to earn that much.

Rose Marie and I were idyllically happy, painting and writing, cooking in garlic and olive-oil, and finding our way eventually to

Thoronet Abbey, which made an indelible impression on me. It is like the *Symphony of Psalms* in stone. But we often squabbled at Cotignac. One quarrel had a consequence, though I have entirely forgotten the cause of the scene. However, eventually it ended with Rose Marie announcing that she had had enough of living with a bloody genius and was going to leave me for ever, there and then.

"It's dark," I said.

"And I'll never come back!"

"There are no buses or trains," I said.

"I'll walk. Anything's better than living in the squalor of your coffee-cups and cigarette-ash while you daydream about other women, pretending to be too much of a monk to marry me."

"You're being hysterical."

"I'm not," she screamed, snatching up her handbag, "and I'm doing what I ought to have done months ago: walk out and leave you to your bogus ideals."

She turned, opened the door and walked out into the night.

There was an enormous splash. I rushed out. The poor girl had forgotten the stream which ran like a moat round the place. She was stretched out in the water.

"That spoiled my exit," she said, smiling through her tears.

The next day, to celebrate our reunion, I decided to take her to Marseilles so that we could feast on lobsters. But we must have quarrelled again because I can remember that neither of us spoke to the other on the four-hour drive to our celebration lunch. Strange that though I have forgotten the cause of the row I can recall the size of the roe of the lobsters.

I had intended to winter at Cotignac and finish *The Unburied Dead*, but after about six weeks there was the Munich crisis and everybody urged us to pack our bags and run for home. This should have been easy, since I always travel light—or at least when I *leave* England. Then a toothbrush and a pen are all I consider essential. But my acquisitive instincts make the return journey another matter. Then only a caravan will suffice. My luggage comes to consist of various vines, trees, cuttings and animals; a crate or two of pottery, a dozen gallons of olive-oil, some iron lamps, vials of vanilla, books, bougainvillea-cuttings, more books, more bougainvillea, and a smoked ham. And on this occasion I had acquired a bottle of ninety-per-cent alcohol too, which Rose Marie carried, besides her other burdens, successfully through the customs.

Munich provided a breathing-space in which we found a false security. We spent the summer in Devon at West Mill, trying to make the cottage more habitable, dig the garden, edit *Townsman*, write a play, break in a horse, grow up, and entertain the people who descended upon us.

Among these were Max Plowman and a friend of Gandhi's called Professor Malkani from Delhi. Henry Boys too found himself hacking at the undergrowth and building a wall to act as a wind-break round an unreclaimed extension of the garden, while Frank Smithson and his girl-friend Angela came down from Holmwood for a holiday and found, I think, that the mine was a vacation-centre in comparison. My habit was to make use of people. They must have enjoyed the work, for I remember counting fourteen people to sleep in the cottage one week-end, although we still owned only one double bed.

My sister and I had always been so close that at first she felt defeated when Rose Marie and I went to live at West Mill. Partially from umbrage, she left Devon and went with some friends to the cottage at Cotignac. I hoped that this move towards independence might lead her to develop her own talent. She had abilities and could write, but for some reason she had always preferred to prop me rather than strengthen herself. I was glad to hear that she was now writing herself, but her independence was brief. Soon after her return to England she was sucked willingly into the West Mill vortex: there was a magazine to help edit, print and circulate; besides assisting in my other activities which had now become as varied as unmanageable. No wonder my sister felt constrained to help. Of course I was wrong to allow her to live her life on the periphery of mine. I suppose I did this believing any person's existence was wholly justified if they helped me. I have always needed the assistance of at least four women—and thought they were happy if they were too busy to complain.

And in addition to people there were the animals. I had bought an Arab mare, Dil Fareb, from Lady Savile, picking her out of a herd of twenty. She is outside the door as I write this—and is now thirty-three. I have been riding her for twenty-five years. And I had also bought another horse: a bitch of a mare called Judy, which had been sired by a Derby winner called Flying Fox. She was the most bad-tempered, thieving horse I ever knew and she eventually hanged herself on a thorn-bush. There were also three unbroken Exmoor ponies, which I had bought at Bampton Fair to prevent their being slaughtered for cats' meat. I called them Bovril, Oxo and Marmite.

Gerald Brenan literally fell into our life. He did this by slipping on a rock on the beach at Welcombe and falling flat on his back at Rose Marie's feet. For him it was a happy and not unpremeditated accident: he had admired her from a distance for some time: introductions inevitably followed. We discovered that Brenan and his wife Gamel had known Welcombe for much longer than we had, and had returned to it after they had had to abandon their home near Malaga at the outbreak of the Spanish Civil War.

Brenan had lived at West Mill before the First World War, when Lytton Strachey had rented it and shared the place with the Carringtons. His description of this household and their tangled emotional relationships kept us fascinated for many evenings.

Brenan was the best-read man I ever met, and by that I don't mean he had just read the most: he was a man of letters, not merely steeped in English literature but in European too. He was self-educated, having attended an English public school, and then went to Mons instead of Oxford. He was of that generation which produced Wilfred Owen, Henry Williamson and Siegfried Sassoon.

Wiry and sprightly, erect of bearing, with a small moustache, he seemed to carry an invisible swagger-cane and brought to his writing the thoroughness and discipline he had acquired in the army. In Devon he was writing his *Spanish Labyrinth*, and the method and learning he brought to this monumental task made me feel an illiterate amateur in comparison. Cut off as we were, the Brenans were good for Rose Marie and me. In a sense they adopted us and educated us.

Gamel Brenan published her poetry under the name of Woolsey. She had been born in the Southern States and always carried with her an atmosphere of the leisured elegance which she had known on the plantation. She was extremely beautiful: black hair, white skin and slow eyes: but it was not these features that held you so much as some mysterious gentleness, almost sadness, which surrounded her. Whatever she said her voice seemed to caress you. When we first met she was in her forties and I was only twenty-two. I think we both felt the same frustration immediately. It remained unspoken. But it was a sense of resentment that fate should have separated us by a generation.

The tide was just on the turn. A faint evening wind blew from the land, turning the backs of the waves as though they were the leaves of a book. For a few moments I stood watching, almost mesmerised by their monotonous sound as they broke on the indifferent beach. Then, suddenly, I saw something bobbing up and down about three waves out from the shore. For a moment I thought it was a seal; I had often watched them along this coast on a calm day. Then the surf seemed to roll itself up into one great wave, which flung the object towards me. It was a small wooden keg. I rolled it out of the sea, far too excited to notice that I was now almost soaked to the skin. Then, with hands as clumsy as a crab, I began to claw at the lid. I could tell by its weight that it was full—but of what? In desperation I looked for a sharp pebble, and with this bashed a hole in the lid. I smelt. I stuck my finger in. I sucked. It was fresh butter—about fifty pounds of it. Like a prospector who had at last found gold by tripping over a mine, breaking his nose on a nugget, I began to giggle hysterically. Then, finding the strength I did not know I possessed, I carried the keg back to the cottage.

"Butter from beach," I announced, placing it before Rose Marie, as though that now completed her home.

She dug her finger in. "It's perfect!" she said. "What a pity we haven't got any bread."

That's how it began; and for the next seven years the tide seldom turned but I was there to meet it. And the tide turns twice a day. The fascination of finding something for nothing now completely dominated me. Often I would wake up at four o'clock in the morning, hearing the wind moaning over the cottage. For a few seconds I would lie still, wondering what might have been cast up on the rocks. Perhaps another keg? This time some tea? Could I risk it and go to sleep again? But, if I did, wouldn't some neighbour find it before me? Sheer predatory greed would then fling me out of bed, and curiosity hurl me out into the cold, wet night. My flickering lantern would make the mist seem solid. My feet grew eyes of their own and would lift me from rock to rock with a sleep-walker's sureness; my hands, too, got to know the surface of the granite cliff with an almost indecent intimacy. I had become an addict. And the drug drew me slithering over the wet rocks every twelve hours, whatever the season, whatever the weather.

Many mornings there was nothing but seaweed. On such days I would return home with only firewood and sit sullen through breakfast, having already exhausted myself before the day began. I would then resolve to give up this mad pursuit and get on with my work. But on the very next tide the sea would yield something to me, as if unwilling to let me go. I remember the morning when I promised Rose Marie that I would go no more to the beach if there was nothing washed up by the next tide. But I knew there would be; I knew that the sea had no mercy.

The wind had been blowing from the south-west, so, instead of going towards Gull Rock, I went towards Chizel Reach. As soon as I turned the point of the cove I saw it. The tide had only just dropped it; its side was still flecked with foam. I raced across the rocks, terrified that the object for which I had waited and watched for so many tides might turn out to be a mirage, or, worse, be claimed by a neighbour getting his mark on it first.

But nobody was there before me. For a full minute I stood still, letting my eyes caress its lovely shape, appraising its full-bodied depth, its compact, buoyant lines. I stood in awe as though before an idol. Indeed it was my idol. I had dreamt it, wished it, willed it—this barrel. For this was no mere brewer's barrel which you often see rolled into a pub's cellar; this was the Emperor of all the Barrels. I was reminded of a great ebony Buddha which had suddenly confronted me in an Indian jungle.

I tapped one end. It was full. If it had been empty I know I should have wept with disappointment. It was full. But of what? Oil? Treacle? Pitch? Brandy? What else goes in barrels? A panic of speculation seized me. I put my nose to it but could smell nothing, only the sea. Then I began grovelling for the bung and, breaking my penknife-blade, gradually eased it out. A scarlet flow spurted into the night. It was as though I had let its blood; as if I had severed the artery of a wild boar. I put my mouth to it as one does to a fountain, and the wine gushed all over my neck. "My God!" I cried aloud, never so fervently, "it's Burgundy!"

And I dived frantically to replace the bung. This secure, and my initials scratched on the end, I raced home across the rocks. As I went I tried desperately to remember all the elementary mathematics I had learned at school in an effort to work out how much wine was in the barrel. The nearest I could get to the formula for volume was to remember the name of the mathematics master's wife. No matter; the problem was not to measure, but to salve, before the tide washed the barrel out again.

I ran upstairs to Rose Marie, who was still in bed. "Oh, what have you done?" she cried, mistaking the wine on my shirt for blood.

"Quick! Quick!" I yelled, "give me a bottle, dozens of bottles," and, for a start, I grabbed her hot-water bottle and emptied it out of the window. Then I tore round the cottage, grabbing every jug, basin, pitcher, pot or po.

All day we went to the beach, back and forth, carrying our jars of wine until even the sink and the child's bath were full. At last we counted eighty gallons of the sea's red mercy.

After this haul there was no stopping me. And though no more wine came in, the sea kept me faithful to her tides by casting an occasional favour.

One morning I found the beach littered with airtight tins—each full of American coffee in perfect condition. And soon after the invasion of Normandy two American supply-ships collided in a fog off our coast. Like a greedy vulture I waited.

Sometimes I had to wait a week, impatiently watching for the wind to change. When it eventually did, I found a man's leg lying bootless on the beach. I knew the rest of the cargo would soon follow.

Sure enough, the next tide was profligate: cartons and crates were squandered on the shore. There must have been fifty thousand cigarettes, all perfectly dry. There were cigars too. One could pick them out of the sea and light them, bless the packers. And all the comforts of a bathroom culture followed, including hundreds of tubes of shaving cream, toothpaste, chewing gum, and, of course, contraceptives. The village children used them as balloons and carried them gaily to school.

Then weeks would pass and I would find nothing but a mere slab of tallow, a dozen pit-props or a bale of raw rubber, for which the Custom and Excise would pay me £3 a bale.

And sometimes the tides would tease me pitilessly. I remember, one sullen November, spending all the morning watching a barrel bob up and down on the backs of the waves. It seemed as if the tide just lacked sufficient strength to land it. I could tell it was full by the way it floated. I decided to wade out to it and push it ashore. I stripped; the water was maliciously cold, but I kept my eye on the barrel and waded on, up to my neck. Then I began to push the barrel ashore. Just as I had almost succeeded in landing it, a great Atlantic roller came up behind me unawares and wrapped me helplessly round the barrel. As it turned, so did I. And in this ridiculous fashion I rode the surf—with the slight difference of being underneath it. At last the great wave flung us on the beach: I on top of my prize. Before I could break from this compulsory embrace, the wretched thing began to roll backwards over me. I turned, chasing it as it trundled back, faster and faster down the shingle, towards the sea again. Then a small rock arrested its mad career and I caught up with it, only to watch sixty gallons of Guinness seep into the thirsty beach. Few experiences have moved me as much as this did. I almost wept over the waste of it.

It is not that I like beer. I never drink it. But when the sea presents one with a gift, one is inclined to cast both taste and principles to the winds. Some years ago a keg came in just below Hartland, and was picked up by a family of Wesleyan teetotallers. They abandoned their principles and yielded to the temptation of drinking the wine. In spite of finding the taste rather bitter, they persisted and drank regularly with their meals rather than waste the stuff. Their reward for overcoming their prejudices was that their teeth gradually dissolved away in their mouths, which served them right, I suppose, for if they had known what good wine was, they would not have mistaken dilute hydrochloric acid for Sauterne.

Then, in spite of the healthy life I led on the beach, I began to suffer again from bouts of indigestion and migraine which I have had occasionally all my life. Nothing seemed to alleviate the ailments, and eventually a doctor diagnosed a quiescent appendix as a possible cause. A specialist confirmed this and advised me to have the operation, "because the thing might one day blow up into acute peritonitis when you were on safari or somewhere." I couldn't understand how he could have possibly mistaken me for a big-game hunter, but saw his point.

Within a couple of days I entered a London hospital. I have always dreaded hospitals. I am terrified at the thought of surgery. But there were consolations; I took a portable gramophone in with me and several new Stravinsky records, including the *Octet* and *Jeu de Cartes*. I read *The Book of the Dead* and composed a ballet. Rose Marie visited me twice a day with peaches and prawns, and a pretty night-nurse brought me tea every hour and kept me amused by telling me stories of her life in Australia. Even so I dreaded the operation: my indigestion disappeared: I could find no trace of a headache: only acute funk remained. My fear was that I would one day recall the pain of the experience several months after the operation. I realised the anaesthetic would prevent me from feeling pain at the time, but I was suspicious that my muscles would then have memories which they would involuntarily recall. It was a ridiculously irrational fear but none the less terrifying for that.

After the operation the surgeon came into my room and presented me with his account for eighty guineas. This brought me back to consciousness.

"We got it out just in time," he said.

After he had gone, my nurse confided in me that she had been present at the operation.

"I suppose I shouldn't tell you," she said, "but your appendix was as clean as a new born babe's. All you wanted was a couple of alka-seltzers, and they don't cost eighty guineas!"

"That surgeon will get on," I said ruefully, and he did.

I left the hospital within ten days and immediately took Rose Marie and my sister to Fez, where I thought I might find some sun in November. We did, but the girls were not happy there because they were frightened of catching ringworm, which they saw on nearly every Arab in the town.

In spite of this I was fascinated by the old city and insisted on dragging them in and out of the bazaar round the famous water-clock. One day while I was pursuing a bottle of musk, an Arab mullah came up to me and began upbraiding me angrily. A crowd gathered round. The three of us were nonplussed: the priest continued his tirade against me: we understood not a single word. I couldn't think what harm I had been doing—merely walking with Rose Marie and my sister in search of a shop to buy some scent. Eventually the priest snorted with disgust and strode down the street.

"And what was all that about?" I asked Rose Marie.

Then somebody in the crowd told me.

"The mullah mistook you for an Arab. He objected to your being with two white girls."

This pleased me. I like to boast of the fact that in Spain I am mistaken for a Spaniard, and in India for an Indian—at least so long as I keep my mouth shut. I have no gift for languages.

We left Fez for Paris. The city was snowbound and the slush had frozen. Stravinsky asked me round to his flat. He seemed depressed and worried: he told me that his wife was ill. To try and cheer him up I told him how much pleasure I had derived from his recording of *Jeu de Cartes* when he had conducted the Berlin Philharmonic Orchestra. He seemed surprised that I had heard of it. He knew that only a handful of people either enjoyed or respected his work. Concert programmes excluded him. The press used his name to describe any music which they wished to deride. And if any of the so-called serious quarterlies referred to him it was in a similar vein. Only a month before I had been angry when a Mr Wilfred Mellers had sneered at Stravinsky in *Scrutiny*. I had written a letter of protest to the *New English Weekly* only to receive a pained letter from Leavis taking me to task for trying to spoil Mellers's reputation as a music-critic. I didn't tell Stravinsky any

of this: it would have depressed him further. Instead I asked him
if he would consider the idea of coming over to London to conduct
the first performance of *Jeu de Cartes* for the memorial concert the
Peace Pledge Union was arranging for Dick Sheppard. Stravinsky
immediately agreed.

"Of course I'll come," he said, "if you can arrange it."

"That'll be easy," I replied naïvely.

"I'm not so sure."

"We could do a whole programme of your work—*Jeu de Cartes*,
Symphony of Psalms and ——"

"Maybe I could write something specially for it?"

I could hardly believe the offer. I doubt if I have ever been so
excited.

"Only the deaf can fail to agree that Stravinsky is the greatest
composer since Schubert," I told Rose Marie and my sister when I
met them, and they tried gently to curb my confidence that the
concert could be arranged.

I cut all appointments in Paris and returned to London. The
next day I wrote to the Royal Philharmonic Society and told them
the great news that Stravinsky himself was prepared to come to
London to conduct the first performance of *Jeu de Cartes*, *Symphony
of Psalms* and a new work especially written for the occasion. Two
days later I received a reply from the Secretary of the Orchestra to
say they were not interested. I kept this letter. Maybe the Royal
Philharmonic Society would like to display it now.

That same afternoon I decided, since the Orchestra wouldn't
co-operate, to go and see Ralph Hawkes of Boosey & Hawkes,
whom Stravinsky had told me was his London agent.

Mr Hawkes listened to my news without any enthusiasm.

"Yes, we act for Stravinsky," he said sadly, "but he hasn't
written anything since *The Firebird*."

I reeled off about twenty titles.

"Nothing of any interest, I mean," he said.

His door must have had strong hinges.

I then approached two daily newspapers with the suggestion that
they might sponsor the concert. This was perverse of me: of course
they evinced no interest. The idea was precisely twenty-five years
too soon. Stravinsky was not a name then. Now the same papers

devote a double-page spread to his laundry-list. I was disgusted with their damned indifference. My fury made me decide to sing high and aloof from London. At least there were no bogus artistic pretensions in Devon. I could not understand how even the music world of London could be so besotted with mediocrity that they couldn't appreciate the *Symphony of Psalms* or realise it was a masterpiece. I didn't understand then that it takes precisely twenty-five years, one full generation, for any new idea, either in music, literature or paint, to perforate the island fog.

I could do nothing but write to Stravinsky and tell him that I was having difficulties. He replied with a sad note: but his sadness was not because of the disappointment about the concert.

"My wife has died," he wrote.

In the autumn of 1938 Pound wrote suddenly and unexpectedly to say he was coming to London. He suggested that we should meet after dinner the day he arrived, at some Italian restaurant which he named in Dean Street. Rose Marie and I went along, but found that Pound's restaurant was long bankrupt and had closed eight years ago. It had been a long time since the self-appointed exile had been in England.

We had arrived a little late and there was no knowing whether Pound had already been there. We hung around for ten minutes and then I noticed a bit of paper stuck on the wall giving an odd clue to Pound's whereabouts. "Where it says: *no dogs or Japs admitted*," we read. This baffled me. It was Rose Marie who solved the message and led off for the nearest Chinese restaurant. The notice was in the window: Pound was inside ordering a meal sufficient for sixteen.

(Twenty-five years later when Pound was, I thought, dying in a hospital at Merano, he turned to me after half-an-hour's silence and enigmatically said, "No dogs or Japs admitted." Then he lapsed into silence again. I had no inkling what he meant. I put it down to his delirium.)

During the meal I asked Ezra what had brought him to London.

"Business," he said mysteriously. "When she's eaten those lichees you must both come and help me with it."

We got a taxi and drove to an Edwardian flat in Kensington.

The rooms were stuffed with the ivory and brass trophies of colonialism, silver photograph-frames, ornaments à la Harrods, and all the bric-à-brac of a predatory dowager with an assured income. Ezra looked cornered in these surroundings, as he glanced hopelessly round at the clutter.

"As I say, I need your help. A pity you haven't got a car."

We discovered that Ezra's mother-in-law had died. And for some inexplicable reason Ezra's wife, Dorothy, had been foolish enough to ask Ezra to dispose of the furniture and effects, so that the flat could be sold.

At any rate that was Ezra's story. I never believed it. Dorothy Pound was not stupid. I suppose the truth was Ezra had seized on his mother-in-law's death as an excuse to get to London for a few days and had offered to dispose of the flat, and left before his wife had time to protest.

For Ezra's method of doing business was simple but hardly profitable. He merely asked his friends to help themselves. That evening Rose Marie and I staggered off, our pockets bulging with Chinese ivory and jade, fish knives and forks, an inscribed copy of Yeats's poems, several cushions, and a stool ornamented with quotations from Virgil.

These presents were heaped on us, in spite of the fact that Rose Marie had just trodden on Ezra's feelings. While she was going round the flat indulging in her usual curiosity, Ezra had picked up the volume of Yeats and amused me by giving an imitation of Yeats reading his own poems. Then a few minutes later he had tipped out a drawer of his mother-in-law's desk on to the floor.

"I must start getting some order somewhere," he said.

Among the pile of papers on the floor he espied a volume of *Personae*. Opening the book, he now began to read some of his own poems to me in the extraordinary sing-song voice which he always affected whenever he read poetry. When he had finished reading, Rose Marie gaily congratulated him on his "hilarious imitation of Yeats reading his own work." Her mistake was understandable: there was no difference in the style of the reading.

He put his book down, for a second silenced. Then he studied her twenty-two years of dumb-blonde insolent beauty.

"I'm glad you found it—ah—funny, Madame," he said, and

then, seeing the fear in her face that she'd said the wrong thing and hurt him in some way, he jumped to his feet and grabbed a picture from the wall. "And I'd like you to have this, since you admired it." It was a Chinese painting on silk.

"But why did he give me this if I had upset him?" she had asked as we walked home.

"Because he didn't want you to know you had."

"A pity you haven't his politeness. And why did you kick me under the table at dinner when I told Ezra I'd just been reading Henry James's *Ulysses*?"

"Because it was written by Sir Walter Scott."

"You're teasing me. Anyhow, if you can be in love with anybody as ignorant as me, it shows you're really only interested in sex."

During the next week or two Pound and I tried to find some method of staging one of his Noh plays for our own private pleasure. I managed to persuade Ashley Dukes to lend us the Mercury Theatre. Britten produced a musician who could play gongs, and Henry Boys, who had composed some music for Michel St Denis at the Studio Theatre, suggested a dancer. She was a girl called Suria Magito, very dark and beautiful. Eventually we ran through the play one afternoon at the Mercury, with Ezra reciting while the girl danced. He and I constituted the entire audience. After this performance Ezra asked me if I would send the girl a couple of dozen red roses. I couldn't think why he could not do this himself. I think he felt less guilty by doing it at one remove. At his request I sent several other bouquets. He never paid me for these flowers. By not doing so I suppose he kidded himself he was not sending them. The girl eventually married Michel St Denis.

The pre-war political scene was grim and serious. But its grimness took on the qualities of a charade and its seriousness could only be commented on in satire. I wrote a pamphlet which purported to be the Manifesto of a new political organisation, which I named the Rexist Party. I used the nom-de-plume of the Bishop of Marsland. Marsland is the name of the valley in which West Mill is situated. An imposing list of mythical sponsors of the new Party graced the front page. Among these was one character whom I called the Rt. Hon. Lord Gifford, borrowing the name of a neighbouring farmer.

The body of the pamphlet contained the aims of the Rexist Party. Writing in careful political clichés, I pointed out that the social stability of the State was being threatened by the menace of continued unemployment, which problem could not be solved while the working classes were allowed to multiply so tediously and indiscriminately. This thesis was written in the style of a *Times* leader, and the conclusions were set forth in exact sociological terms. They amounted to the proposal that, since the working class bred in such places as Hampstead Heath, Brighton Pier and upon open heathlands, these amenities and temptations should be withdrawn by the simple process of closing all of them. The Bishop further advocated sterilisation and wholesale circulation of birth-control material. This alone, he maintained, could reduce the numbers of the working class and solve the problem of unemployment for ever. Which problem, he added, threatened the stability, not only of the established State but of the Church too, and even of Peace itself.

The pamphlet contained about ten pages and I had several hundred copies printed. I sent one to every M.P. and to all members of the House of Lords. I had enjoyed the joke of writing this squib and as soon as I had posted the copies I forgot all about it.

Incredibly I received not only serious replies from several Members of Parliament, but application for membership of the Rexist Party poured into the headquarters at West Mill. Every day we would open the mail and roll about the floor in hysterics. But one day a letter came which was less amusing. It was from the Rt. Hon. Lord Gifford himself, stating that I had taken his name in vain, and in doing so had committed a slander, and that he was instructing his solicitors to sue for damages. Meanwhile would I recall my Manifesto from circulation.

I replied suitably, regretting that he in fact existed, apologising that reality should prove more perverse than my imagination, and explaining that I could not withdraw the pamphlet, as all copies had been given away. I never heard any more from him. No doubt his solicitor advised him not to sue for damages but merely repair his sense of humour. Many years later I met Lord Gifford, but he did not know he was standing a drink to the late Bishop of Marsland.

But unfortunately the Bishop had a brother, Brigadier-General Marsland, and his pen really got me into trouble.

In 1937 only a blind worm hibernating under a glacier of complacency, or a Neville Chamberlain sheltering beneath an umbrella, could have failed to see that war was most probable. We listened with morbid fascination to Hitler's rabble-rousing perorations on the radio; we saw the storm-troopers cross into Austria; the papers carried almost daily pictures of another submarine or pocket-battleship being launched at Kiel. One day in 1938 when I was in the Peace Pledge Union office in Regent Street, impotently fingering my pile of pacifist pamphlets, a young man walked in and announced that he was a German soldier who had deserted because he had learned that certain military preparations were in hand in Germany which made "war too horrible for him to contemplate." We questioned him further. He told us that Hitler had ordered the Luftwaffe to research into rockets, and that one "as large as a London bus was already on the drawing-board." He actually produced a drawing. Naturally this information was passed on to the War Office by the Peace Pledge Union. Nobody there believed it, since they suspected the validity of information received from a pacifist organisation. But it was not even the blue-prints of V2 which made me see that war was now inevitable. I became convinced of that when the bishops began to talk vehemently of the virtues of peace.

My reaction to this was to enlarge the vegetable-garden at West Mill, buy some dustbins and fill them with sugar. I also bought half a hundredweight of Cadbury's milk-chocolate as an iron ration, which Rose Marie succeeded in nibbling her way through before hostilities began. My panic was justified: I knew the bishops. For I had been in correspondence with every one of them, asking each a number of questions relating to pacifism, and received their evasive and jingoistic replies. I think it was the Bishop of Coventry who had written and told me he looked upon Britannia as a Saint.

As General Marsland surveyed the scene he was appalled by the way the War Office was reacting to this threat by merely piling up conventional arms as though they were going to fight Mons and Passchendaele over again. Nor did the press do anything to prepare the people for the fact that a new kind of war was in store for them. Guernica had been ignored by almost everybody except Picasso.

The General therefore wrote a pamphlet *Our Strategy in War*, which was published by *Townsman*. Five hundred copies were printed. Rose Marie, my sister and I sat up all one night addressing envelopes. We sent them off free—to M.P.s, generals, to anybody we thought might be irritated by the contents.

My real purpose in writing this pamphlet was to demonstrate that there could be no victor in modern war; and that the only way we could "defend" ourselves against Hitler was to adopt means that were as low as his own—which I wished to imply was no defence, but imitation. I wanted to shock people into realising that war could no longer be a sort of Gentlemen *v* Players contest. Consequently General Marsland postulated his strategy: he advocated the creation of what he called a Fifth Column to work behind the enemy lines; the creation of battalions of parachute troops who, in mufti, would be detailed to sabotage the enemy's railways and poison his water-systems. This style of fighting, the General pointed out, was the logical result of total war. The next paragraphs tried to stress the importance of psychological warfare and of destroying the enemy's will to survive. In this the General made specific suggestions: advocating that nothing would reduce Germany so quickly to complete moral apathy and cultural disintegration as being gratuitously presented with some of our artists and so-called leaders of thought. He advocated that Edith Sitwell, Stephen Spender *et alii* should be dropped on Berlin, where they could lecture and rot the Wehrmacht's will to live from within. And to add to the disintegration the General urged that the music of Delius and Vaughan Williams should be broadcast incessantly over the Ruhr.

Again, having posted this squib, I forgot all about it. We continued to reclaim the valley, buying rusty ploughs and discovering nineteenth-century ditches lost in the undergrowth. But about four months later I suddenly received three mysterious visitors at West Mill. They asked me if I was the author of the pamphlet *Our Strategy in War*. I admitted that. They looked very grave and told me they were from M.I.5 and would have to ask me some questions. They said they wanted to know where I had obtained all the secret military information which the pamphlet carried? I found it impossible to take their enquiry seriously. But they said a vital secret was at stake; and they solemnly closed the doors for further grilling. After a great deal of probing about my background and asking me whether I had been to Germany, etc., one of them came out with this question.

"What the War Office wants to know is: how did you come by the information that parachute battalions will be used in another war?"

"I didn't. I suggested it," I said, "but you're welcome to the idea."

"What we want to know is what made you think of it?"

"It's obvious. The Russians have been using parachute battalions for years on manœuvres."

"Ha," said one of my inquisitors, standing up so that I could almost see the handcuffs in his raincoat pocket. "How do you know this?"

"Because a year ago," I replied, "I went to a cinema and saw a film of one."

"Where?" barked the other man.

"The Academy Cinema, Oxford Street, London," I replied. "You could probably borrow the film to show the War Office if they're interested."

There was a pause.

"What was the film called?" the first man asked.

I told him. They made a note of it. The questioning had taken a couple of hours. They eventually rose to go, leaving me feeling a sort of spy.

"We advise you in future not to write about military matters, and to refrain from mentioning secret armaments," they warned me.

"Including Edith Sitwell?" I asked.

They were not amused. I think they imagined she was a pocket battleship.

Having finished *The Unburied Dead*, the long verse play set in a coalmine, I immediately began a play in the style of a lampoon which a busker, whom I'd met performing outside Covent Garden, had asked me to write. I called it *Pimp, Skunk and Profiteer*. It was written to be performed in the gutter, but it never was. In the published edition it is described as: *A Lampoon to be performed in the open, before a theatre queue, outside a cinema, along a dole queue or a bread line. No stage, scenery, make-up, agents, London managers or money necessary. No rights reserved.*

Before presenting this sketch several of the actors, buskers, troupe, should join the queue, the audience, unobtrusively. For it is the author's intention that the sketch should not be announced or presented as such, but merely imposed upon the audience's idleness.

Naturally I dedicated this to Ezra.

After this essay I decided to write a play within the framework of the Order of the Mass: *Ora Pro Nobis*. This piece was eventually played in St Thomas's, Regent Street. And these three plays were published under the title *The Dull Ass's Hoof* with the quotation from Ben Jonson:

> *And since our dainty age*
> *Cannot endure reproof,*
> *Make not thyself a page*
> *To that strumpet, the stage;*
> *But sing high and aloof,*
> *Safe from the wolf's black maw and the dull ass's hoof.*

Disgusted with Shaftesbury Avenue I intend to write no more plays. Not altogether unfortunately, the edition was mostly destroyed by a bomb a few days after publication. But one copy somehow found its way into Eliot's hands and he reviewed it in the *New English Weekly*.

After this I collected together a few poems which had been printed in various magazines, and these were published by the Fortune Press under the title *Postcards to Pulcinella*. I don't know what accident befell this edition: maybe it was used to fill in the hole made by the bomb that had fallen on the other? All I know is that copies are rare, which is not the same thing as precious.

As I have confessed, I have never read very much, since I have always preferred to write. But about this time I did enjoy reading one book; it was a text-book on horticulture with illustrations of vegetables—large onions that I too hoped to grow, and cauliflowers that caterpillars hadn't devoured. This book was seldom out of my pocket. I used to go to sleep at night thinking of my seeds growing, and when people thought I was composing a poem because I looked abstracted, I was in fact generally day-dreaming about whether to transplant my beetroot. I became totally absorbed and entirely fascinated by growing vegetables. Indeed I still am, and I get more satisfaction from growing a row of peas or beans than I do from writing a scene for a play. I wouldn't say I was a good gardener or farmer, but I just can't get over the wonder of seeing some of my seeds come up. It is much more of a miracle than stringing words together.

But at this time another book somehow came into my hands. I think it must have been part of a lot at an auction sale, when I had bid for something else. It was a *History of Texas*. I was very interested in the cycle: how the land there was grazed, fenced, ploughed and turned into a dust-bowl within a century. Here was a decline and fall of a civilisation concentrated into one territory and within a brief period—an ideal subject for a poem, I thought. And I was fascinated by the subject for two other reasons: horses were part of that history, so were cowboys and Red Indians: and though I had never been to Texas, I had spent a good deal of my childhood being a Red Indian, shooting with a bow that lacked a string, until shot or captured, then tied to a pole by my sister.

I decided to write the poem because I saw two challenges in it. Could I get poetry out of its rut of exclusive "subjective hosannahs" and write something lucid and concise about something? If poetry has the ability to be immediate and vivid, is it not, I asked myself, basically a better vehicle for history than prose? I looked at the four hundred and eighty pages of the *History* before me and liked the idea of trying to get the essence into a dozen pages. I also decided to use an established verse-form. I had long been nauseated by the current mode of free verse, the cult of verbal diarrhœa, much of it written, not because the writer needed the freedom, but because he lacked the ability to submit to and write within a form. I saw that a verse-form, far from limiting the content, heightened its expression. The precise analogy on this subject occurred to me one day while watering my garden: the hose I held in my hand caused the water to come out at a pressure: without the form of the hose to contain it, the water would have trickled over the page as impotently as *New Directions* and most of *Transition*. I realised that the intensity of verse was obtained by running the rhythm *against* the verse-structure. So for this poem I chose Dante's *terza rima*. I realised from reading Pope that the rhymes need not puncture each line if the sense of the line was carried over each rhyme. I wrote the poem quickly, occasionally taking liberties with the form: but that was a different thing from having no form at all.

I printed the poem in *Townsman*. The copies were eventually pulped as we could not afford to advertise the magazine, and no distributor would handle it. Our subscription list was almost the same length as our list of contributors. And Rose Marie and my sister now had to print the magazine on a Gestetner machine at West Mill, since we could no longer afford to have it printed. But by some accident, in this age of mass communication, the poem did within twenty years reach Texas and was used as the commentary to a documentary film about the state. Finally the University of Texas gave me £150 for the manuscript.

I used to go up to London about once in every three months on *Townsman* business, and sometimes had lunch with Eliot. We used to meet at the Etoile in Charlotte Street, and discuss the problem of finding a style for verse-plays which could carry the colloquial run of everyday conversation and, at the same time, could be heightened when required. Eliot didn't seem to realise how much he had already achieved in *Sweeney*. On one occasion he said he thought I ought to meet the French producer, Michel St Denis, who had established the Studio Theatre. He gave me a note to St Denis, and that afternoon I went round to his flat. While waiting for him to come into the room, I picked up a book from a side-table. It contained reproductions of Hieronymus Bosch. These made such an impression on me that I hardly heard St Denis, even though he was discussing *The Unburied Dead*. He invited me round to his theatre and suggested I should write him a play. But I was unable to listen. Bosch obscured everything else. I could not understand the impact these paintings had on me. All I remember is leaving St Denis's flat and going off immediately to buy a copy of the same book. I had no thought of his invitation to write a play for him. But some years later Bosch and his invitation came together. The unconscious is very economical: it uses everything and connects anything.

The next day I went to see my Aunt Henrietta. She was dying: and she knew it. She was dying of starvation. The humour of this didn't escape her. She looked like a bandaged skeleton. The growth in her throat had prevented her from taking any food for a fortnight. She sipped brandy, refusing artificial feeding, intimidating her servants and relatives to the end.

PART FOUR

A Sandwich for the Wind

MY horse, on heat, had broken out. Banging a pail of oats, like her lackey I looked for her, up through the overgrown valley. I met a couple of hikers, who were lost and tired and without a match. He was of my generation; we the warriors. He said "Is there any news?" as though he had been lost for a month instead of since lunch. I put them on their way, and he said "Perhaps we'll meet in the army."

I continued up the valley, pushing the brambles aside, but thinking in my mind of the Voice of God announcing that this is the six o'clock news. Vox Populi now says that England is prepared. The Oracle announces, the horizon darkens. Bishops coin epithets, the Bank Rate is raised. And in twos and threes the politicians come beating the Anthem on their own bombastic drum. The Thing approaches: we wag our spoons. On a scenic railway going down for a fascinating thrill. They say the conductor is Hitler, he the deceiver, he the Original Cause. But England that June was lying and loved Adolf Hitler, for he was the man on the flying trapeze, the man who dared, who thickened the headlines. To any depths for a thrill.

In this spirit of sad facetiousness the Oracle warned England that the Forty Years War of the twentieth century was about to change its name again. From 1914 to 1918 this war was known as the Great War, or as it is now called the Four-Year War. Then the war from 1918 to 1925 was known as the Post-War Period, and from 1925 to 1931 it was called Should a State of Emergency Arise. Now it is going to be called a War again, perhaps a Crusade. They say a condemned man feels nothing but relief towards the rope.

The Box sings "England, Land of Freedom." Whatever the pattern was, it had little to do with freedom. The Box says "England, Land of Tradition, Equality and Justice."

As to equality, I do not think my generation believed equality was an English attribute, even if they were romantic enough, or vague enough, to wish it to be. But justice stood higher in our esteem: there was something there. I am trying to show what were the average reactions to the improvised jingoism which was broadcast in the months preceding the garrulous Crusade. Most of us had joined or toyed with some ineffective party movement or society; many of us had spent our late teens and early twenties wholly absorbed in these abstract diversions, all of us were affected by a vague political restlessness, and many had precise social grievances. We did not pray for salvation, we wished for a revolution. Few of us had any ties with any established religion; if we prayed we did not admit it to ourselves; we made our own priesthood, which we venerated, in small magazines whose arrogance was in inverted proportion to their circulation. And I had often noticed how many of my acquaintances had lost touch with their own family, either through differences of political opinion or on account of sheer restlessness and a distaste for anything that was an established institution. It was a period of barrenness. We wished to organise life but hadn't the vitality to submit to it.

And the appeals to England's Empire carried very little weight with us. For we were able to distinguish between the Imperial Chemical Industries' interests and our own. I had felt ashamed of a British passport in India and had gone down the gold-mines in Johannesburg to observe the realities of Imperial Glory. Many of us felt the necessity of some form of economic repentance rather than an enthusiasm to fight for our grandfathers' gains. Nor did we understand what the word "duty" meant; for though we had allegiances they were to trends of thought rather than to territories. Some of my acquaintances were Welsh Nationalists or Scottish Separatists; others were still talking vaguely about Internationalism. All were equally incapable of singing the National Anthem. And even when the propaganda focused on the ideological differences between Germany and England, few of us were roused, for we had some sympathy with the German attempt to establish goods as opposed to gold as a financial base. And for the word Democracy we had derision. I could see that many of us would not defend England until we found it.

My horse was almost hidden by the bracken through which I waded. She was eating gorse. There was no grass. There were bracken, brambles, ragwort, nettles, thistles, and thorn-bushes about which bryony climbed. The job was to get out of this wilderness. I led the horse first this way and then that, but could not coax her through the maze. I remembered that my riding-whip had a blade inside it, and using this I cut my way out. This brought me to a bank and I noticed that it was walled. Somebody had once walled this bank. This wilderness was once a field. Somebody had worked this field. Here was England. I decided to found a community, an order based on agriculture.

I knew very little about farming, no more than the average person who has spent a good deal of time in the country but has not participated in its activities; in other words very little indeed. By a community I meant first a group of people co-operating instead of competing. The need for some form of monasticism becomes apparent whenever civilisation lurches towards the abyss. By "based on agriculture" I meant that it should grow its own food, bake its own bread and weave its own clothes. I felt that these activities would not only impose the precise economic repentance which we required, but that they contained some of the elements of a spiritual communion. Besides which we were sick of ideas which produced only tepid flat pamphlets bulging with abstractions and suppositions. The sharp hook and the steel scythe, these were the ideas which satisfied me. Their shape showed their integrity. Better to start here, where I was, than wait for a vague millennium.

As soon as I got on to a track again and had taken my bearings, I realised that the wilderness must be part of the land belonging to a small farm of some thirty or forty acres, which had been abandoned for fifteen years. I had visited it as a child twenty years ago to steal apples.

The place was suitable, for it was utterly derelict. We could not spoil it: I thought each day's work would improve, clear and encourage. Whereas if, as a novice, I took a farm in good heart, hedged and gated, my inexperience would be expensive in depreciations: we would see the land slide back, not creep forward. But this place was ideal for a social experiment, being wholly isolated:

the nearest house a mile away. On one side Darracott Hill, up which no average car could climb; on the other side Gooseham Hill, down which no normal driver dared descend. And therefore there would be less likelihood of diversions. The valley is a geographical unit, with a mill at each end and woods as a scarf to it, and this too would be an advantage.

But I began to realise that I was suffering from the worst and most dangerous of all mental diseases—the habit of seeing things as we wish them to be, not as they are. Foreseeing about four per cent of our difficulties and failing to assess the extent of my ignorance, I decided to attempt the experiment, for the only way of seeing things or people as they are is to attempt to change their nature. I decided that I had only money to lose, and little of that, and whatever happened the result would be valuable.

Tracing the owners was almost as difficult as cutting a way through the thorn. Eventually I discovered that it had been left in trust to two sisters and their brother, all old people, farmers who had not visited the place for several years. I was told that they were willing to let the farm for £20 a year, the rent it had fetched twenty years ago, before they let it go into dilapidation. In other words they were angling for me to clear their land for them and pay them for the privilege. But I knew nothing of this, nor had I any knowledge of land-values or legal procedure. It is strange that an educational system which is no longer classical but commercial does not contain any tuition on this subject of Common Law.

Fortunately I was called away during the second month of the negotiations, with the result that the owners thought my enthusiasm for the place had abated. So on my return they offered to show me round the farm, which was an admission of their willingness to sell at a reasonable figure. The male owner was a horse-dealer with the grin of a fox. It was he whom I met on the property. First we surveyed the buildings. The old mill stood, that is all one could say. The windows had fallen in, the doors had fallen out. Slates had slid into gutterings, gutterings swayed in the wind. Pigs had been kept in the living-room and, as though it were an advantage, the owner pointed out that a concrete trough had been made on the living-room floor. With his stick he pointed at it through a foot of dung. The mill-stones were still in position on the second floor, which we reached from a bank at the back of the building: the stairs had collapsed and lay like a folded concertina on the ground. On the walls of the mill were pencilled calculations which the miller had made to keep account of the grinding he had done for the neighbouring farmers. But the water-wheel had been sold for scrap-iron, and about the whole place was that atmosphere of complete futility which derelict machinery always accentuates. The other farm-buildings were in a worse state of disrepair. Only one had a door and that was not hung; only one had a roof and that was not waterproof.

The cottage had been lived in more recently. The last tenant had moved in the middle of the night because he could not pay his rent. Nettles lolled up against the walls like unemployed dockers: an improvised galvanised-iron porch lurched into the lane, a hideous contraption, a sentry-box. The cottage itself looked like an old charwoman with two hats on, for its roofing was several ratted layers of sodden thatch surmounted by the usual galvanised iron, red with rust and broken at the eaves. And in place of a chimney-pot some ingenious person had placed an upturned earthenware bread-bin. Ivy crawled, sprawled, choking the whole place with its unnumerable fingers, and at the same time supporting it. Where there was a bare patch, the cob walls could be seen, cracked, decorated with rats' holes and festooned with birds' nests.

The Fox pushed the door open. We had obviously intruded. Each of the four rooms was very much inhabited and there was a general scurry of livestock towards the non-existent wainscoting. Wallpaper flapped in the draught. I tore off the gargantuan green roses, to find a fleur-de-lis: there were eight thicknesses of a decorator's delirium, and one tenant had economised by sticking up copies of newspapers. I read of the atrocities of Boers.

"The place needs a coat of whitewash and a bit of cement and it would soon be as good as any cottage round here." He was more or less right, for this monument of haphazard galvanised improvisation, sloping from the scandal of a deserted house into the respectability of a ruin, was typical of the average English labourer's home. Thoroughness had built it, poverty inhabited it, and ingenuity maintained it.

The land consisted of four rectangular marshes which cul-minated in a swamp. These fields ran along the bottom of the valley, and on either side the valley steeped with bracken, gorse, elder and thorn, an occasional bank proving the Fox's contention that these were once fields. I had seen the cottage with both my hand and my eye, for I had had some practical experience of reno-vating a ruin. But although I walked over the fields I did not see them as anything but scenery. That is to say, I did not examine a single drain or dig my stick in here and there to see what the soil was like. My mind was dominated by the idea of clearing this land, but I did not consider whether it would be possible or profit-able to do so. The cow-shippon, now derelict, had plainly not been built for nothing; and I guessed that where gorse, bracken and weeds grew to such monstrous heights, and brambles spewed so prolifically, other things would grow if planted. I knew that it was possible to drain a marsh, but had no idea how to go about it. An occasional gatepost reinforced my optimism. Obviously something had been kept here since the dinosaurs. I thought of the colliers' immaculate gardens of two square yards.

And my companion said, "I mind the time when my father kept eight cows here, and that meadow turned out a master rick of hay."

"Then why did you let it go like this?" I asked.

The Fox stopped. He grinned, not out of embarrassment. He just grinned.

"But surely," I continued, "even if this place couldn't pay you to run as a farm again, if you had kept it cut and the hedges steeped, you would have been able to let it or sell it to me at a higher price."

"How was I to know you'd come along?" he answered. Which was precisely the same as telling me that I was a bigger fool than even he, the horse-dealer, thought existed. The point was that he was a farmer who had found horse-dealing more profitable than cultivating indifferent acres. He was not the type of man who would do anything that was not immediately profitable, though he was very far from being poor. It was a matter of attitude, a question of responsibility. Plainly there is a type of man who should never own land, and another who would maintain it though doing so would impoverish him. A matter of character, not of class. An observation I would keep up my sleeve for the Comrades.

We crossed the stream which divides Cornwall from Devon into the field where I had found my horse some months before. "And I suppose," the Fox said, "if you buy the farm and they meadows [marshes] you'll want to buy this field from me. This don't go with the other: I bought it privately." In other words the Fox owned three fields in the middle of the farm. He mumbled something about how they'd give a right of way if I bought them to go with the lot.

"How much do you want?" I asked.

"Well," he said, looking around, "they're useful plats, turn out a whole heap of corn, proper for potatoes, it's no odds."

"How much have you got?" he replied. We were at deadlock. Finally he said:

"Three acres and a right of way, what they call accommodation ground, couldn't take less than £75. I gave £70 for them." I told him I had only £525, so I could obviously not afford to buy these three fields which he owned entirely. He seemed surprised and we walked on in solemn silence. Then he said, "Well, if you buy these three fields and give me £75 that'll be mine entirely, I'll persuade my sisters to take £450, which will make your total of £525." In other words he was willing for his sisters to drop £66 between them so that he would gain £40. The matter was settled. I owned forty acres of weeds.

I bought a hook, and decided to begin methodically. The neighbours shook their heads; "It'll take ten years and will bust your pocket and break your back." Half-blind with hope and half-deaf with enthusiasm, I hardly heard them. I will start on the vegetable garden, I thought, for I have plenty of plants that can go right in there; I will colonise it with surplus autumn broccoli which are crowded. Yesterday I found England, today her Empire.

I begun by swiping at the nettles at the gate and then cut my way into the garden. The weeds were nearly six feet high, the sharp new hook took its delight out of docks and cow-parsley, a dance easier to begin than to control. I was soon lagging behind the thing, hot, stung and entangled. A pity I had not cut up one side and then down the same side again, as I have seen hayfields. A pity I have cut a figure of eight. But already something is clean, something better, and there were strawberry-plants buried there, now visible. Too hot to continue and too impatient to rest, I went into the cottage and tackled the gargantuan green roses. I had better get on with the garden. A pity, for it is surely possible to make one tear right round the room and show a past generation's yellow geraniums. By doing this I will do the other quicker. For I can then carry all the wallpaper out and burn it in the garden and so destroy all the weeds. I am already lost.

Lost like every farmer floundering with too many jobs to do. You go to shut a gate; and on your way to the gate see a spade in the hedge; you go to pick up the spade and you see a drain blocked; you go back to the gate carrying the spade and a field-pipe, and perhaps you even leave the gate open. I have seen a carpenter wielding a plough-plane, wholly absorbed in the wood curling off the blade. He did not notice or care about the tarpaulin behind him which had blown off the straw-stack. The carpenter has a much more contented, unworried, tranquil look than any of the successful farmers. For he has one job to do; he is not lost in an avalanche of diversions.

I persuaded Spottiswoode to abandon his job at the headquarters of the P.P.V. to join me; also Smithson, the collier, was absent from his morning shift and with great enthusiasm had gone to a Cornish farm to learn milking. Then there was Horst von Kleist: he came from a Prussian military family. He was eighteen and at school in Bavaria. Although he was a member of the Hitler Youth and regarded Der Fuehrer with a certain amount of hero-worship, he was no National Socialist. This was chiefly because, as a student of architecture, he was shocked by the palace Goering had built, which, he said, was like a cream bun; as a Prussian he resented the *parvenu* Nazi officials; and though he disliked the Jews, his principle point against National Socialism was its Jewish persecution, which, he said, made Germans reviled by the whole world. I do not know whether his training as a Hitler Youth had anything to do with it or not, but he could use an axe and a pencil with equal dexterity; he was not unacquainted with farm-work as he had collected several harvests.

I think he was attracted to the community solely because it provided him with an outlet for his destructive energy and satisfied his pleasure in doing pioneer work. He had worked on German roads. He made a chicken-house out of driftwood, and later, when he ignored his call-up to the German Army and joined us, he frequently showed the same ingenuity with materials. He was most anxious for us to begin building a shippon, but his parents were trying to persude him to join some academy for architecture.

Unfortunately I was the only member with any money, about £400. And so every old tool stood up from any junk-heap and announced that it would be of some use to us. Pieces of board took on a new quality and were no longer used for firewood; and we kept watch with a lantern on the tides slithering over the rocks, and picked up planks, ropes, barrels and an occasional foot or head or hand. The farmers said it was a pity the boats were made of iron now, for they didn't break up so quickly, and lay at the bottom, only vomiting up their deck-cargoes.

The so-called Period of Emergency moved inevitably towards War. There was a feeling in the country that the actual declaration would come as an anticlimax. Meanwhile ultimatums shuttled to and fro; on the radio politicians exhorted the nation through a bushel of platitudes to "stand firm" and "row together to get out of the wood." Meanwhile we waited for Hitler to cross the Polish Corridor.

West Mill was not on the mains, but at week-ends Spottiswoode had helped me fit new buckets to the old water-mill and gear it to a dynamo. This gave us electricity—when there was enough water running along the silted-up leat. But in the early part of September 1939 there was a drought, and not enough water to turn the wheel fast enough. While I sat by the radio, Spottiswoode stood outside kicking the mill-wheel round with his feet, adding just enough thrust for me to hear Chamberlain's speech declaring war.

I was shocked by the elation which the news released in me. I had spent three or four years writing and talking about pacifism, and now that war had been officially declared, I observed my own glee with some guilt and more bewilderment. I tried to analyse the reason for my emotions and was forced to some lamentable conclusions. I discovered that we get pleasure out of any catastrophe, so long as we have foretold it; that human suffering is no suffering to us if it confirms our perspicacity. And behind these reasons for our excitement was the fact that we preferred the bang to the whimper. My generation had been so dissatisfied with the *status quo*, we had foolishly concluded that any change would be for the better. And with stupendous self-satisfaction we didn't mind what those changes entailed for others, so long as they didn't touch ourselves. I recall being personally irritated by the inconvenience of putting up the blackout curtains. Even so, for the next few months we continued to be elated: the war was a challenge; it meant that my foresight in buying dustbins and filling them with sugar had been justified; real purpose was now given to my farming and reclamation schemes along the valley. All my principles which I had inflicted on Rose Marie against using coal, tinned foods or cosmetics were now reinforced: they were now unobtainable. My passion for beachcombing was given purpose and became ' 'helping the war effort." It was as if Robinson Crusoe had suddenly been presented with his island and had at last inherited his own identity.

Wars are not caused solely by economics and politics; they happen because people want them: however much we may protest, people did and do enjoy this escape from their own personal vacuity. War is a way out from the burden of being an individual into the khaki luxury of mass unconsciousness. War is destructive; we are destructive. I am certain there will be another: maybe it will be mass-suicide. People want mass-suicide.

But within a few days of the declaration my elation was punctured by the realisation that war means more officials, more regulations, more boring red-tape. This was brought home to me when I had to take Horst into the Police Station at Horns Cross to register as an enemy alien. The local bobby thought it strange to have a young German of eighteen staying with me. He would have been even more alarmed if he had realised that Horst had once been a Hitler Youth. But the bobby gave Horst his papers and thanked us for calling so promptly.

A week later we both had to go to a tribunal at Barnstaple which enquired into Horst's credentials, to decide whether he should be interned or not. The tribunal was held in the Mayor's Parlour. I vouched for Horst and offered to stand surety for him. I informed the bench that he had evaded call-up into the German Army and had stayed in England because of his antipathy to Nazism, which, he maintained, with its Jew-baiting and violence was betraying Germany. But the officials were unimpressed. Somebody asked me what my own credentials were—whereupon a police superintendent remarked aloud in the court that it was plain I wasn't a gentleman, or I wouldn't have a German living in my house.

That was the beginning. For the next four years I was the fox. The M.F.H. was a man called Jackson. He had farmed in Canada, and then had come to England to be a timber-merchant in Exeter. I had not met him. Jackson was one of those little men who thrive in wartime: from a nobody he became a V.I.P. overnight: an Executive Officer of the War Agricultural Committee; Special Constable; Air-Raid Warden, and Big Wig on the Rural District Council. He was a highly competent person, who was, as they say, self-educated, and he resented me deeply for having had those advantages which he spurned. Within a few days Jackson, in his special constable's uniform, led a posse of police down to West Mill. It was a raid.

Without asking permission, they poked round the cottage—gathering up back-numbers of *Townsman*, and then some stooge called out from the barn. They rushed in for the kill.

"So!" cried Mr Jackson. "Your protestations of loyalty amount to this?"

I looked. There, in an old school tuck-box, were a few rusty condensers, antiquated valves and coils of wire—the pathetic remnants of Spottiswoode's and my attempt to make an electronic movie-camera, which we had abandoned some years before.

"Your transmitter will be confiscated," Jackson threatened, "and reported to the proper quarters."

"Get a wireless engineer down and ask him if it's possible to make a short-wave transmitter out of that junk," I suggested.

But it was already on its way up the hill.

Within a few days the bush-telegraph had informed the whole

219

of North Devon that I was a German spy who had been caught red-handed with a transmitter talking to Goering. Nobody asked themselves why, if this were so, I was still at large, going about Bideford and Bude in my old Sunbeam, collecting bins of fish-heads from Mac Fisheries, and sacks of stale bread from the R.A.F. camp, with which we fed half-a-dozen black lop-eared sows.

Mr Jackson now visited us about twice a day, either in his capacity as Air-Raid Warden to see that our blackout was up, or as an Executive Officer of the Agricultural Committee to check on our ploughing. And at odd times he would be found standing out-side the door in his special constable's uniform. He was a quick-change artist with a consistent character.

Other officials, snoopers and busybodies descended the hill in droves. North Devon was determined to make a contribution to the war effort: and persecuting me seemed to be as good a method as they knew. West Mill became as secluded as Piccadilly Tube Station. For days at a time it looked like a film-set for the Key-stone Cops.

Meanwhile rumours and gossip multiplied: most of the stories were too ridiculous to cause anything but merriment: we heard that a woman in the village of Gooseham had decided to stop buy-ing milk from us, and was advising others to do the same, be-cause I was putting poison in it; we learned that it had been stated in Exeter that I was the leader of a spy-ring, had chosen to live on the North Devon coast so as to facilitate an invasion there, and that I had agents all along the coast at various coves; and the reason why I kept so many pigs was to feed the Wehrmacht when they arrived.

The Community was in fact composed of S.S. members; and to top all it was reported in Bude, as proof of my German sympathies, that I had once said I would rather hear one page of Bach than all the music written in England in the last three centuries.

But none of this worried us. It was not till seven policemen in uniform and two in plain clothes came trundling down the hill that we got seriously alarmed. This pack was led by a Superin-tendent. For an hour or so Rose Marie and I sat and watched them tapping walls, peering into the cloam oven, and even removing broody hens from coops.

I asked the Superintendent what his men were searching for.

"A radio transmitter," he replied.

"Surely," I said, "you have electrical means of knowing definitely whether or not any signals have been transmitted from here. If you have such proof, then arrest me."

He made no reply.

"I suggest you put me in the Tower or leave me alone."

He made a rude reply.

"What are the grounds for your suspicions?" I asked him.

"You've printed Ezra Pound in your magazine: you've got a young German staying with you. And——"

"And?"

He didn't answer, but led the way upstairs to the bedroom. Two policeman started to burrow in a chest-of-drawers, removing Rose Marie's underclothes.

Suddenly they unearthed a bundle of papers neatly folded beneath a pile of nightdresses. The Superintendent grinned triumphantly. Here was the missing code. For a second I must have looked surprised. I couldn't think of any papers Rose Marie would keep—let alone in such a place. The Superintendent was reading: he seemed pathologically absorbed.

"Did you write this?" he asked eventually.

"I can't say, as I don't know what you're reading."

"This," he sneered, showing me a page of my own handwriting.

I recognised what the papers were.

"I must ask you not to read private letters," I said.

But he read on.

"My God," he exclaimed eventually, licking his lips, "you've got a bloody filthy mind."

It had never occurred to me to ask him whether he had a search-warrant. I thought Regulation 18B made such formalities unnecessary.

When this Superintendent assembled his troupe to march them up the hill again, I naturally expected that I would be accompanying them on my way to Wormwood Scrubs, the Isle of Man, or some other hostelry of enforced leisure. But no arrest was made. Rose Marie and I were surprised, too dumbfounded to express any relief. The Superintendent turned back to her.

"We shall be picking him up some day," he threatened, loading her with an uncertainty which she had to endure for the next five years.

As soon as this raid was over, I sat down and wrote to Sir Samuel Hoare, the Home Secretary. I told him that I was being persecuted with suspicion and urged him to have my loyalty investigated. "If I'm a spy, please deal with me as one," I urged. My letter was never acknowledged. The petty persecution continued. For five years I never went up the hill without feeling I might be arrested at the top of it. I began to develop the psychosis of a criminal, almost reverting to childhood, dreaming of fright, nibbled to death by policemen. After this police raid I decided to frustrate any further curiosity in my correspondence. I gathered together all the letters which I had received from Pound and, though there was nothing incriminating in them, I put them all in a box, and wrote to Eliot to ask if he would look after some papers of mine which might, in the present circumstances, cause me trouble. He replied that he was only too willing to do this, so long as he didn't know what the parcel contained. I sent Rose Marie to London with the letters, and Eliot put them into a safe at Faber's. For years I forgot that I had deposited them there. After Rose Marie had gone off with Pound's letters I came across some which Gandhi had written to me on his hand-made paper that looked like Bromo. I decided to hide them and did this so effectively that I never found them again.

From the start it was plain that this wreck of a farm could not be run by us on the normal economy. Even if its land had been clean and we had had the capital to stock it, the amount of produce it could have exported up the precipitous hill would have paid for the labour of only one man. And what we had was sour derelict wet land, little stock or buildings, capital depleted by legal charges, and three of us dependent on it for a livelihood. Not three competent land-workers, but three ham-handed enthusiasts. And the land needed the labour of a dozen: ditches to be dug, banks to be mended, gates to be made and hung, buildings demolished, an infinity of multitudinous jobs. It was clear that this farm could never pay for that labour in cash.

The land was fertile under the weed. It could have produced

within a year sufficient food for at least a dozen people. Good land can grow good food, but it is a rare piece of clay that grows gold. And anyway, who eats gold? We decided to attempt self-sufficiency, to share produce and profits, to do without a cash wage. There was no other practical alternative. We were not merely trying to turn ourselves into farmers but also trying to establish an economy and a social base. We were not going to try and make a quick cash profit. We were going to grow our own wheat, even though it was cheaper to buy it. We intended to grow it, grind it and bake it. To see loaves in the stooks, to watch our breakfast and supper going gold in the drying wind. We knew we could not assess the value of that. It is an asset a farmer always has which does not show in his unhappy balance-sheet. It is, too, his most valuable possession. I maintained that to grow one's own bread was the minimum base for political morality, and used to say that a nation which lived on the rest of the world, and had turned itself into middlemen, insurance agents and brokers, was putrid.

Realising that the war was largely due to this international sponging and that we individually had participated in it, we did our best to take up the hook with the minimum of priggishness and the maximum of humility. We sowed as a penance. This attempt at self-sufficiency was the base of our home-made theology: no doubt it was inadequate but it was all we had. "If you cannot find a horse, ride a donkey."

With these aims we were fortunate in having very little money. And consequently I hoped that our stomachs would lead us to our hoe, and our pockets not tempt us to the tin-opener.

Early in the autumn Leonard Connelly, a communist, arrived. He was very much a Londoner, wore hat and gloves and carried a portable typewriter. Among his luggage was the Communist's portable dogma: the works of Lenin, Mr and Mrs Webb, Strachey and the poems of various fashionable sentimentalists of the proletariat. Connelly himself had no striking features or characteristics. As far as I could gather, his parents owned a large number of automatic cigarette-machines and Connelly had previously been occupied in looking after these things. I was anxious to know the precise reason why he had joined us. He was equally anxious to know what I "stood for." Our conversation was cautious. Then I took him round the farm and gave him a picture of our achievements and intentions. He showed some general enthusiasm, though it was obvious that he was quite strange to the world of things and had always sheltered behind ideas. But I hoped that in spite of his being a communist he might still be interested in a small practical experiment in community.

Soon after Connelly's arrival a Mrs Welling, or Mrs Yatter, as I called her, rented Rose Cottage, a hundred yards from the farm cottage. Her husband visited her occasionally. He was a solicitor in some south-coast town. This woman became a menace. She continually ran across to the farm, asking one of us to go and mend her stove or some other gadget, and in return for these services, and to guarantee their continuance, she baked us cakes or let one of us have a hot bath. On the surface one might think that this was a sensible arrangement and a matter of ordinary social neighbourliness. But this Mrs Welling, trivial as she was in herself, was an important disruptive force to us. Why she bothered about us is a matter which could only be revealed by burrowing into her own pathetic history. She was the sort of disintegrating influence which any community meets in actuality but not on paper. She was a woman of enormous curiosity, intrigued by the fact that a few men should have cut themselves off from the world to do their own washing. She resented our attempts to do our own cooking and to live without the domestic assistance of the opposite sex, although I told her explicitly that certain amenities and a good few kinds of unrationed foods were taboo to us, that we were trying to form a community, and the washing of our own clothes was part of our embryonic discipline. So Mrs Welling went to any length to wash Horst's shirts and coax Spottiswoode into dinner—which was not very difficult.

There must have been three or four books always concealed about her person, for whoever met her found her just laying aside a book on his particular subject. Spottiswoode interrupted her reading Einstein; Heine was dropped in front of Horst, and for me she was to be seen lost in the *Ta-Hio*. But the only subject which interested Mrs Welling was the autobiography of Mrs Welling.

As poultry hadn't run here for so many years the land was clean of disease and the birds found plenty of insects. For milk, butter and cheese we had a cow. Horst looked after the pigs. Spottiswoode looked after the cow and undertook to learn from a farmer's wife how to make butter. After one lesson our butter was made. With no dairy, or anything approaching one, it was difficult to keep the cream clean. But nobody in the district knew how to make cheese. Several farmers showed us wooden presses which had been used in their childhood. And they gave us good accounts of the quality of the cheese and the bacon which used to be produced from the whey. But dumped Dutch cheeses had put paid to all that, and the farmers sent their milk to the factory, eating margarine themselves. The factory made the milk into plastics to be used as knobs in aeroplanes. We had to look further afield for a cheese-recipe and bought a small press for fifteen shillings. There was no difficulty; it was excellent. After the invasion of Denmark the neighbours came and borrowed our recipe. Less milk went to the factory. Pigsties were patched. (Few farmers were sorry when Copenhagen fell, for that city had been sitting on English farming for half a century.)

And along those lines we hoped within three months to be self-sufficient in eggs, milk, butter, cheese and pig-dung to go to the hungry hopeless pasture. Honey, wheat and wool were to follow the next year. That way we tried to feed ourselves and the sour acres. But it was not the way to fill our pockets. Which meant we had to do without innumerable things, or learn to make do with substitutes. It was a new "puritanism" in favour of what was produced there, against goods which had to be imported down the hill. But we could not grow nails, or plough-shares. We hadn't the skill to make boots. So pigs were chosen as the export, and I tried to prevent the milk from going to the factory. If the milk went up the hill, the cream of the farm left for London. In time that would have meant no cheese for us, therefore less labour, no whey for the pigs and therefore no dung for the land.

But quite apart from any reason for doing these things, we soon discovered that we enjoyed doing them for their own sake. To take a loaf from the oven, a cheese from the press, or even the finding of a nest of eggs, were real pleasures, sure joys, much more reliable and satisfying than most of the abstract fiddling we had toyed with. Contact with things is infinitely more satisfying than contact with ideas. And if we are honest we must admit that few of us are capable of holding abstract conceptions in our heads. If we manage it, it gives us little pleasure. Somehow or other we have fallen into the rot of thinking that pigs and poetry are incompatible. They are not.

As no cash wage was paid to the members, I made enquiries whether the title-deeds could be placed in our joint names as a corporation, but I was told this would be complicated. I was assured it was unnecessary. Perhaps it was, I thought, for to own is to use. And I believed each person would own the farm in proportion to the amount he felt it was his creation. When there were any cash profits, they were to be shared, meanwhile to each a part of the produce. But profits on paper were one thing; after a few months our one and only cow got red-water. We drenched it, tempted it to drink, gave it lard and salt. The poor great thing stood in abject patient pain. Its guts baked, it could pass nothing. This disease used to strike one farm or another in North Devon every year. They said it was a spore picked up from rank old pasture. Our neighbour Yeoford left his own cows unmilked, pulled at the ribs of the beast and said that we hadn't seen the symptoms soon enough. I ranged every kind of cow-food within her reach from cabbage to rolled oats. But she was as obstinate and determined to die, and stood there patiently waiting; her forlorn eyes knew it, her tail knew it, and nothing could be done.

Her great gaunt ribs showed like a half-made boat. I mixed her an egg-flip composed of two quarts of milk and half a dozen eggs and poured it down her throat to keep her strength up till the drench freed her bowels.

The next day I went over to see the cow as soon as it was light, knowing the animal would be dead and hoping it would be. She was dead all but for dying. She lifted her head occasionally and then breathed hard from exhaustion. Then she lay still with her wide eyes open. When she was on her feet and there was a chance of her recovery, she seemed obstinately inclined to die; but when there was no hope for her, she put up a pathetic struggle. She reared her head and got one leg up, ready to take her weight. Then she collapsed and her tender fluid eyes went instantaneously solid. This meant no milk or butter for us. I stood wondering how to shift her unwieldy body? Then I got a spade. It was hard work digging a grave, harder still dragging her into it.

After the First World War a Gloucester gunner was demobbed. He was stone-deaf, and perhaps this, together with a certain nervousness as a result of gas, prevented him from finding a job. So he visited his sister who was married to a farmer in Welcombe. To help pay for his keep, he did a few repair jobs. Gradually other farmers gave him work and he was soon the local mason, rebuilding cottages, plastering chimneys and walling up shippons. After a year or so he married; nobody knew where the girl came from. The longest tongue said she was gipsy. They were not natives of the place, and in a district where everybody is related to everybody else, a certain lostness was their lot. Although Whyle was now a very competent mason he had nowhere to live. He could have built a cottage for a couple of hundred pounds in four months, but he had neither the capital nor the time to work for himself. A shrewd farmer let them live in an old lorry which was left on its wheels (to avoid paying rates); Whyle put a stove in and walled up the back. This was their home, and the farmer had first call on the mason, besides charging him rent. Soon the lorry was sprawling with children, one a year; some died, some survived, but every year Mrs Whyle was carrying two, one in her arms, and one under her apron. They had eight, clothed with ingenuity and a disregard of modesty. For years the local doctor and the Council tried to persuade the farmer to do the lorry up. He did just sufficient to comply with an order, by adding a sheet of galvanised iron here and there. Then suddenly the lorry was condemned as unfit for human habitation. Whyle never complained, although he had spent twenty years building other people's houses and was now without any sort of roof over his head. Two of his daughters went out to service, his wife to a relative with the youngest, as usual with another already protruding. Whyle sat by his stove and told me he he wanted to know whether I'd buy some wreck-timber from him which he'd got hidden under the lorry. He offered me his tools too, and said he was going back to Gloucestershire to see if there was anybody there who would help him. There was an obvious alternative, so he moved into Gooseham with two of his sons, a few blankets, a trowel, level and plumb-line. Soon he was showing Spottiswoode how to hang a door straight, and the kids were out catching rabbits. Leonard regarded this intrusion of the working class into our community with much disfavour. Whyle was under no obligation to work, as he bought his own food, but he worked while it was light, and in the evening sat and read the memoirs of Marshal Foch.

Our first job was to find the field, trace out the hedge, and locate the gateway. Then we used to saw down the hedge-trees and drag them out to make enormous bonfires. Slowly the banks showed themselves; one tree felled let the light in as though one had opened a window. Gradually the shape of the field became apparent; seldom straight, not even following the contours of the land. We found small fields walled round, of no particular shape and less than half an acre. They were too small to plough with a tractor and if worked with a horse half the area was taken up with turning. The banks of this farm took up at least a tenth of the total area. And they were a menace, as rats and rabbits sheltered in them, and the roots from the hedge-trees stretched far into the field.

It is possible to write a sonnet or a *canzone* with hedge-wood. A neighbour showed me how to do it. He first cleared the bank of brambles and bracken, taking his time. Then he sharpened his bill-hook till it would divide a straw if lightly pushed upon it. Next he ruthlessly removed all the dead wood, taking his time. Then he cut a hedge-tree close to its stub, leaving about an inch uncut to act as a hinge and hold the trunk which he pushed down to lie along the bank running from west to east away from the prevailing wind. He hooked the branches, keeping ash-sticks for pegs or posts, which he drove into the hedge at intervals. These kept the first trunk down and in place. Soon other trees were felled and cleaned, with their supple boughs woven in and out of the posts. Gradually a definite pattern was apparent. So many branches and then another post, and in each section there was a design, an internal rhyme. Four limbs going straight to the post, one diagonally. After several sections were complete with their posts, he went along the whole with his hook, shaving it, getting it to one level and entwining pieces into the top of the fence till the whole was an impenetrable barrier. There was no need for this rigid design: the same system of hedging would have been equally effective with haphazard crossing and entwining. But, as he said, there's great pleasure doing it this way, if you can take your time.

And eight or ten yards from the hedge trees had grown out in the field. They were mostly elder or ash which had been cut sometime and had then grown into clumps. Where that had happened it was much more difficult to remove the stump, for there was usually no trunk sufficiently high to act as a lever. The only thing was to dig round the base and sever the roots with an axe. Then we used to sway the stump till it released its hold. I wondered how they removed the great stumps when clearing land in America or Australia, for they had no tractors then to lug them out. And you cannot burn them below the ground. I experimented with concentrated sulphuric acid, boring several six-inch holes in the stump with a brace and bit. As soon as the acid was poured in these holes the wood blackened. But it took years before the stumps rotted away. We had to dig them out.

My sister lent me the money to buy another cow to replace the one that had died of red-water. At the sale there were a dozen cows and calves to be sold. I got to the farm early, as I wished to have a good look at the animals before the fluster of the sale. The vet was also there, and rather than rely on my own judgment I thought it wise to give him half a guinea to pick me a good second-calver. This he did and assured me that she was a good heifer, sound in all quarters. So I made a note of her number and managed to get her for £28. She had a bull-calf with a good flat back. And I arranged with the farmer to have her driven to a cross-roads three miles from us, where we would meet her. Spottiswoode and I were cutting gate-posts in the woods. Leonard went to meet the cow and drive her home. He should have returned by three o'clock. He arrived about eight, having lost the cow, his temper and his spectacles. He was nearly in tears, for he had not only lost

his temper with the animal, which had then become quite unmanageable, but he was full of righteous indignation. We immediately set off and eventually found the cow and drove her
home. Leonard complained that he didn't see why he should have
had to drive the cow, since it was I who had bought it. But the
question of who had bought the cow did not worry him when it
came to drinking her milk. Here is a fair example of the depths of
stupid childishness to which so many moderately intelligent people
are brought when they are involved in any sort of communal activity. It seems that the intelligence of our community was the
lowest common denominator of the members. It was all very
pathetic and ridiculous. But that is how it was.

Some people said that our attempt to create this community
was an escape from what they still call civilisation. Do we call a
man an escapist who moves out of the road of a steamroller before
it obliterates him? At any rate, it is impossible to withdraw from
the worst aspects of society, for we carry its weaknesses in one
pocket and its faults in another. All the pus, warp, and rotten-
ness which exist in the social elephant could be observed in our
microscopic mouse of a community: there was a chance there
that by concentrating ourselves into one small unit we might observe some of these frailties more precisely and assess their nature
more accurately. We were not quite so stupid as to imagine
that any of these frailties could be cured. It seemed to me as
rational to believe in Original Sin as it is to believe in gravity.
But we had a chance of finding out precisely where barbed wire is
required to prevent us from trampling our own growing corn. The
carpenter used to say you could get a good surface on any board if
you planed with its grain and not against it. But the snag there
was we were not even able to hold a plane.

As I owned the farm and alone had any money, I was the
"capitalist," the landowner. Horst, being a member of the Hitler
Youth and coming from a Prussian military family, was cast as the
"fascist"; Leonard, the "communist"; besides which we had
Spottiswoode, a "conscientious pacifist." And so if one took these
silly labels seriously we had the characters for the gutter-press
charade. Whatever those labels stood for, they had this in common: the assumption that the party was capable of imposing a

230

better order on the world than the one which existed at the moment. I used this to suggest to Leonard and Horst that it would be as well if they, as Party members, began their political training by attempting to create order in our tool-shed. Plainly, whatever one may think of these doctrines one must be suspicious of them because they postpone the personal reformation until the millennium. When they replied that they were interested in politics and not in saints, I replied that only saints had had any permanent effect on politics.

Whether the farm would become a communist cell, a fascist gang, or a pacifist group, did not matter, for what worked, got the seed sown in time, would have been valid. I was certain none of them were valid. And could see too that whatever ideas our community was based on, they were false, too. But I persisted because a practical experiment is worth a ton of theory.

Frank Smithson, the collier from Holmwood, who went to learn milking as a preparation for joining the Community, threw it up and returned to the mine. Yet he said that he loathed his industrial rabbit-hutch. His whole life was a longing to get out of it into the country. From which one may conclude that we cling to our tyrannies. Without them we are lost; we sulk in silence till we return to rejoice in the complaints of servitude.

In less than a year enthusiasm died; the novelty of the work decreased and it became necessary to rely on routine. The pigsties went uncleaned, tools unsharpened and everybody hoped that somebody would hang the gate. These were our political realities. The communist had taken over the milking. At nine o'clock he was still in bed. The cow should have been milked at eight. Spottiswoode called up to him "Comrade Leonard, the communist revolution has arrived!" Snores. At nine-thirty he called up again "Comrade Leonard, the counter-revolution has arrived!" More snores. He milked the cow, and called up—"Comrade Leonard, the *status quo* has been re-established!"

After this incident Spottiswoode abandoned his pacifist opinion that man being reasonable would act accordingly. (Previously he had said that since it was obvious that certain things had to be done at certain times it was unnecessary to fix a time-sheet.) A time-sheet was therefore drawn up with fixed times for everything throughout the day and the week. That way the pigs enjoyed clean straw for a week or so. We were handicapped by inadequate education.

One day I asked Leonard, who was then the horseman, to be sure to give the horse some hay. He replied that there was none. I asked him what he intended to feed the horse on. "Straw," he answered. I looked in the stable and saw that a couple of wads of barley-straw had been thrown in for the morning feed. The horse had not eaten any of it, of course, but had trampled it. The rack was empty. We had brought half a ton of hay down the hill only a fortnight ago, and there had only been one cow, a year-ling, and a horse to eat it. But I did not have to look far for the hay. Spottiswoode had not kept the cow's stall cleaned out daily, with the result that the cow had trampled most of her ration into the dung and wasted it. Leonard had not bothered to put hay into the horse-rack, and so the horse had wasted it also. This was the sort of thing which was constantly recurring. If I went round the animals like any ordinary farmer, the others thought I was spying on them, being officious, and a sulk ensued. I asked Leonard what he intended to feed the horse on, since a horse would not eat filthy barley-straw and required good hay or oaten straw if it was to continue to drag firewood for us. He said that the hill was too icebound to get the cart up, and inferred that the horse would have to go hungry. Within a few minutes he was sitting by the fire, thanks to the horse's efforts, reading a communist penny pamphlet on "What Agriculture Needs." Spottiswoode, too, was sitting by the fire reading. But they could not be left there. I was not in a position to order them, so I spent an hour trying to urge them into reasonableness and activity. Spottiswoode produced his usual schoolboyish excuse that he had forgotten that there was no hay. And Leonard's final statement was that, as I paid for feeding-stuffs, it was not his province to tell me when more was required. I had arranged this, for I thought that by leaving the choice of foods to them, it would give them a feeling of responsibility and interest. Leonard tried to turn the conversation into generalisations about remote political issues. Whatever he

232

said, his inner conviction was that it was very kind of him to feed the horse every other day, and neither I nor the horse could have expected him to do it every day—since he was not getting a cash wage. But he lacked the guts to say this outright and resorted to examples from political utopias to make his point. He thought that he had the moral right to eat the rations I paid for and to live in the cottage without doing anything in return, all by the divine right of Karl Marx. "At any rate," he added, "nothing can be done about getting any hay, as the hill is too icebound to get the cart up."

So I suggested that, since he was interested in imitating the Russians in so many ways, he could not do better than construct a sleigh; this was done, and by this method the horse eventually had her dinner. But the effort and energy required to lift that dead weight of obstinate personality was about five times that required to move one ton of hay up and down Ben Nevis. It was eleven o'clock by the time I got to Gooseham the next day where the social atmosphere and the thermometer stood below freezing-point. But the workers were both sitting by an enormous fire reading. As the ground was frozen hard, the job in hand was supposed to be plastering over the old cob walls of the living-room. After a few minutes I asked the "workers" whether they thought we had reached that stage of either affluence or order which might have justified the morning being spent in reading? Spottiswoode said that the lime was too frozen to mix into plaster; I asked if it were not possible to apply heat to it. The reply was: "if you want to"; which I did, for I suppose that there was this distinction between myself and Spottiswoode and Leonard. They lived in the cottage, I owned it. They didn't see why they should go out of their way to plaster it. If it had been their property I suspected they would have been very active. I was glad of this discovery. The Community taught me a lot about my own failings and other people's too. If I had not made that experiment, I should have made bigger mistakes about people by building on false assumptions. I had already made the stupid error of assuming that people will do a thing because it needs to be done, irrespective of who owns, who directs. That was nonsense. Perhaps I was looking for the cohesion and virtues of the British Navy?

233

Certainly the monasticism of a battleship was nearer to what I was looking for than the hotch-potch of intellectual nit-wits which we were.

While I boiled the lime on the fire, the "workers" sat in a sulk. They would have liked all my plaster to fall off the wall (some of it did, for I had not mixed any hair in it). One of them giggled. I suppose I was regarded as a schoolmaster. I realised that unless we could get on to a better basis, it would be better if we abandoned the place and let owls and rats move in again.

I asked Leonard and Spottiswoode to come over to West Mill for dinner. This they did, and I spent the whole night going over what we were trying to do and seeing if I couldn't get their enthusiasm to persist into the day. It is always too easy to make people interested in a project while discussing it over a good fire and coffee. We see things done before they're thought of or begun. They agreed it was a good thing to reclaim the farm and support ourselves entirely from it, and I said that if we could not do that, we ought to join the army; for we ourselves would have failed in finding any practical alternative to a national economy of imported food, exports to pay for it, and wars to maintain the market. One could have gone on endlessly talking round and round the point, forcing agreement by avoiding issues. It was a waste of time. Perhaps I was not temperamentally suited to deal with other people and direct the farm. For I really didn't care a tinker's damn who decided, so long as grass grew where there was bracken. So I suggested that perhaps Spottiswoode would in future decide who did what, and when. He agreed to get out schedules, and I asked Leonard to type them and pin them up where they would be permanently visible.

Since Leonard may have had some class-war grudge about the comparative livings of West Mill with Gooseham, I showed him Rose Marie's housekeeping bills and gave him a sum in excess of them to spend as steward along the valley. He, as steward, decided what we ate, who cooked it, and the time of meals. Horst was to control feeding-stuffs, and I took my orders from Spottiswoode, who decided what farm-job I should do each week. And so we tried again.

Spottiswoode got the schedules out. Leonard became cowman

and steward; Horst horseman and woodman; Spottiswoode pig-
man and transport; I the gardener. Every hour was accounted for,
meal-times fixed, and Spottiswoode was to direct us to specific
farm-jobs each morning. For the first week I was told to hedge.
The cottage looked clean and neat. Leonard and Spottiswoode
were cleaning stables soon after it was light.

My sister said that the Community would go better if the cottage
itself looked more comfortable and set a standard for the rest of the
farm. This was obviously true, for the cottage was the centre; and
if that was not clean it was highly improbable that the shippons
would be.

So Rose Marie and my sister redecorated the entire cottage and
painted all the woodwork, providing cushions, desk, kitchen-
furniture and innumerable washing-up material, brooms and new
towels.

About a fortnight after this renaissance, I noticed the horse was
lame and discovered a great cut on her leg. She was limping round
the field. As Horst had been doing the carting, I went and found
him. He was putting more energy than was necessary into breaking up a pigsty-door. From a distance it was obvious that he knew
something about the horse's injury. Apparently he had gone to
catch the horse that morning; as usual she had trotted up to the
pail and then, cunningly, cantered off as he reached to halter her.
She had done this several times and eventually just galloped round
the field. Horst had lost his temper and had thrown what was in
his hand at the horse. It was a bill-hook.

A woman is never so foolish that she does not know how to
manage a man. Perhaps it is because instinct always prompts her
to an infallible method which requires only a tongue to put it into
effect. And it is certain that, if all men are vain, flattery is certain
bait for all men. Horst was soon cutting firewood for Mrs Welling when he was supposed to be doing some other job. But
the loss of time was nothing, and the loss of wood was very
much less.

Horst's guardians decided that he should leave us to become a
student at London University. It was just as well, for he was so
much within the orbit of Mrs Welling that he might as well have
been in London as in the Community.

After he left, the lady's attention switched towards Leonard. I suspected this would happen when I overheard her singing the words of the Internationale to an air of Sullivan—a not incongrous combination.

Whyle built a granary and a pigsty and found all his materials except sand, lime and cement. He did not seem happy unless he was squaring a stone off or tapping it with the side of his trowel until it sat tight in the mortar. It was as though he was building his way out of this life which had treated him so meanly. He built with fanatical energy, and, although he could not have expressed it, it was all for a spiritual reason: *Dei Gloria* one pigsty and a chimney-stack. He then offered to build us a shippon. It was his idea, he chose the site and sketched out a plan and dimensions. He could see that the question of costs worried me, and insisted that he could find the stones in the stream and would work for very much less than the regulation pay, so long as I said nothing to "those bloody labour officials." Before the matter was settled he was already digging the foundation and yelling to his kids to start carting the muck away. It was a tie-up for ten cows with a tallet above.

Cleaning wasteland, I sometimes disturbed more than I bargained for. It was my intention to cut out some of the useless hedge-trees such as elder and alder, and replant with damson or gooseberry. The more fruit the better, I argued, and gooseberry makes as good a hedge as bramble and a better jam. I thought it was quite an original idea. And so I cut out some old wood from an overgrown hedge and found some gooseberry bushes, white currant and damson trees there already, strangled by ivy. I had done it all a century ago and must have forgotten to prune them. I also discovered the ruins of a house while clearing wasteland. We are like paste between the bread, the dead: a sandwich for the wind hungry from gathering ruins.

At last the blacksmith mended and sharpened the awkward harrows. We soon found that the horse could not pull the pair, even though they were not much heavier than seed-harrows. This was due not only to the gradient of the field but also to the tangle of bracken, which the plough had broken and brought to the surface. This meant that one of us had to manage the horse, and the other clean the harrows of bracken-roots at each turning. But for all that, we got good tilth, due as much to the frost as to our efforts. I looked up the feeding-value of bracken-roots and found that they were similar to potatoes; but the pigs wouldn't eat the stuff, nor would it burn; still it made a good monument to our efforts, and was something to show to the County War Agricultural Committee's pedlar.

While we were harrowing each field, Rose Marie and my sister were cleaning another for ploughing. This made a visible result which was encouraging. And that had a good effect on Spottis-woode, but Leonard seemed almost annoyed that some of our plans were working out. This was because Spottiswoode intended to stay, whereas Leonard was looking for an excuse to go. This was apparent when we started talking in terms of political generalities which amounted to the statement that ploughing little plats in North Devon was not likely to turn the world over; and that the true way to salvation lay in fomenting industrial strikes, pamphle-teering and the stirring of oceans of coffee in dreary cafés. I tried to point out to Leonard that if one had any belief in one's power of improving society, it was surely expedient to start where one was, and that when we had ploughed one field we would then clear another. But discussion at this level was sheer waste of words. And of course these were not the true reasons for Leonard's restlessness.

Whyle's only complaint was the scarcity of good quoin-stones. If he saw one lying by the road or in a ditch, out it came and soon his kids were hauling it to him. As Whyle was stone-deaf, one had to write one's comments on a piece of slate which he kept handy, but I think he heard more than people realised. I wrote many lines on the slate trying to persuade him that Mussolini was not the King of Italy. He talked a great deal about the last war and used to say "Haig" and then spit and get on with his wall.

The harrowing continued, and we found an old stone roller buried in a ditch. This was wonderful, a timely prize. Spottis-woode soon made a frame for it and melted down some lead, which I had found on the beach, to fix in an axle. We were doing this when suddenly Leonard appeared wearing coat and gloves to announce his immediate departure. Apparently he had received some communication from his communist superiors to the effect that he was to be flown to Dublin. The purpose of all this was to evade his call-up to the army. And so Leonard left in the triumphant company of Mrs Welling, who was giving him a lift. He left his unmade bed and his improbable story behind him. Later when Comrade Stalin graduated to Mr Stalin, Leonard went into the army and was eventually killed at Tobruk.

The education authorities discovered the existence of the Whyle kids and two of them had to attend school. So then only Spottiswoode and I were left to do the planting. Our schedule broke down. Spottiswoode became the sole inhabitant of the cottage, and this depressed him; he thought himself into the part of the hermit, the failure, the unloved, with the usual result that he tended to bring his position to one's notice by accentuating it and isolating himself still further. What discipline we had established fell away. Spottiswoode's washing-up remained undone; the cottage became filthy again—the whole scheme looked hopeless.

There had been four of us to sow; there were two of us to harvest. It was one thing to sling the seed in but another to pick it up again, binding and binding till the last sheaf was stooked. What we thought four of us could tackle at a stretch, two of us had to attempt without adequate knowledge, implements or experience. The labour this derelict farm of forty acres required was more than a farm of several hundred in good condition. For it was not merely a question of feeding the pigs and milking cows; without a single gate or fence we were the animals' jailers and could not give both eyes to any job.

Plainly the way to tackle this profligate wilderness would have been to spend a year clearing, a year hedging, ditching and gating before acquiring a single pig or sowing any seed. But that we could not do, even if we could have supported ourselves during the period of clearing; for now the various Committees with innumerable officials and multitudinous forms descended with small cars and large fountain-pens. We had a certain acreage to crop irrespective of whether it was profitable. Admittedly the land needed ploughing, but it would have been better to fallow it till the hedges could keep out the invading cows and the infiltrating rabbits.

The wind was blowing a north-west gale and I could not stand up on the cliff-path for fear of being blown over. I found a baulk of Oregon pine just left by the tide, eight inches by eight inches and thirty-two feet long. I immediately ran home to get my saw, worrying lest the Coast Watchers or the Home Guard had seen it and were running to get their saws. Fortunately I found Harry Whyle and told him of my find. Together we slithered over the rocks and were soon knee-deep in the sea, sawing the baulk into eight-foot lengths so that they would saw back for gate-pales. We were both soaked by the time we had made the first cut, but no matter. Soon we had the four pieces and with great effort landed them high above the tide, leaning them against the cliff. Now the problem was to get help to lift them up the cliff, and yet not leave them. Whyle said he would guard the pieces and would be glad if somebody challenged our ownership. I went to get Spottiswoode and some rope. When I returned Whyle was sitting smoking a cigarette, and for the first time I saw him without a cap on. I asked him where it was. "It must have come off," he replied, "when I was telling those Hocking fellows that we had found the timber afore they." He had enjoyed the fight and no further mention was made of it. And though it took us all day to land the timber, it sawed up for several gates and was worth the work and the wetting.

Many people applied to join the Community, but it was difficult to know whether they were genuinely interested in farming or merely wished to escape into a reserved occupation and obtain a funk-hole from air-raids. The necessity of a novitiate became apparent. Many of them enquired into our beliefs. They expected a credo to be handed to them like a sandwich.

One afternoon when we were harvesting, Peter Card and Victor Wells arrived. They had cycled from their homes in north-west London. They had never been in a cornfield before, but within five minutes of their arrival they were binding up. We knew very little about them. Wells had been a clerk in a City office. Card was employed in the office of a London warehouse. Both had lost their jobs after registering as Conscientious Objectors. Card was very well-built, fair and stocky: Wells, a few years older, was dark and sallow.

The question was whether they had come to join the Community only so as to comply with their Tribunal Order to take up agricultural employment. We could do nothing but wait and see. Wells had the habit of alternately singing little-known excerpts from *La Traviata*, of which he seemed to know all the words, and quoting speeches from Shakespeare.

While I was binding up the sheaves of oats, I was certain I believed in oats. The stalks fell behind the cutter which we drew behind an old car, a monk who had joined us for a month was binding methodically, the new members more enthusiastic but less effective. Gamel and Gerald Brenan also helped at the stooking with Rose Marie and my sister. The women wore coloured scarves round their heads. It is impossible to glean ungracefully. Here was the whole of it.

By six o'clock one field was in and the weather still held. Tiredness said it would be dry again tomorrow, but Yeoford's man said it would rain, and so it was decided to carry the other field right away. Energy is not the same thing as urgency, and it was quite dark before the field was half carried. As we threw up the last sheaf on to the stack Yeoford's man caught it, held it up and shouted: "Ah! this be the one we been all day a-looking for!" He had waited all day for the privilege of making that traditional gesture. It was nearly midnight and we were too tired to get any supper. But much more than corn was carried; a dead weight of social frigidity has been lifted. If we could have worked like that every day, something would have been built.

A week later the Battle of Britain was raging. Card and Wells read newspapers which were sent from their homes and, as they read them, they announced to each other the destruction of some street or building in their locality. Their parents refused to leave for a safe district and sent parcels of cake or darned socks to their pacifist sons in Devon.

Each day brought three or four applications from young men wishing to join us. Some were merely looking for funk-holes, though they did not know it, and others wrote priggishly about "always wishing to get back to the land and a spiritual way of life." Others had simply been ordered by Tribunals to take up agriculture and honestly admitted it. As they had no experience, few ordinary farmers wanted them as labourers, even if they could have tolerated their opinions.

But there were some applicants from whose letters it was plain that a more genuine interest prompted them.

A Henry Stone followed his first letter by visiting us before I had time to answer. He was most enthusiastic about all our plans and intentions, in spite of the fact that I described the realities, difficulties and shortages of the place in the grimmest colour, so as to discourage those who sought a retreat. He saw that we lived largely on rice and lentils. And I told him that, were he to stay for six months' novitiate, he could expect no cash, receiving only his rations and milk, butter, cheese, potatoes, and a share in anything else the farm produced.

The difficulty in his joining us was that he had a young wife and baby. I told him that although he might be prepared to live on short rations, his wife might not, and furthermore we could not produce any of those innumerable necessities from napkins to perambulators which his wife obviously required. But he said that even under these conditions the Community would provide him with a life as opposed to a mere living. He was a fragile-looking person, about twenty-five, with a degree in Classics and a live interest in the Chinese alphabet. But it was plain that, with his theoretical culture, he was short of a very great deal. He was a natural research student, born to become a curator or a don. Perhaps he saw in the Community a college in embryo, some shelter for his studies and an escape from the travel agency in which he had worked. Finally I tried to discourage him by pointing out the social difficulties: his wife would be isolated, and I told him I doubted whether women were ever interested in communal experiments. They pull always to their own homes and resent their husbands' efforts being shared by other homes. But of all that he would hear nothing, and eventually he persuaded me that his wife, who had some knowledge of poultry, would fit in with the place and possibly increase our income.

241

The owner of Rose Cottage was unwilling to let the house to Stone but was prepared to sell it. There was no other alternative accommodation. By shuffling deeds and visiting the bank, I managed to buy the place. The Stones moved into it. They arrived with child and furniture. It fitted into two rooms of Rose Cottage, which left half the place empty.

One morning I went to see how the pigs were doing on the arish. One of the black sows was missing. Unhappily she was not far away but lay on her side dead. She was only a young sow, due to produce her second litter.

We had half-dug the grave when Spottiswoode suggested that it might be an offence to bury an animal which had died from an unknown cause, and that we had best telephone the vet, who said he would have to come out and make a post-mortem, as there was swine-fever in a nearby district and, as we had several other pigs, it was better to be on the safe side. Eventually he arrived at 10 p.m. We had only one lantern, but the sow drew us to her corpse on the rails of her smell. She no longer had a side to lie on but was blown up like a balloon. The vet took a pocket-knife and punctured the enormous round thing, which exploded like the shot of a gun, making me drop the lantern. Then he got to work and put the knife in between its front legs and slit it down to the tail. Out spilled yards of obese silvery bowels. The vet's rubber-gloved hand rummaged, making a vast sucking noise till he cut out the stomach, which he divided. It was tight with grass. "She died of internal combustion," he explained, "due to eating too much roughage with the dew on it. Never turn pigs out till the sun's well up." I remembered that I had a bet of a shilling with a neighbour on how many pigs the sow would have. So I asked the vet to count the embryos. There were sixteen slippery bags; their feet, heads and hair were already there.

A friend of Card and Wells, called Eric Finch, wished to join us. He too had a wife and child. I stressed our difficulties and the long time it would be before they were lessened. I also told him that we worked to a time-table and schedule. I said that we intended to share profits and it would be a year or two before there were any, and that they would be small then by urban wage-standards. He still wished to join us; it was arranged that he and his wife should share Rose Cottage with the Stones. Fortunately there was ample room, and the cottage, with two sitting-rooms downstairs and a kitchen, three bedrooms and a bathroom upstairs, was easy to divide. Finch had about £100, which he was willing to invest in our funds. This was welcome, for, apart from the money, it assured his efforts. He was good-looking; those who had never seen Rupert Brooke probably saw some facial similarity between them. But what struck me most was his broad straight back and the unnatural stiffness with which his head was attached to his slight shoulders. He walked like a missionary through a world of lepers. His wife, on the other hand, had no moral rigidity in her appearance, though she supported her husband by talking in a low serious voice. He was a clerk and she a school-teacher. They had met at a political meeting. The dull everydayness of their jobs had permanently embittered them; they were interested in all reforms and were the type of people who worked hard as unpaid secretaries and treasurers to little-known movements.

Their furniture was hardly unpacked before he asked me where the nearest chapel was situated, and within a week he had arranged to preach there.

The Community would, I thought, appeal to their moral seriousness: the only question was: would they be sufficiently flexible? I wondered about this, for any person who had such belief in his own rectitude to enable him to preach to the locals before he had time to know them was probably rather a prig.

However, like many people, they were grateful to the war for breaking their office tyranny and they threw themselves into rural life with an enthusiasm which their energy could not maintain.

After a few days it was apparent that the Rose Cottage effort at community had started most unfortunately. It began with the arrival of the Finches' furniture, massive leather suite, writing-desk and bookcase containing many volumes of theology and psychology, besides innumerable objects of urban comfort such as pouffes, coal-scuttles and ornaments. Although Rose Cottage divided up easily, the parts were not quite equal in size. On the right hand side of the house there were two small bedrooms upstairs with a very large sitting-room downstairs. And to the left there was one large bedroom upstairs and a small sitting-room downstairs. The bathroom and kitchen conveniently abutted on to the main part of the house and these were to be common to both families. The Stones, who arrived first, had naturally chosen the half with the large sitting-room; and they were comfortably settled there with their few pieces of home-made furniture when the Finches' pantechnicon arrived. It was immediately plain that their furniture would not fit or squeeze into the smaller sitting-room but would suit the larger one. An obvious solution was immediately apparent to everybody but the Stones. The Finches then showed neither tact nor patience, and a great deal of bad feeling was precipitated into the house within a few minutes. In other words, neither party had been able to accept the reality of community: in spite of all the verbal idealism, each was imbued with the idea of each for himself and what is mine is mine. Betty Stone was in tears, Mrs Finch bit her lower lip. Spottiswoode and I moved the furniture round and round and tried to console the Stones by informing them that the smaller room would be warmer in winter.

There were nine of us then, all dependent on the produce of this marginal farm. And with that amount of labour, even allowing for our inexperience and the precipitous hill, we should have been able to swipe down the undergrowth and create an area of fertility there. But whereas enthusiasm will hang a gate, it requires some rarer qualities to hang it straight and keep it shut. And those qualities were the tools we lacked. It was one thing to cut the nettles and uproot some of the docks; but after three days' work together, it was apparent that unless we could achieve some sort of discipline and direction we might just as well have replanted the weeds.

The sequence in which we should do jobs was largely determined by the necessities of the season. But as the work was uncoordinated the haphazard energy of a dozen only achieved unprofitable chaos. On an ordinary farm the farmer is the boss, the men are employees, doing as he directs. Our relationship was not so simple. I bought the farm, stock and implements, and paid the steward's weekly account for provisions. The others invested their labour. If there had been a profit it was to have been shared equally.

We were people of some education, that is to say, we knew enough to question but not enough to accept the answer. If one were to define intelligence as the ability to understand and accept the nature of men and things as they are, we should have been excluded. For, like most of our generation, we saw ourselves and things as we would have had them, and not as they were. A peasant does not make this mistake. The experiment might have succeeded had we had sufficient mental discipline to discard prejudices and dreams as they proved inadequate. We were people used to dealing with ideas which are infinitely pliable, and for the first time were in contact with things which are rigid, brittle.

That we were pacifists was also a considerable disadvantage, for among the current fallacies which many of us read into this dogma was the postulate that discipline was of no value unless it was self-imposed. As soon as the members had joined the farm I asked one to tend one job, one another, and various officers had been elected, such as a steward, an accountant, etc. But this amount of order proved to be entirely inadequate, for it did not fix a time for any job to be done. I had thought that ordinary farm-routine would fix that. The cows had to be milked at a certain time to meet the milk-lorry. But I soon discovered that the problem was what was to be done when the cows were not milked by that time —when this was forgotten, and that left in the hedge. It was assumed that people could not be sacked, and without money it was impossible to fine them, and who was there to impose the fine? Gandhi had told me that the only thing to do in these circumstances was to fast oneself. Perhaps I did not fast enough or was unable to control the irritability of hunger.

A farm does not exist merely in the fields. It slops over into the house. The cleanliness of milk-pails is as important as pasture. I found the cottage a respectable ruin but its cultured inhabitants soon gave it the untidiness of unwashed cups and unmade beds. And to alter these conditions by persuasion was difficult, for like most of our generation we affected untidiness. I believe that the picture of Beethoven composing in a filthy shirt at a piano littered with cups lies at the bottom of this myth. It is one to which not only adolescents and undergraduates cling. I know of one internationally famous artist who deliberately performs hourly the ritual of forgetfulness and untidiness.

Another pose of a similar nature is the casual off-hand manner which goes with studied bad manners. The word "gentleman" is frequently derided, but everybody hopes to be mistaken for one. It is interesting to trace the origin of this sort of thinking and values. People behave without restraint for fear of "repressing" themselves; which nonsense no doubt is due to their mis-reading or not reading Freud. Similarly, a mis-reading of Lawrence left us a heritage of licentiousness, the impact of Joyce ended in the windbag of Miller. What happened to poetry was worse—the man who coined the phrase "free verse" should be condemned to the perpetual editorship of a literary quarterly. There is a very great deal to be said for mass illiteracy.

Widow Yelton was a hunchback. She was seventy. One could not imagine her ever being younger. Most people's characters remain constant, only their age alters, but for a few years their character and their age seem to coincide. It is as if some men were intended for middle age and some condemned to a life of adolescence. Widow Yelton was born a crone, and her deformity was not her only cronish attribute, for her voice was a Cornish falsetto, a cross between a turkey's gobble and a goose gargling. And on top of this she had a wispy beard, a long black apron, and was never without her hat, a greenish trilby without a brim. There was always a broom in her hand. She kept a shop, for it is certain that the shop did not keep her. She sold potions and pills, but they were not compounded of owl's liver or ferrets' tongues, but just the usual soap and sugar or milk of magnesia. The only sign marking her cottage as a shop was a large advertisement for some brand of cider which she never stocked. Inside the emporium, which was also her kitchen, there was everything from pig-powders to shoe-laces. Interesting as this variety of objects was, one was aware of something else and did not know what it was. It was a pair of blue eyes watching you. Widow Yelton's daughter was also a hunchback, but whereas the old woman was as active as an ant, the daughter could do little more than cut the beans and sit and watch for people coming into her mother's shop.

We were registered with Widow Yelton: she held our ration-books, took our points and cut out our coupons. In return for matches, candles, etc., she took logs, plums and apples. Coins seldom entered her accounts; had she restricted her trade to them, there would have been little indeed.

One might have thought that two women of a similar age, each with a child to interest and a husband to attend her, could have lived peacefully in Rose Cottage. Especially since their accommodation was adequate and separate. But there they were, safe from air-raids, scratching each other's eyes out, while other women only as far away as Plymouth were crawling out of the debris of their homes with one hand holding the remains of their child and the other stretched to the aid of their neighbour. Yet here Betty accused Joan of stealing her napkins, and Joan accused Betty of not sweeping the common staircase. The communal experiment in this house started badly and deteriorated daily. With the result that their respective husbands were late for work, distracted, and hardly on speaking terms.

As I passed the house, I heard the two girls nagging at each other, doors slamming, sobs, and the whole cannon and fire of two women having a scene. I remembered once watching two harridans outside a pub in Brixton having a hair-pulling contest, and the noise from Rose Cottage was similar; I went in and listened to each accusing the other and eventually left them, both for a moment brought together by a mutual dislike of me. I suppose each girl was trying to drive the other out of the house. One hankered for the big bedroom and the other for the big sitting-room. I had to tell them and their husbands that if these domestic brawls persisted they must all leave.

It occurred to me that men choose their wives with less care than they devote to the selection of a threepenny book from a second-hand barrow of throw-outs. And while all this sort of dreary waste went on, weeds grew up again, and rats returned.

For a week we dug potatoes; six of us on a field not more than an acre, and the work went as slowly as if paralytic moles were at

247

it. This was most depressing, for the work did not require skill, so we could not excuse ourselves on that score. In this case it was nothing more than sloth that was the cause. Although the diggers would eat the potatoes, and share in the receipts of the sale of the surplus, there was no interest or enthusiasm. It was half-past ten before Spottiswoode arrived in the field, walking towards it slowly. The male members of Rose Cottage followed separately half an hour later: Stone had some excuse, for he did many of his wife's jobs: Finch made some excuse and relied on his pompous preaching voice to give it veracity. Victor and Peter next arrived, the former at least showing signs of having hurried. At last we were all in the field and for a moment there was a great show of labour. The scheduled time for everybody to be in the field was nine o'clock. This was ridiculous. Had these people been in the army, they would have been punished; had they been paid employees they would have been sacked. I thought of the time when I had stayed with Gandhi at his *Ashram* and the way he had dealt with similar incidents. And so when lunch-time arrived and the others stopped work, I stayed and said that I would work on through the lunch-hour as a practical protest against the way everybody had arrived late for work. The only person I could punish was myself. But it was a most difficult method. No sooner had the others gone to lunch than feelings of indignant self-righteousness rose to smother me. And if this feeling is shown, the method is useless. I had to try and root it out. But it would have been easier to skin the hill like a rabbit or control the traffic of migrating shrimps—that is much simpler than steering oneself from one mood to another.

Alfred Stoyes joined us. He informed us he was a poet. Within his first week he wrote at least six elegies and five and a half yards of free verse; and not a rat or a rabbit died without Alfred's hurrying to some corner to salute the unimportant event. He had a talent for rhyme but no ear for rhythm. He was the most unhappy of all creatures, the ambitious and unnoticed artist: a person tiresome to himself and to his few friends: if he is not persecuted he imagines he is disliked. He made a hobby of failure and dreaded nothing so much as success. All this was there, written lucidly on his worried face, shown in his blink and occasional stutter. But in spite of that, he brightened the cottage by his skit on surrealist sculpture, an arrangement of stones picked out of the ditch he was digging. But what was most hopeful was his effort to show a communal spirit. He rushed to wash up, and that was a contribution.

There were now ten of us; our average age was twenty-four; before the war we had all been pen-pushers, either paid or unpaid; none of us had had any farming experience. Most had no money; a few enough to last a month or two. The money was pooled. For most days it was chicken-rice for lunch, which we bought at a penny a pound. But we had plenty of milk, eggs, bread and vegetables. The two babies thrived. In spite of our muddle and chaos the land did get reclaimed. As a community the experiment looked like a failure; but so were the social patterns around us failures too. At least we were not dropping bombs on each other. And our attempts at self-sufficiency had some meaning, for it was plain that we could not eat American food without a fleet to convoy it here. Tinned beans, Kentucky Ketchup, Canadian Salmon —these were our taboos and they had the advantage of giving a precise breakfast application to a vague philosophy. We had all chattered for years about the evils of industrial and imperial exploitation, and now that all the products of that system were rationed we had the excellent opportunity of doing without them. The assiduous cultivation of kitchen-gardens is the only realistic alternative to the singing of Rule Britannia. We cannot have it both ways. Civilisation may have followed the trade-routes, but so did syphilis.

The unwieldy traction-engine clumsied its way into the farmyard about 5 a.m., and in the uncomfortable and oyster dawn the monster manoeuvred, getting its rump close to the stack, and there eventually we staked it. We had no need to announce to neighbours that we were going to thresh; they could hear, and they arrived with their prongs—putting off other jobs and waiting for direction. We had two on the stack, two at the back with the straw, one on the thresher, one carrying water to the ludicrous rhinoceros, and he stood by changing the sacks, the strong carrying

I   249

the grain up tortuous ladders. There were eleven of us in all, plus a boy dealing with a mountain of dust. As soon as the drum started and the first sheaf was cut and the hard barley began to trickle, then pour bountifully, abundantly, each man came round and thrust his hand into the fall of grain on the excuse of taking a handful, but really to feel the pleasure of its running over the hand, and then they would bite a grain or cut one with a pocket-knife and say: "Running well. Not a bad sample. Broad Acre always does turn out well, especially if you get a dry time." They will always work furiously, it does not matter whose corn it is. They count the sacks and work out the yield, and over the enormous threshers' lunch they will congratulate you and encourage you, and at the end of the day when the last rat has been walloped, the loose rakings are put through, not a handful wasted.

Hedging is the most satisfying of all farm-jobs so long as the hook is sharp and the saw set; otherwise it is as exasperating as writing with a broom. And though a great deal of skill can be put into laying a hedge, only sharp tools are required to cut out the surplus wood. Alfred complained that he felt constantly exasperated, as he was clumsy at it. So I asked him to cut out the hedge between two fields and armed him with a Swedish bushman's saw with a new blade. I showed him what was to be done, and told him that it did not matter how long he took over the job. If any time-limit had been mentioned, he would have been sure to seize on that and let it persecute him. I left him working on that hedge, hoping that he would soon be able to see that his efforts had made some improvement. After an hour I returned; he was thrashing at the hedge, and using every stick as a ledge on which to climb up to a crisis of exasperation, frustration and helplessness. His whole energy was directed into persecuting himself. He was sitting in the hedge, drugged with self-pity. I tried to encourage him, pointing out that it was now possible to see across the hedge, and how useful the work was. But he complained that it was all drudgery and that it gave him no time to write. I restrained myself from asking him why he had joined us, and pointed out that we had taken on the job of clearing a derelict farm and that our living depended on it. His reply was that poets and priests should be supported by the society in which they lived and could not be expected to dig with the others. All of which may have had some truth in it, but it was expedient, I suggested, to consider the realities which existed rather than talk about conditions which did not. I said that after a few years we might be sufficiently established, as a community, to allow shorter hours in the fields and more in the library which we were already collecting. But these conditions did not obtain then, and privately I held the opinion that poetry was not a whole-time occupation. I can think of no worse drudgery than being confined as a whole-time writer. However, Alfred was dejected and there was nothing left but to try an extreme course with him. So I said that we quite realised it was a waste of his time to work in the fields all day, and that in future he would be expected to work outdoors only in the morning. I added that all the field-cultivations were forward and the rest of us could easily manage. And he believed me. I hoped that when he saw us doing his share of the work outdoors, he might decide to write his poetry in the meticulous arrangement of field-pipes. He didn't.

I instituted a community chapter. This met every Sunday afternoon. The procedure was that the minutes of the last chapter were read, so that we could see whether we had done what we had resolved to do the preceding week. After this the cowman made his report giving the statistics of yield, services, etc., and stated any requirements for feeding-stuffs; then the pigman-poultryman made his statement. The steward then commented on food-rations and the members made any complaints or suggestions. After which I had before me the requirements of the various offices and, since all could not be satisfied, decided on the priorities. Then the jobs for the next week were decided. Finally the chapter was thrown open to the hearing of complaints and suggestions. With ten members, this took a considerable time, but I was trying to establish the idea that it was taboo to complain about a job, or a person, unless the complaint was made at the general chapter. This was an attempt to stop the chitter-chatter of communal spitefulness and resentment. And this method of dividing responsibility according to ability to accept it was the only way: in theory the position was that the horseman and cowman were wholly responsible for their departments. If I said we were to plough, and the horseman said the horse was not fit, obviously his word carried. But if both the horseman and the cowman laid claim to the last truss of hay, I arbitrated. This worked for a month or two. During that time some of the members of the community showed dissatisfaction at the method of government. They considered it not sufficiently democratic. They wanted every issue decided by vote. I vetoed this idea on purely practical grounds and avoided treading on any ideological toes. But Victor announced that he resented my saying that the bedrooms were kept in a filthy state. I had suggested that we should fold our bed-clothes in precisely the same order and arrangement as they do in the army. Victor and Peter maintained that their bedroom was their private concern and I had no right to issue suggestions or orders concerning it. The question of what is private cuts across the whole idea of community. Since I was trying to found a small ordered society I did not recant. Therefore Peter said he would leave. Victor then took the line that, by deciding major issues, such as what should be grown and when tilled, I was liable to make mistakes which might jeopardise his and the others' position. This was obviously true and inevitable. But Victor's alternative was that there should be a sort of committee. At this dreadful word I resigned from all "official" capacity and said I would in future only work on the place and accept orders and would take no part in the chapter until invited to do so. And I left the merry crew squab-bling among themselves. Spottiswoode then said that since they wanted government by vote, would they vote on the issue of whether they would return to the method I had established. This they did and the next day I was asked to return. But unhappily Victor left us altogether. Now there were nine.

The feudal Court functioned adequately and appointed officers who levied fines. Reading many of the Court Rolls and reports I came across several instances where a peasant appointed by the Court to some manorial office such as a reeve had summoned the Lord of the Manor in his own Court where he had subse-quently been fined. The sort of office and regulation required by these Feudal societies is most interesting, and there was no doubt that if we were to achieve any order we should have to make equal provision.

Accordingly this was attempted. But without any success, for many of us not only lacked a background of discipline but on "ideological reasoning" or "moral grounds" would not submit to the censure of an officer and would not undertake such a responsibility ourselves. These problems which we met are, I think, worth noticing, for they had implications outside our own experiment. At these chapters it was no longer relevant that somebody decided who had the corn if both the pig-keeper and the cowman wanted it. Perhaps a farm is unlike a nation and one cannot be permitted to draw a parallel and make conclusions. But in a farm efficiency is largely a matter of quick decisions, often against advice, and anything like democracy is entirely inadequate.

The adequacy of a law or a rule in a society seems to depend on assuming that the law will be broken, and framing it on that basis. Nonsense about freedom and liberty and rights will not only ridicule a group of people but can bring a nation quickly to the tyranny of indecision. Liberty is the discipline you accept.

Sooner or later it was plain that a decision might be made which would go against the wishes of a member of the Community. But this issue was reached theoretically. Finch asked me what I would do if, by vote, the Community wished to sell a tractor and I wished to sell a horse. I replied that the horse would be sold. The fact that I had purchased both was irrelevant; the matter hinged on whether the decision should be reached by a number of people who knew nothing about farming, or by one who knew a very little. Accordingly the Wesleyan left. Now there were eight.

Whyle had been unwell for a few days. He complained of giddiness and lay in bed reading *Mein Kampf*. Then he came down the hill carrying his jug of cold tea and was soon hard at it again, lifting the stones up to the walls of the shippon, which were now eight feet high all round. In the afternoon he complained of a pain in the head and went home. There he collapsed and the doctor sent him to Exeter Hospital. He had a burst blood-vessel, due probably to the last war. They loaded him into the ambulance; he was already unconscious. He was dead in the morning. And by this everybody lost, except Harry Whyle. Every farmer, myself included, was without a mason. When the news of his death came, his kids were cleaning out the stable and both of them sat and cried pitifully. After a few minutes the elder, who was thirteen, said: "I suppose I shall have to be my mother's husband now." His death upset me. I wrote this for his epitaph:

> He was neither prince nor politician,
> no priest and no poet,
> as the world knows them; but he was the man
> to smoothe stones, make each fit
>
> straight to his quoin, and thus used less mortar
> than contract masons waste,
> with the next job as their present master,
> in their slow toil of haste.
>
> He worked no fixed hours, he just came and went,
> carrying a jug of cold tea;
> he'd stay till he'd used up all his cement,
> then leave, with no temerity.
>
> His work was such that each action contained
> its own contemplation;
> the more he gave his work, the more he gained
> in strict meditation
>
> on stones of infinite shape. He weighed
> their neat rigidity.
> Disciplined by working with these, he made
> his own philosophy
>
> which was as sound as any Analects,
> —at least, in application—
> all men and things to their own nature fit
> with or without salvation.

"Larch is no good for a lintel," he said,
"it warps young and rots old
true to its nature; and from friends," he said,
"expect from friends their colds."

Protected by these exact measurements
he spent his evening home.
Freed from resentments and disappointment,
married—to be alone.

His wife, a woman of monotonous lust,
without one attraction.
He kept her pregnant, for he knew this must
assure some relaxation.

But to assess his solid character,
words do not weigh enough.
Observe his walls, they maintain his nature;
see where he smoothed the rough

and how his beam's mortised. Then you will see
that civilisation
exists where men work for posterity
and build from sheer passion

for durability. Whyle built that way;
this shippon here proves it.
Living, he gave us this, and now we say:
He died to no profit.

The Whyle family dispersed; the children to an institution.
I herited the tools and still have some of them. But we could not
build a place with twenty-eight quoins—a pity, for we had just
purchased a good Shorthorn and another Devon, and could have
milked six or seven if we had somewhere to milk them.

The blacksmith was old and needed an apprentice. He was the
only blacksmith for a radius of ten miles. There was a living for
at least five more in this area—at his estimate. Half the work went

undone. The carpenter was two years behind with his jobs; the thatcher had a hole in his own roof; and the mechanic had gone to assist in "that mess in Libya." At the end of the war it was difficult to distinguish between what had been bombed and what had merely slid into disrepair. I saw barns and a cottage collapse through the lack of labour and the price of timber. At this time a public school moved to the district, and instructed its pupils in the carpentry shop. They were making peculiar small boxes which were meant to hold playing cards for those who play bridge.

I think that the word "husbandry" is better than "agriculture." One of the chief delights of farming is that it brings you into contact with a whole series of good sounding English words, words derived from the shape or use of the thing they describe: hook, scythe and sickle; dung, load and lintel. I have found farming terms to be most precise; the meanings have not slopped over into each other or got worn into counters. Philosophers can no doubt afford to get their terms muddled, so that they can talk of one thing and mean another, but it would be awkward for a farmer were he to order a tractor when he wanted a drill, or send for a mattock when he needed a pick-axe.

We reached a financial crisis. There was no money coming in. Our weekly outgoings were £3 and our income less than 30s. I found a merchant who took logs at 38s. a ton if they were sawn up into nine-inch pieces and stacked at the top of the hill. We had about fifty acres of oak which needed thinning and a lorry that could carry half a ton up the hill. Nobody had an alternative plan, so it was decided that we should work in the woods in pairs on alternate weeks. This arrangement and the financial position's obvious complication made things critical. Alfred took advantage of the situation and left. A similar impulse which drove him to throw up his job and join the Community was bound in the end to make him leave the Community also. Now there were seven.

I produced a quarterly balance-sheet and this grim object was pinned up for everybody to see. A farm account is difficult to assess; especially items such as the value of unexhausted manures. Also the value of our improvements was not easily judged. However, whether a cash loss showed or not, the account which interested me most was one in which what came down the hill was balanced against what went up as exports. For thirty years the farm had produced nothing but what we exported—something like 2000 gallons of milk a year, a hundred and fifty score of bacon, a hundred tons of logs, two tons of fruit, besides eggs, poultry, potatoes and other items. Against which we imported army-camp swill, a few hundredweight of oilcake, petrol, sand, lime and manures.

The Stones were having another baby and since there was no way of getting more cash to meet their increased expenses, they decided to leave. Henry was reluctant to do this but his wife was relieved that circumstances gave them no alternative. With both married couples gone, Rose Cottage was empty again and a rather expensive experiment ended with a definite conclusion: that marriage and community living do not go well together. Now there were two.

Only Spottiswoode and I remained to do the work that was planned for a dozen. We had to stop clearing land and concentrate on preventing what was reclaimed from going back again. The general plan was to concentrate on milk and to get those queer-shaped fields back into three-year or five-year leys. And to keep up fertility, and balance the export of milk, we collected swill from two camps and Bideford. This meant we could keep about twenty pigs, and with dung and lime we hoped to improve the grass and to keep the churn full. But this much was done: thirty acres were reclaimed, six acres drained and fifteen acres seeded out after cleaning with potatoes, and where only rabbits had been there were eight cows, twenty pigs and a mountain of dung.

The Community failed. But I learned from it some things which other people knew from the start. I always had to discover everything for myself, even the alphabet and my own stupidity.

PART FIVE

Flotsam or Jetsam?

WHEN our prayers are evil, they are answered more promptly. Is this because we have more reliable means of communication with the devil? Or merely that when our meditations are malevolent, we are not so easily distracted from them? Whatever the reason, I know that the most evil wish I ever had was granted with alarming alacrity. It was as if my call had been given priority over all others.

We never know our temptations until they come arm-in-arm with opportunity. It is comparatively easy to remain honest if you live in Kensington, for instance. There you are hardly likely to find the High Street littered with objects which are yours for the taking. But when the Atlantic foreshore is at your back, and each high tide strews other people's property at your feet, and the nearest coastguard is ten miles away—it is not quite so easy to keep your hands in your pockets.

Beachcombing is a drug. But one that never satisfies. Some appetites can be fulfilled, but to greed there is no end. And no sooner had I dragged my first hatch-plank out of the breakers, than I was off searching for some of the deck-cargo. For a short time I was content with finding driftwood with which to light my fires; then I salvaged my first teak plank; after that nothing but seasoned timber would satisfy me. And from timber I graduated to bales of raw rubber; then to tins of American coffee and barrels of wine. This was my downfall. Once having moved into the category of goods proper, my greed sought nothing but cargo—and not merely deck-cargo. I began to hope morbidly for a wreck.

At first my wish was inarticulate: I pondered the prospect of finding a small coaster cast up on the shore with all its hatch-planks and brass-fitted teak doors easily accessible. But those idle and modest daydreams soon solidified into a secret wish that one day I would awaken to find a great liner irretrievably holed on the rocks. As I composed myself to sleep, listening to the great Atlantic rollers bullying the shore, I used to speculate on the contents of her hold and the variety of her cargo. Some night I would imagine myself exploring treasures of silk and cargoes of wine; another time I would have the boat filled with typewriters. It would all depend on my most pressing need at the time. But I was consistent in this—I always prayed that the wreck should be a total loss and that the cargo should be portable and easy to handle.

To my delight my prayer was attended to with the utmost dispatch. And within a week of formulating my evil wishes I was awakened one night by the mournful sound of a ship's siren giving a distress signal. I sprang out of bed and peered at the blanket of mist. I could hear the repeated moan of Hartland foghorn and the noise of the waves breaking on the shore. I flung on some clothes, grabbed a lantern, and ran out into the night just in time to see a rocket soar into the sky.

Even from the cliff-edge I could not see the ship through the mist, though the sound of her siren came from dangerously close inshore. I stood and waited. Other ghouls joined me. True there was nothing we could do—we had no lifeboat to man. So we stood and waited.

"Let us pray for those on board," said the Vicar, who had a blanket round his shoulders. We bowed our heads. "Amen," I mumbled. Then we sang the first verse of "For those in peril on the sea" with one eye on the Vicar and the other on the bay.

"Here she comes!" cried the village postman triumphantly as the outline of a funnel and a lighted mast broke through the mist.

The second verse of the hymn was never sung. We rushed down the narrow donkey-path to the shore, the Vicar following. As we reached the shingle, we could see the prow of the ship heading straight for the rocks.

"She'll hole all right," shouted the carpenter.

"They'll never get her off no more," he added with complete complacency, as we heard the first terrific impact and saw the waves lift the helpless boat by the stern.

"I wonder what she was carrying?" I said, articulating each man's thoughts.

"I wonder," my companions repeated, as though making a fervent response.

"Think of those poor souls on board," said the Vicar.

Then, as the dawn came up, the mist lifted enough for us to see that the prow of the ship was wedged in between two rocks and her hull was listing badly to starboard. "She's holed all right," the carpenter concluded. "No tug'll ever shift her again."

"But think of those on board," repeated the Vicar. Sure enough we could now see some figures crowded together on the bridge.

"They'll never be able to launch a lifeboat in this sea," the carpenter said, no longer thinking of his deck-planks. "We'd best go up and git that there apparatus they sent us."

At this we dutifully climbed up the cliff again and from somewhere beneath a heap of wood-shavings at the back of his untidy shop we unearthed a life-saving rocket, coil of rope, and breeches-buoy. The coastguards had sent this equipment out some years ago for such an emergency. We loaded ourselves with the gear, then set off to the cliff.

"Drat it!" exclaimed the carpenter, turning back. "I've forgotten to bring the book of instructions."

We waited for him on the beach. It is now quite light enough to read the name of the boat, S.S. *Maud. Trondheim.*

"Ah, a Swedish vessel," said the Vicar, airing his geography.

"No, Danish," I said, forgetting mine.

"She must be three thousand tons at least," mused the postman.

Just then the carpenter returned, slithering down the cliff-face as a short cut from the zigzag of the path.

A dozen figures clustered in the captain's cabin on the bridge, while the great rollers swept the decks. The list to starboard had increased by five degrees. At that rate the ship would heel over in less than a couple of hours if it didn't break into two halves before then.

"S.O.S." signalled the desperate sailors.

Drenched with spray, we set to work to erect the equipment for firing the rocket, the Vicar reading the instructions, the carpenter carrying them out, the rest of us correcting one or hindering the other. After half an hour the rocket was in position with its rope attached.

"Now ignite fuse and fire rocket over vessel," the Vicar read. The carpenter borrowed my lighter, adjusted the angle and lit the fuse. There was a slight splutter. For a moment we thought the rocket was a dud. But just as one of us went to touch it to see if it was damp, it scorched up into the air. And, to our intense surprise, it went straight towards the wreck.

"How's that?" the carpenter grinned proudly. "It's going to hit the bridge."

But he was wrong. The rocket zoomed straight through the window of the captain's cabin, where all the crew were huddled. Sparks and smoke belched out behind it. Then the door was flung open and a sailor signalled: "Get doctor. Rocket has taken off the captain's leg."

Never had Trinity House Life Saving Instructions been more accurately followed.

One of us ran up the cliff to phone for the doctor and ambulance while the rest of us helped pay out the lines of the breeches-buoy, which the crew made fast to the bridge. We then staked our end at the foot of the cliff. The boat was now breaking up rapidly: a great gash showed in her steel plating and the sea was awash right over the stern.

When the first man climbed into the breeches-buoy and we began to haul him ashore, we saw that we had not got our end of the line fixed high enough up the cliff. We were dragging the man through the water instead of above it. At some moments he was immersed in the waves.

"Bet he wishes he'd stayed on the boat," someone said as we waded out to lift the half-drowned man ashore. His legs were cut and bruised by the rocks we had dragged him over. Two of us gave him our version of artificial respiration but, in spite of that, he soon recovered. The rest fixed the line higher up the cliff, and the next survivor arrived safely on the beach without getting a ducking. He was holding a hideous-looking cat and told us that all its fur had been burned off by the rocket.

"Did it really take off your captain's leg?" I asked incredulously.

"As clean as a whistle, right at the knee. He didn't feel it when it happened. In fact, he went to . . ."

"Quite, quite," I said, feeling a little sick and wondering what they had done with the booted limb.

"The first mate's fixing a tourniquet on him to stop the bleeding. When they've fixed that, they'll send him over."

We hauled away; and, after another hour, had rescued six more. They lay exhausted at the foot of the cliff. We gave them what dry clothing we had and made a fire of driftwood. We did not ask them that question which scratched at the door within each of our minds.

There were still five on the boat, including the injured captain. And the list of the vessel was increasing—each greedy wave seemed to push her a little more. It was feared that she would turn right over before we could rescue all the others. I began to regret my prayers.

I sent a message over, telling them they'd have to risk coming in couples, though we knew this would strain the breeches dangerously and perhaps foul the line altogether. There was no time now to fix it again still higher up the cliff.

And all the time one question barked within our minds.

We pulled the next two in on the sagging line, their heads just above water. The postman and I ran down the cliff to help them up the beach. As we began to wade out through the surf, a great roller broke, flinging splintered spars, lifebuoys, and two rubber mats on to the shingle. Among this jetsam lay the captain's leg. We stared at it mutely; the postman solemnly removed his hat.

"Looks like a case where a man's put his best foot forward," he said. "Let's hope he'll follow it. I can remember when the *Maggy* sank, the other side of the bay, some ten years agone; then we only had three heads to bury. These rocks are as sharp as razors, and when they do let a body float in, it's not so easy as you might think to be sure you're giving a man his own head and not someone else's."

We helped the two Norwegians up to the bonfire just as the local policeman, two coastguard officers and the new doctor hurried down the cliff-path. The next thing I knew was that the doctor had thrust the neck of a bottle between my lips. I gulped contentedly at the brandy.

"This poor fellow looks as if he needs that," the doctor said.

265

"Yes," drawled our bobby. "But why didn't you give it to one of the crew? They deserve it more than he does."

The bottle was pulled from my mouth: "I thought you were a sailor," the doctor snarled.

Meanwhile the captain was in the breeches. We carried him safely on to a stretcher which we made up out of a blanket and a couple of spars. The tough Norwegian still smoked his pipe as we carried him over the rocks.

When we returned from the ambulance, the four other sailors had been safely rescued. The entire crew now sat round the fire, solemnly drinking and staring out at their broken vessel as each wave edged her over. A dozen empty rum-bottles littered the beach. Apparently each man had been rescued fully armed.

We locals gathered round like vultures. "What were you carrying?" I asked, as casually as I could. The sailor did not speak English. I tried another. "What was your cargo?" Misunderstanding, he passed a bottle.

So I sought the sailor who had arrived holding the cat; for he, I remembered, spoke English. I repeated my question with unfeigned urgency; now that the poor souls on board had been rescued, I was once again up to my neck in predatory greed, visualising the hold packed with buoyant booty, a sort of cross between Harrods and Aladdin's Cave.

The pause was pregnant. The carpenter edged nearer. Then, for answer, the sailor merely hiccoughed in my face, then rolled over on to his side. He was completely drunk.

Furious, we stared down at the crew, who were all too sodden to satisfy our curiosity. But we could not leave them there. So we decided to split them up among us and take them to our homes to give them food and dry clothing.

I chose, in spite of his condition, the fellow who could speak English, believing that I might then get the precious news before my companions. I helped him to his feet and, with another sailor at his other side, we staggered up the cliff path to West Mill.

It was to my interest to sober my guests as quickly as possible. I therefore told Rose Marie to start getting them a meal of ham, eggs and black coffee, while I ran and fetched my two suits.

Returning with these, I found that the men had already made themselves at home and were drinking neat whiskey out of the neck of the decanter. They managed to tumble into my clothes, but only to fall asleep in them. "Let them," I whispered to Rose Marie, shutting the door on the two drunks. "They're bound to wake up sober."

No doubt they did, but we never got there in time. No sooner were they awake than they began drinking again. When they'd finished my whiskey and gin, they fell on my port. Eventually a police-car toured the village, collecting the crew to take them to the station, where their documents and rail-tickets were waiting. I accompanied my couple of drunks up to the car.

"Now then," I begged, "tell me what's in those holds."

The sailor hesitated. "Cement," he said.

Thus did my prayers solidify. And even to this day, though nothing remains of the S.S. *Maud*, a stack of concrete in the shape of the hold stands in the bay. It is a monument to malevolence. And whenever I look at it I am reminded that even the devil cannot be relied upon to answer prayers completely.

As a Conscientious Objector I expected to have to go before a tribunal. It was necessary to have two sponsors to confirm that your principles were held sincerely and were of long standing. I informed the tribunal that my sponsors would be Major-General Fuller, the strategist, and Lt.-Colonel Creagh Scott, both of whom had contributed to *Townsman* and agreed, if necessary, to go before the tribunal to speak on my behalf. This impartial gesture from the military so impressed me that I nearly joined up instead. But no tribunal was held. Being a farmer I discovered I was in a reserved occupation. This frustrated the local *Gauleiters*, who now sought to prove that I was incompetent as a farmer and should accordingly be evicted. Not a furrow was ploughed without one of the Committee's stooges being there to see if it was straight; our weeds were counted, and if our corn was laid, that was proof of bad husbandry and no allowance made for the weather.

This sort of petty persecution reached such a point that I saw the farm would soon be taken from me unless I could get some impartial authority to inspect it and state that the yields from derelict land in the process of reclamation could hardly be expected to compare with those from farms in good heart. I appealed to my friend Lord Portsmouth, who had invited me the year before to join his Husbandry Circle, which met periodically at Farleigh Wallop. Portsmouth asked Colonel Hayter Haymes, the chief Executive Officer of the Devon Agricultural Committee, to look into my case. He came and walked over the farm himself.

"You need a couple of dozen prisoners-of-war to help you," he said, surveying the jungle where we were yanking out tree-roots with a rope tied to my Sunbeam's axle. He congratulated me on getting barley to grow in a swamp.

This reprieve meant I could go on spending my days ditching and swiping at the all-embracing hedges. While I did this I found two images kept recurring to my mind. One was the Bosch painting of St Anthony with a sow at his feet, and the other was of a ruin in Portsmouth's park at Farleigh. A lot of poetry kept coming into my head too. I didn't write any of it down immediately, but it wouldn't go away. Eventually I started to scribble out some of it in the evening, hoping that it might make a masque which the Community could perform in one of the fields. I called it *The Masque of Saint Anthony* and naturally dedicated it to Lord Portsmouth, since it was he who had helped me get this interval from persecution in which to write it. Later, at the suggestion of Mrs Martin Browne, the title of the masque was changed to *This Way to the Tomb*.

But though the thought of imminent arrest didn't worry me unduly during the day, it was another thing at night. During this period I used to wake up and find I was soaked with sweat. I was always pursued by Law and cornered by Order. These dreams reduced me. I became ill: acute lethargy, migraine and indigestion returned. I went up and down Harley Street. Nothing organically wrong could be discovered. Finally one doctor decided I ought to go into the London Clinic for metabolism observation. They measured the oxygen I consumed, gave me drugs to make me sleep, drugs to make me wake up, and drugs to enable me to relax.

The treatment triggered off even worse dreams. On the second night there I dreamed that my own feet were rats. I ran from them in vain. The doctor came and told me that one test had revealed that I needed an abnormal amount of oxygen and sugar and should be fed every two hours. I told him of my nightmare. He said he would give me a sedative that would guarantee deep untroubled sleep. I swallowed his pills. That night I dreamed I was being pursued down Regent Street by packs of hands (after an air-raid in London I had seen a severed hand lying like a glove on the floor). The hands moved like crabs: I ran from them. As I did so it began to rain and then to hail: then I saw that it was in fact hailing human eyes. The eyes settled on the pavement and in the gutter, making up a fixed and fantastic bank of stares.

I decided that there was no point in staying in the Clinic to suffer from the hallucinations of DT's, though I was almost a teetotaller. And while still wobbling from the drug I found my dressing-gown and escaped. I found a taxi, vomited in it and, still wearing my dressing-gown, knocked up an aunt in New Cavendish Street. Britten came round to see me in the morning. I told him my dreams: they frightened him almost as much as they troubled me.

I had refused to marry Rose Marie, not because I did not think that our affections were stable, but because I was certain that they were. "Our marriage is between the eyes," I used to say; "to reduce that to a legal contract is unnecessary. Vows and promises can't make anything permanent. To bind affections is to mistrust them."

She listened unconvinced. I loved her all the more for staying with me in spite of this, bearing her parents' disapproval and her girl-friends' pity. It is one thing to stick to your own principles, another to maintain somebody else's. But she did this with good grace and occasional petulance. "I should have thought you'd want to marry me to prevent my marrying anybody else," she would sometimes say. But I was far too conceited to have doubts of that nature.

But early in 1941 she produced another argument. She was pregnant. Rose Marie was confident this would convince me. It didn't: I wanted her to have a child but its legality seemed irrelevant. But eventually I saw that it was also frivolous on my part to be as obstinate about not getting married as I thought she was in urging it. And on top of this I could see we would run into the complications of ration-books and identity-cards. So, with the sort of grace you might expect from a convinced teetotaller who has just been offered a flask of whiskey, I agreed to take her into a registry office in Bideford.

My mother and sister came as witnesses. It was irrational of me to be so depressed by the dingy little office where we signed and I bought the licence. But I felt I had betrayed something precious and intangible for three half-crowns and a rubber stamp. With complete insensitivity to Rose Marie's feelings, I had indulged in mine. I looked as if I were attending a funeral, except that one usually tidies oneself up for those occasions. I kept my Wellingtons on and remained unshaven and sulky. I even failed to buy her a wedding-ring, and the poor girl had to run off by herself and buy a utility ring for eight shillings and slip it on her own hand. I didn't even notice she was wearing it. In the jeweller's shop she had also bought me a wedding-present: a shaving-mirror: it was all she could afford. The price was irrelevant: it was a present. But I was in such a mood at having been caged by bureaucracy that I never thought of even giving her a flower. My mother had bought us a bottle of champagne. I said I didn't like champagne.

That evening Rose Marie and I returned to West Mill, married. While she got the dinner I started to write letters. We hardly spoke through the meal. After it she began to cry. I thought this was very inconsiderate of her. After all, she and the world had made me conform. She went to bed. I stayed up writing letters. They ought to have been all addressed to myself, for the day had proved I was obsessed with myself, and in love with myself.

After the Community dispersed, I went on reclaiming the farm. I did no writing beyond a quarterly editorial for *Townsman* and the weekly column called "Husbandry Notes" for the *New English Weekly*. But phrases and images kept coming involuntarily to me: I found I would, especially when alone beachcombing, say a couple of lines aloud while my conscious mind was thinking about something else. I remember one morning in the half-light leaping across the rocks before breakfast looking for some planks to mend the door of the shippon. I was worrying whether we had enough seed-potatoes to plant out a field called Oman's Land. My conscious mind began to work out the sum, how many hundredweight required for three and a half acres—and instead of producing a figure I heard myself say:

> And my mind clings to the past,
> Like a velvet train dragged on wet grass.

I stopped short, to see if I was being followed. But the words had been mine. The image impressed me. But I was convinced that the lines were a quotation. When I got back to the cottage I repeated them to Rose Marie to see if she could place the author. She couldn't. I began searching fruitlessly in anthologies. For some reason I cannot explain these two lines obsessed me. Eventually I wrote to Leavis and asked him to name their author.

"You," he replied.

A year later the rest of the poem suddenly emerged as one of the meditations of Saint Anthony.

9 September 1943 was my daughter's second birthday. We were carrying barley, making the most of a change in the weather. A light breeze blowing up over the cliffs had dried the stooks during the night. Now the sheaves rustled and rattled with ripeness as the stack rose in a sheltered corner of the field.

The tractor reversed and went off again with the empty trailer. I climbed down the ladder, threw up an odd sheaf which I had missed with my prong, and then sat smoking my pipe, waiting for the next load.

The country looked very peaceful. An occasional Spitfire crossing the valley passed unnoticed. The war meant little more to us in North Devon than an irritating shortage of petrol. In the distance anti-aircraft shells from a practice-range puffed idly up into the blue sky.

I had promised Rose Marie to go home early for tea, as she had arranged a little birthday party. Glancing at my watch, I decided that there was still time to do one more load. I knocked out my pipe carefully and mounted the ladder again just as the tractor came towards the gate. But when I looked down I saw that there was no corn on the trailer. Instead there stood a policeman.

"Never been so glad of a lift in all my life," he said, removing his helmet and mopping his bald head.

I assumed he had called for the usual donation to the local police ball, and went on arranging the sheaves round the stack.

"Are you busy?" he shouted up.

"Sure, come up and give us a hand."

There was a puffing and blowing on the ladder. Then he sat down beside me.

"Not bad corn at all, sir," he said, rubbing out a few ears. "Daresay it's fit for malting."

"Too good for your chickens," I replied, anticipating the purpose of his visit. "Still, I might give you a bag of seconds again if you keep it under your helmet."

I went on arranging the sheaves.

"It's not exactly about my chickens that I've called, sir."

"Isn't it? What is it, then? You know damn well I've got a dog-licence."

"Nor is it on account of your dog, sir."

Something in his tone made me turn round. There he sat, sweating not from heat but from sheer embarrassment. I felt quite sorry for him. "Well, what is it, man?"

"The sergeant, sir, and the inspector, would like a word with you," he said, glancing towards the road. There they were, both standing beside a car.

It even crossed my mind that they had come to ask me to become a Special Constable. I slipped on my coat and went down the ladder. The constable followed.

"Are you Ronald Duncan?" asked the sergeant, who had known me since I was a child.

I was about to make a facetious reply, but something in the inspector's expression made me hold my tongue. I had not seen him before; a little wedge of a man, all profile and no fullness to his face. But, to the relief of my two friends, he took over.

"Are you Ronald Duncan?" he snapped.

"I am," I replied, now quite bewildered by his manner.

"Then I must ask you to come along with us," he said.

"Where?"

"To the station."

"Why?"

"You're under arrest."

I should have said "Why?" again but I didn't. I was too surprised to speak. And, before I knew what I was doing, I found myself getting into their car. The inspector got in the front; Sergeant Lipscombe and the constable sat one each side of me in the back. We drove off. Then suddenly I remembered.

"Stop," I said; "I've just remembered I've promised to go home to tea for my daughter's party." I moved from my seat as though to alight.

"I'll call in and see whatever all this is about tomorrow." But the car didn't even slow down.

Now the bobbies each side of me looked most unhappy.

The constable tried to make conversation. "Have you carried most of your corn, sir?"

"No, we've just started."

"Been a catchy time with so much rain about, hasn't it?" he said affably.

I agreed automatically. My mind refused to realise my predicament, let alone speculate on the reason for it.

For a few miles we continued this idle and awkward conversation about the harvest as though nothing were amiss. Then, when we were passing through the village of Kilkhampton, I realised that I had run out of cigarettes. I asked if they would mind stopping so that I could get some.

The car drew up at the village square. The sergeant nipped out. "What sort do you want, sir?" he asked as though he were my butler.

I then realised that I was not to be allowed out of the car myself. I was, in fact, a prisoner.

"You'd better get a hundred," I said jokingly; "it looks as if I shall need them." But I couldn't quite see the joke.

When the car started again, I settled down to speculating on the cause of my arrest. I racked my brain for any offence I might have committed. I started by considering the most likely possibilities. As a criminal I was quite modest; and, indeed, I could think of

273

nothing more dreadful than that my gun-licence might have lapsed. My conscience was too clear. Indeed, its very purity began to alarm me. Was I, I asked myself in all seriousness, an absent-minded criminal? Had I simply forgotten my crime?

The car drew up outside the police station at Stratton. I was escorted in, the sergeant making way for me as though he was my host and I his guest—which indeed I was. I was asked to produce the contents of my pockets. I did this as though in a trance.

"Now, sir," said the sergeant, playing the valet to perfection, "may I ask you to remove your tie and your braces?"

"My braces!" I exclaimed. "Whatever for?"

He did not answer the question but added, "And I'm afraid it's my painful duty to ask you to remove your shoes." So saying, he was down on his knees like Jeeves himself, undoing my laces.

I stood in my stockinged feet.

"This way, sir," he whispered, trying to hide the large bunch of keys which the constable passed him. "We'll try to make you as comfortable as circumstances permit."

He led me down a corridor to the cells.

"Here you are, sir. I'm afraid it's not quite what you're used to, but it is clean."

It was now I who felt embarrassed, as though I were a guest in a small house with an over-apologetic host.

"I shall be very comfortable here," I said, looking at the bleak, unfurnished cell as though it were his best bedroom.

"I'll go and tell the missus to make you a cup of tea."

"Please don't trouble."

"No trouble at all, sir. I expect she has it all ready for you."

So I was expected here, I thought, as I walked towards the shaft of light which fell from the small barred window three feet above my head. The door closed behind me. The keys rattled. The lock went home.

"Do you like sugar, sir?"

I spun round to see where the voice came from. There was the sergeant's face, framed in a little grill in the door.

"Yes, please."

"One lump or two?" For a second I pondered this question, clinging desperately to the normality which it suggested.

"Two, please." The grill closed from outside. I could hear the sergeant clumping off down the corridor to his own married quarters which adjoined the station.

My first impression was of cold feet, for I stood in my socks and a draught blew from under the door. I lay on the wooden form which, covered with one army blanket, constituted a bed. I lit a cigarette, now determined to make an effort to remember the crime which had apparently caught up with me. I could think of nothing. My conscience remained so clear that I was surprised at my virtue. Was it a motoring offence? No, I had a licence, and had had no accident. A black-out offence? Surely people weren't arrested for that, but merely fined. But they had even taken away my tie, braces and shoe-laces, so that I couldn't hang myself. Plainly I must be guilty of something.

I arose from the uncomfortable bed, which lacked a pillow, and, like every prisoner in every romance, I paced my cell. It measured six feet by four. I worked out how many turns I would have to do to walk a mile. The answer made me feel giddy.

Then I noticed that the wall had been scribbled on by previous guests. I read the lewd confessions of various members of the United States Army Air Force, who had apparently passed out in the local and been brought here to sober up.

And on the wall by the door I deciphered a crude plan of the police station with facetious directions on how to escape. In another hand another inmate had written: "Why bother?" underneath.

This display of cave-drawings distracted me; and, when the little grill opened and a cup of tea was pushed through, I had still not succeeded in tarnishing my conscience. Nor had I been sensible enough to ask for a solicitor. But the sight of the tea reminded me of my daughter's birthday party. I now felt guilty for the first time.

"Can I telephone to my wife?" I asked the sergeant.

He unlocked the door and led me to the instrument.

Rose Marie answered. "I'm afraid I shall be a little late for tea," I said.

"Where are you?"

"Stratton."

"Whatever for?"

275

"I don't know."

"Well, what are you doing there?"

"Nothing."

"Then come home."

"I can't."

"Why not?"

"I'm in prison!"

"What for?"

"I don't know."

"You don't know! Then ask them."

"All right, hold on."

I turned to the sergeant. "What is the charge against me?"

The poor fellow blushed. "Larceny," he said.

I repeated the charge to my wife.

"What's larceny?" she asked.

"Stealing," I said.

"Stealing what?"

"I don't know. I'll ring you back when I find out."

"Yes, do," she said, "and let me know where you've hidden the swag." The poor girl was a little hysterical. I had quite ruined her party. I replaced the receiver and returned to my cell to brood over a cup of cold tea.

As the sun set, the cell was immediately darkened. There was no artificial light. It would be a long evening. I settled down, trying to recall anything I had ever stolen. At least the scope of my crime had now been narrowed. But I could think of nothing at all.

The keys rattled and the cell-door opened to admit the inspector and a police constable, the latter armed with a large notebook.

"You are charged with larceny," said the inspector coldly. "Would you care to make a statement?"

"Yes, if you tell me precisely what I am supposed to have stolen?"

The inspector read from his notes: "On the 17th instant an examination of the fuel tank of a Sunbeam lorry, the property of Mr Ronald Duncan, revealed that it was filled with octane, i.e. aviation fuel."

My conscience woke. Yes, I remembered now how suspicious the bobby in Bideford had looked when I drove past him with my exhaust making a noise like a super-charged Spitfire.

"Do you admit that your petrol-tank was full of aviation petrol?"

"Yes."

"From what aerodrome did you steal it?"

"I didn't steal it." The inspector smiled. Even the constable looked dubious. "About a month ago," I explained, "I found an old drum of petrol floating in the sea, so I waded out and rolled it ashore."

The constable grinned warmly like one old Devonian wrecker to another, but continued to write in his notebook.

"And why didn't you report it to the coastguards?"

"I didn't think it was worth it." I paused. "It was nearly empty," I lied.

"It was nearly empty," the constable repeated my lie somewhat unnecessarily as he painfully wrote it down.

"How many gallons were there in the drum when you found it?" the inspector asked.

"About six," I said, and found it a little difficult to swallow.

"Then how do you account for there being eight gallons in your tank?" the inspector shut his eyes.

"I was only making a rough estimate." This time the inspector repeated me.

"Where's the empty drum now?" he fired.

"At my farm, in one of the barns."

"Hidden?"

"No, just surrounded by straw."

"Empty?"

"Of course."

The inspector went to the cell-door and ordered the sergeant to go to my farm immediately and return with the drum. "Take three men—you'll probably need them to lift it," he added.

But I smiled; for I knew that there wasn't a single drop left, though there had been sixty gallons when I had laboriously rolled it out of the waves. Guilty as I was, I felt nothing but relief, for this was not very serious—well, not compared to those crimes which I had imagined I might have committed.

The inspector left my cell. I heard voices in the passage. It was Spottiswoode, being locked up in the adjoining cell.

277

As soon as the police had left him, I tapped on the wall. But it was too thick for him to hear. So I tapped on a pipe. This brought a response. Contact established, I made a desperate effort to recall the Morse code. It was necessary for me to warn him to confirm my statement concerning the amount of petrol there was in the drum when we found it.

"SAY THERE WAS ABOUT SIX GA . . ." I tapped, failing to remember the Morse for 'L'. But it was to no avail. Spottiswoode merely thought I was fidgeting from nerves.

"Go to sleep," he bellowed, loud enough to cause the bobby on guard to shine a torch through the grill of my cell-door.

The next morning I was woken by the constable, who stood before me holding a pail of water.

"What's this for?" I asked.

"To wash in, sir," he murmured apologetically.

I glanced at the dirty water. Spottiswoode had used it first and washed his feet. I refused to wash. "The water's not clean," I said petulantly. "Anyhow I've no soap, razor, toothbrush, towel."

Within a few minutes the sergeant appeared with soap and his own razor. As I shaved, I wondered whether his giving me a cut-throat razor was quite consistent with depriving me of my dangerous tie, braces and shoe-laces.

When we were clean, we were taken before a magistrate. The inspector pleaded that we should remain on remand, as investigations against us were still proceeding. This plea was granted and we were promptly returned to our cells for another four days and nights.

But that afternoon Rose Marie was allowed to visit me. She arrived with a suitcase of solid reading: *Paradise Lost*, *The Prelude*, and three novels of Dickens—"all things you're unlikely to read in happier circumstances."

She looked worried, for she had discussed my plight with my solicitor and discovered that, if I were found guilty, I could be sentenced to six months.

This was a very sobering thought. Indeed for the next few days I sat in my cell pondering my future. During this time I read nothing but the *News of the World*, noting the sentences that different crimes received.

The only use I made of *Paradise Lost* was to underline certain letters of the text in it as a crude code, and have the constable pass the poem to my friend in the adjoining cell. I shall always be grateful to Milton.

I did not find that the time dragged at all. I had never had so much leisure in my life. The sergeant provided me with pens and paper, and his good wife cooked to perfection.

Thinking of Gandhi in prison, and wondering where Ezra was too, I started to scribble a poem on the cell-wall which I called *The Ballad of Stratton Gaol.*

I copied these verses out neatly on paper and the sergeant posted off the copies, one to Eliot to indicate my predicament to him, and the other to Philip Mairet, editor of the *New English Weekly,* who immediately published it.

I enjoyed the opportunity to write and to read again. And I was just settling down to this monastic and ordered routine when I had to attend to the annoying distraction of the defence for my trial. My solicitor was gloomy. "The best you can hope for is a fine," he said, "but if they send you up the line, I will of course lodge an appeal."

From the dock I surveyed half a dozen of my neighbours sitting on the bench. There was the porter at the station, sitting next to the wife of the local M.P. They were not amused.

The inspector recounted my crime, drawing attention to the fact that I had not only stolen a drum of petrol but, in doing so, had broken the regulations concerning the rationing of that fuel, and —he paused—seriously jeopardised the war-effort. The magistrates were now less amused than ever.

"If you want mercy," I thought, "go outside your own district for it."

At this point I began to wonder what I should look like with a shaven head. But then Rose Marie passed an old Deed to my solicitor. He beamed with pleasure and called me for cross-examination.

"When you found the drum of petrol, was it flotsam or jetsam?" he asked me.

"I had to wade into the sea for it."

279

"In other words, if you had not salvaged it, it would have gone out again to sea."

"All the others did." He coughed to cover my gaffe.

"Are you the owner of the beach on which the drum of petrol foundered?"

"I am."

"Does this Deed convey Manorial Rights to you on the said beach?"

He passed me the papers Rose Marie had found in my deed-box.

"It does."

"In other words, the drum of petrol was yours by right; and, indeed, if the *Queen Mary* itself beached there, the owners would owe you rent for the berth?"

The inspector scowled. The sergeant grinned. The magistrates, thinking of their rights, confirmed me in mine. I walked out of the court free of everything—but a conscience.

The next morning I telephoned the R.A.F. Camp.

"Would that petrol I found have been of any use to you?" I asked.

"None at all," was the reply. "You don't think we'd dare risk putting stuff that had been in the sea into our engines, do you?"

As soon as this legal storm had lifted I was on my beat again. Having missed a dozen tides, there was quite a bit to pick up, including a couple of tins of corn-on-the-cob, which I washed down with Burgundy.

Soon after this episode Spottiswoode joined the R.A.F. As our experiment in pacifist living in the Community had failed, it was the logical thing for him to do. Now there was one.

Emulating an octopus, I had to try and turn myself into an ordinary farmer. I knew I could never leave—my horse, Dil Fareb, had led me along the valley to the derelict farm, and she would always need it. I had bought this mare when she was six. She is now thirty-three. So I am still farming with one hand, writing with the other.

If I only had two arms my life would be simple. If I had only one heart. . . . We write our life when we no longer know how to live it. I see I shall have to write another volume.